In Search
of a Round
Table

Edited by
Musimbi R.A. Kanyoro

In Search
of a Round
Table

Gender, Theology &
Church Leadership

Published for the Lutheran World Federation by

WCC Publications, Geneva

Cover design: Edwin Hassink

ISBN 2-8254-1209-0

© 1997 WCC Publications, World Council of Churches,
150 route de Ferney, 1211 Geneva 2, Switzerland

Printed in The Netherlands

Table of Contents

Foreword:
Making a Difference

PÉRI RASOLONDRAIBE

Opportunities and challenges

What do the promotion of equality between women and men and the full participation of women in church and society entail? What are the issues and challenges we must face together for us to be a sign of an inclusive community?

On the one hand, the promotion of justice and awareness of rights for women brings challenges. We must acknowledge openly that many men feel threatened by talk about equality with women. Like most privileged groups, men fear that equality means in practice loss of power, authority and privilege. Fear and lack of understanding beget resistance, conservatism, and even chauvinism. And our own fear of these reactions is an additional challenge.

On the other hand, we must also initiate and sustain, in all creativity and good sense, the promotion of the involvement of women in all facets of societal life, especially at decision-making and leadership levels. This does not mean *allowing* women to participate, as if they needed permission to do so. Rather, it means that women, together, empower themselves to seize every occasion as an opportunity to share the gift of grace entrusted to them and thus "event" the good news of Jesus Christ in all situations. It is important to keep in mind that we are witnesses in word and deed. We witness to Christ through the words of proclamation as to what Christ has done for us and the world. But we also witness to his love through what we do for the world. When we talk about witnessing through action we must beware of tokenism and acting like bad Samaritans. Tokenism is present when what we do for people is simply a token of our faith and not really meant to strengthen their capacity to stand for themselves. We act like bad Samaritans when we help people to depend on us, so that they lose their dignity and their hope. What we say and do as we witness to Christ in the world must be both faithful and effective: faithful to the call to follow Christ and effective in making life more human.

Throughout the world, individualism, that sickness of the heart, has brought crises to all spheres of life — political, social, and economic — so that peoples and nations are at each other's throats. It has been suggested that racism and ecological destruction feed each other, that the destruction of social ecology is reflected in the destruction of natural ecology and that both are exacerbated by the rise of market culture where value is measured and determined by marketability. Churches are not immune from the sickness: they too are burdened by disunity, dissension, competition, mismanagement of resources and other corrupting factors.

What difference can Lutheran women make to all this? When we talk about the Reformation, we always talk about "his-story" and we learn very little about what women did during and for the Reformation. In the few things written about the women of the Reformation, we can learn, for instance, about Catherine von Bora Luther, who on some decisive occasions and in spite of the prevailing prejudice against women helped Martin Luther move towards the right decisions. I have no doubt that there would have been a great difference in the way the churches of the Reformation were organized, nurtured and structured if women like her had had more room to act.

We can make a difference to Christianity as a whole. In many instances, Christians still confuse denomination with Christianity. We are Christians who respond to the call to follow Christ in the way of Lutheran discipleship. Such discipleship should bring us closer to and not further away from our Christian sisters and brothers. To make an *ecumenical* difference — that is our challenge. We know women continue to make a great difference in many areas of community life and elsewhere in the world at large, but it is up to the church and society generally to expect and receive the gifts of women.

Why women?

Why should the church expect women to bring salutary change and transformation to the world? For a start, the sheer scale of women's presence in the churches (some 80 percent of the total church population) is a considerable force for change if it is used creatively and strategically. But there is also the sustained resilience of women in the face of adversity. The old African American spiritual asks, "Were you there when they crucified my Lord?" Yes, women were there, while the male disciples went into hiding; without the prompting of Christ's women disciples the apostles would not have dared visit the empty tomb. Women's story in the church has shown that women have always been there, often as a transforming leaven, or opening new doors and providing new opportunities for the unfolding of faith.

As many feminist theologians have rightly pointed out, a woman is blessed with the gifts of caring and sharing. There are so many Bible stories that simply did not make it to the pulpit in all their fullness until women started contributing to biblical interpretation. To take obvious examples, the two sisters Mary and Martha help us to see that women, too, belong in the classroom. Even when women have functioned in societies primarily as mothers, their insights are often far more perceptive than is obvious to those in power. Mothers brought their children to Jesus, for example, because they knew that children, too, need to experience God. Remember, also, the Canaanite woman who interrupted Jesus and his disciples while they were on retreat. She wanted healing for her only daughter and did not let the barrier of religion or anything else get in her way. Her concern was to save life.

This life-generating direction to women's lives is the gift the suffering world needs so urgently. Women have the gift of "life- generating faith" and can make a difference. The contributions made in this book by women and men speak to the witness of women and the tremendous gift of self that women bring to the table to be shared by the whole community of God's people. Will our churches and societies accept this gift graciously?

Introduction:
Background and Genesis

MUSIMBI R.A. KANYORO

It was a historic event when 165 representatives from Lutheran churches — women and men from all over the world — convened in Geneva, Switzerland, in October 1995 to discuss what it means to be "Called to Witness Christ", the theme of the Lutheran World Federation assembly in Hong Kong, China, in July 1997. In Bible studies, worship and dialogue, participants searched for new directions to experience equality and partnership between men and women in our societies and churches. They shared the life of their churches and countries. Some of these stories were painful, others were full of vision and hope.

The strong presence and participation of other ecumenical organizations, world communions, non-governmental organizations and the World Bank were special features of this gathering. Ecumenical participants and representatives of world communions shared their experiences, challenging the Lutheran communion to common action in working together in solidarity with one another. World Council of Churches' general secretary Konrad Raiser, deputy general secretary Mary Ann Lundy, and staff working on women's issues Aruna Gnanadason and Nicole Fischer grounded the Lutheran family within an ecumenical setting, reminding us that first and foremost we are Christians and that only as Christians can we live out our confessional lives, always ready to bring back to the ecumenical table something to share with the whole Christian family.

The World Young Women's Christian Association, represented by its general secretary Elaine Hesse Steel, challenged participants to concentrate on leadership training for young people as a priority for the next millennium. The World Alliance of Reformed Churches, represented by Nyambura Njoroge, who heads the programme for partnership of men and women, emphasized that the future of the church depends on the church of the future accepting and nurturing the gifts of both men and women. Other challenges for cooperation in confronting the issues of our time came from the president of the World Union of Catholic Women's Organizations, Maryse Durrer, Wendy Robins representing the Anglican communion, Renate Bloem of the World Federation of Methodist Women, and Irja Askola representing the Conference of European Churches.

Among Lutheran participants were women and men pastors, bishops, teachers in schools, seminaries and universities, lawyers, health professionals, and all categories of women in the church, including those responsible for women's work.

For once, men were in the minority and did not set the agenda. A separate meeting was held for male participants to help build their own solidarity and to encourage each other to participate. They discussed their minority status, which they experienced as a problem and which made some of them get angry or want to withdraw. Some men felt it helped them to understand how women must feel when they are in the minority; for others, their presence at a meeting where the agenda was set by and for women made them feel it was none of their business. It was interesting to note that some male church leaders were happy for this kind of agenda to be discussed in parallel women's meetings but not as an issue for the whole church. A month later one of the men, a bishop on one of the LWF's governing committees, expressed his appreciation at having been invited to the meeting, but added that if he had known beforehand that men would be in the minority he would not have accepted. He felt intimidated by the presence of so many strong women and claimed that although he is a bishop, he felt helpless and powerless because he was not the one setting the agenda. He expressed his frustration at being a mere participant, without a role as leader or speaker. He concluded that if the way he felt was the way women feel when they are in the minority, then there was an urgent need to do something about it and he himself will never be the same again.

Since this conference was partially a follow-up to the fourth world conference on women, the LWF had invited the World Bank to participate, and was able to welcome Minhchau Nguyen, gender adviser at the Bank in Washington. Dialogue between her and the participants provided an opportunity to voice concerns and to hear the Bank's own interpretation of the policies it promotes. There were many questions from the floor, and doubt was expressed about whether the World Bank could ever do anything without putting its own interests first. Once again, we can only wait and see, as news continues to spread that the World Bank is presently giving priority to girls' education and to credit facilities for women.

The conference was graced with art dedicated to the feminine, as presented by Elie Swai from Tanzania and Janis Pozzi-Johnson from the United States. Worship was a feast of spirituality made possible by the leadership of Lusmarina Campos Garcia from Brazil and Stephen and Rebecca Larson from Canada. African women stole the show at the closing worship by demonstrating what drums and songs can do to bring joy, celebration and meaning to the life of a community. Exciting Bible studies by a well-known ecumenical theologian, Milton Schwantes, and a younger pastor, Maristella Freiberg, both from Brazil, meant that the Latin American presence significantly shaped the meeting.

This was the first LWF international conference with significant participation of women from Eastern Europe since the political changes of 1989. Gathering as "one Europe", European women as a whole comprised the largest group at the conference, but the constraints of the new Europe were far from absent. Issues surrounding styles of work, priorities, and the persons performing tasks could be heard loud and clear. Eastern Europe eventually met separately, and when regional reports were received "one Europe" submitted two reports.

Asia was the "focus continent" in discussions about the Lutheran World Federation assembly in Hong Kong. That city was represented by a strong delegation of four, including Josephine Tso, the president of Chinese Lutheran Churches, Hong Kong Association. During the meeting Asian women sought ways to be in solidarity with the women of Hong Kong. The final report from the region called for more women in leadership positions of their churches and more attention to the pressing issues of women in poverty and the international trafficking in Asian women.

The plenary's discussion on the ordination of women is hard to capture in print. It was lively, sometimes painful, sometimes celebratory. From Denmark we learned of the many cases of divorce among clergy persons. This offended some women from the Middle East, and some churches from the South and Eastern Europe could not comprehend how a divorced person could still remain in the clergy. From Eastern Europe we heard how a new wave of young male clergy are building resistance to the ordination of women, specifically within the Latvian Lutheran Church which has stopped ordaining women. Other Eastern European participants feared that the same wave of regression was coming their way and asked for solidarity from the whole ecumenical family. Yet we also heard of rejoicing, with the Lutheran Christian Church in Nigeria preparing for their first woman's ordination. The ordinand, Naomi Malao, was present and shared her joy to be welcomed to the table as the first woman, signifying an inclusive ministry in that church. We also received news from Botswana which had just passed a resolution in the governing council to ordain women.

The presence of regional coordinators from all the continents chairing and providing leadership in group meetings allowed the consultation to come up with one report entitled "We Are Witnesses" (see *LWF Documentation* 34), and also regional reports which will be used as guidelines for work in the regions.

This book cannot hope to capture the rich diversity of the whole meeting. Rather, it comprises edited versions of presentations prepared for the consultation, some of which were read in plenary while others were background reading material. The need to reclaim the Bible as the basis for women's faith and women's spirituality was the focus of the consultation. Hence, the papers in this book are for the most part theologically oriented. It was a privilege to welcome Elisabeth Schüssler Fiorenza as guest speaker, and her two presentations are included here. Biblical hermeneutics featured strongly in the consultation. The work of the desk for women in Church and Society and the three papers by Wanda Deifelt (Brazil), Anna Mghwira (Tanzania) and Nirmala Vasanthakumar (India) show that re-reading the Bible with new perspectives from women is not just a privilege of the West but of the whole world.

Questions of power come up frequently here, demonstrating the complexity of the issue. The church must be willing to struggle urgently with an analysis of power as a hindrance to the realization of God's reign in our lives. These papers should help to get that debate on the table.

The fact that this book has arisen in a Lutheran context makes some of it characteristically Lutheran. In his address to the consultation, the general secretary of the LWF spearheaded something new that churches may wish to follow: taking women's concerns seriously means urging everyone, men and women together, to act. This is what the LWF intends to do; the popular phrase is "mainstreaming gender issues". Among other things, the LWF assembly will discuss the subject of gender and the theology of the church. The papers focusing on Lutheran churches here will serve as examples.

This book is also evidence of the LWF's participation in the Ecumenical Decade of Churches in Solidarity with Women. The consultation heard several church-specific reports and many will be published elsewhere. WCC staff also shared reports from their mid-decade visits and a summary of the issues is presented in papers by Nicole Fischer and Robert Shantz.

It should be noted that the contributions in this book have come from men and women, and from around the world. They herald the hope that it is possible to build a true partnership of women and men, but it takes the will to rethink our structures, to reformulate our theologies, and to create the image of a round table where no one sits at the top or the bottom, but where each of us can hold Christ as the presence that keeps that roundness in shape.

22 October 1996

1. Discipleship of Equals: Reality and Vision

ELISABETH SCHÜSSLER FIORENZA

Mark's gospel tells a story about a Greek woman from Syrophoenicia whose little daughter was possessed by an evil spirit. She asks Jesus to heal her daughter, but Jesus refuses by likening Gentile outsiders to dogs who should not steal the food of the children. Yet the woman does not give up in the face of such an insult. As a cultural and religious foreigner, she rejects the theological argument of Jesus that Gentile aliens are excluded from the life-giving power of God's reign of well-being. The woman turns Jesus' argument against itself, and overcomes his prejudice. No one should be excluded, she insists. God's power of salvation is without boundaries. And her argument wins the day. By opening up a future of well-being for her daughter, the Syrophoenician outsider not only has become the symbolic foremother of those who struggle for the liberation of wo/men. She also is the apostolic witness for a radical religious political vision of a global round table to whom all are invited, or a community of equals in which peoples of different religions, cultures and races can deliberate and take responsibility for the well-being of all of creation.

With this woman as a guide, I begin this theological discussion of an egalitarian re-vision of church and ministry as a "discipleship of equals". This ecclesial vision and incipient reality continues to invigorate her daughters and sons today. I shall then look both at the process and goals of a critical feminist interpretation in and through the prism of her story and at the same time explore the interpretation of her story as a rhetorical site for biblical conscientization in the discipleship community of equals. We must seek to heed the call for a "new", "yet old" vision of justice and equality for the next millennium.

Kyriarchy

The biblical theological vision of the discipleship of equals as I have developed it in my own work aims to respond to this call. It seeks to articulate a radical democratic vision of church and society which is rooted in biblical traditions. The word "disciple" is a translation of the Greek word "learner" and designates someone whose allegiance is to the vision and commitment of a teacher or a movement. Discipleship means not only the commitment to a

---

Note: It is my normal practice to write "wo/men" in order to indicate both that I use wo/men as inclusive of men and to point to the many differences among women and within women themselves. "Woman" is not a unified concept, but an ambiguous one. Similarly, I usually render "God" as "G*d", in order to indicate the broken character, limitation and ambiguity of human language that is not able to comprehend and express adequately divine reality.

message, leader and vision but also to "a way of life". The modification of the word discipleship with that of "equals" must not be understood as advocating sameness under the guise of universality. Rather, it seeks to underscore equality in diversity as the central ethos of discipleship. Throughout the centuries, divine Wisdom has sent an open-ended succession of prophets and messengers for proclaiming and realizing this inclusive radical egalitarian vision.

In the discipleship of equals, wo/men have equal status, dignity and rights as images of the divine, and equal access to the multifarious gifts of the Spirit, Sophia. Each and every one enriches the discipleship community of equals with their different experiences, vocations and talents. In short, the concept of "discipleship of equals" seeks to map a radical democratic vision and reality that articulates an alternative to kyriarchal structures of domination. What do I mean by the neologism "kyriarchal/kyriarchy" which I have coined to displace the widely used expression "patriarchal/patriarchy?"

In contrast to gender feminism, which understands "patriarchal" in terms of gender dualism as global male domination of all women equally, I theorize it as a complex pyramidal system of domination and subordination, profit and exploitation. Such a conceptualization of patriarchy simply in terms of gender, however, is not able adequately to theorize interstructured racial, class and colonial oppressions. Hence, I have suggested replacing the terminology of patriarchy with that of kyriarchy, defined in classical socio-political terms. In antiquity, kyriarchy connoted the rule of the lord/master/father/husband over those subordinated to and dependent on him. Kyriarchy is a socio-political and cultural system of domination that has produced dualistic asymmetric justifications of systemic exclusions and forms of exploitation. However, it must not be overlooked that such kyriarchal dichotomous legitimizations of women's second-class citizenship have developed in interaction with the notions and ideals of democratic equality in antiquity and modernity.

Western society and family are not simply male-dominated. Rather, they are patriarchal (ruled by the father) or, more accurately, kyriarchal (ruled by the master or lord), because elite propertied men have had and still have power and control over those subordinated to and dependent on them. Kyriarchy specifies women's status and way of being not only in terms of gender but also in terms of the class, race, country or religion of the men to whom they "belong".

Kyriarchy represents a graduated elite male status system of domination and subordination, authority and obedience, rulers and subjects in household and state. With the emergence of democracy as an alternative social vision and political order within kyriarchal structures of domination, classical and modern philosophy had to develop arguments as to why people with subordinate status could not participate in democratic governance. Ancient and modern political religious philosophy was compelled to justify the relationship between rulers and ruled in household and state, and it did so by articulating a philosophy of "different" and hence "deficient" human natures.

Consequently, the Western kyriarchal system of domination has produced not only sex-gender ideologies but also colonialist theories of inferior races and cultures. Racist kyriocentric theories have argued that peoples are at different levels of development. In the hierarchy — or better, kyriarchy — of evolution, Europeans were and still are often believed to be the better and more highly developed human beings. For instance, Aboriginal peoples or "the natives" of colonialized countries were seen as uncivilized and inferior by nature. Women, especially, were deemed to be at the bottom of the racial pyramid of evolution. Like white privileged women, all exploited women, men and peoples of colour were deemed to be rationally and morally inferior.

The radical democratic belief that all are created equal and the notion of the ekklesia as the decision-making congress/assembly of all citizens stand in conflictive tension with the reality of classical and modern kyriarchy. As an alternative to kyriarchy this vision of ekklesia understood as radical democracy becomes embodied and realized again and again in the emancipatory struggles to change relations of domination, exploitation and marginalization. This same tension between radical democratic and "malestream" kyriarchal socio-religious visions and projects still comes to the fore in the linguistic notion of the word "church". The Greek word "ekklesia" is usually translated as "church", although the English word "church" derives from the Greek word "kyriak" (i.e. belonging to the lord/master/father/husband). Accordingly, the translation of ekklesia as "church" is misleading.

Ekklesia is best rendered as "democratic assembly/congress of full citizens". The translation process which transformed ekklesia/democratic assembly into kyriak/church indicates a historical development that has privileged the kyriarchal/hierarchical form of church over that of a democratic congress or discipleship of equals. Thus, the same word "church" in English entails two contradictory meanings: one derived from the patri-kyriarchal household in antiquity which was governed by the lord/master/husband/father of the house, to whom freeborn women, freeborn dependents, clients, workers and slaves, both women and men, were subordinated. The other meaning of church = ekklesia understands the equality of its members in terms of citizenship and friendship. This meaning of "church" evolves from the vision of democracy in antiquity and modernity.

-Although in theory Western democracy has promised freedom and equality to all its citizens, in practice it has realized equality only in kyriarchal ways that have restricted leadership for a long time to elite male citizens only. Hence, the radical democratic vision of a citizenry of equals has been realized only partially. Nevertheless, throughout its history this radical democratic vision also has inspired emancipatory movements for full citizenship and justice. These movements, including feminism, have emerged again and again because of the disparity between this radical democratic vision and its actual socio-political and cultural religious realizations.

In the past years, radical democratic movements around the globe have fought for the freedom and power of the people in society and religion. Today, many of these movements are wrecked by ruthless economic exploitation, fundamentalist fanaticism and nationalist strife. At this point in time we seem to confront an alternative: either our "global village" will be fashioned into a radical democratic confederation that is governed by the economic political and religious well-being of all its citizens, or it will turn into a tightly controlled dictatorship that concentrates all economic and cultural resources in the hands of a few and relegates the majority of the people to a permanent impoverished and dehumanized underclass.

Dangerous memory

Does the democratic vision of radical equality from below also still surface as "dangerous memory" in a critical feminist reading of scripture? Do biblical theologies offer a religious vision and communal practice of radical democracy that can intervene in and inspire and empower these struggles? These are key questions which feminist and other liberation theologies urgently raise today in the face of increasing global exploitation and religious dogmatism. In this global struggle over resources, religious communities must keep alive the "dream of freedom and well-being for all", if they are not to legitimate a nationalist "bunker mentality" and to scapegoat the disadvantaged in the interest of those who are better off.

A critical feminist theology of liberation seeks to reflect on the diverse feminist democratic struggles to overcome kyriarchal oppression traversed by racism, class-exploitation, heterosexism, and colonialist militarism and to claim them as the political ecclesial site from where to speak. Since its aim is to recover Bible, history and theology as memory and heritage of the ekklesia of wo/men, such a critical theology of liberation seeks to retrieve Christian history and theology not just as the memory of the suffering and victimization of all women and marginalized men. It also seeks to repossess this heritage as the memory of those women and disenfranchised men who have shaped Christian history as religious interlocutors, agents of change, and survivors in the struggles against kyriarchal dominations. Utilizing such a critical feminist approach and analysis, I have sought in my own work to reconstruct early Christian roots and self-understandings as a site of struggle.

Early Christian discourses, I have argued, still allow one to glimpse the practical theological struggles which sought to realize the radical democratic religious vision of the discipleship of equals in a socio-political and religious situation of Roman colonial imperialism. However, such a reconstruction should not be misunderstood as a factual transcript of egalitarian Christian beginnings or as a theological legitimization of Christian origins. Rather, it must be understood as a reconstitution of those early Christian beginnings that have engendered radical egalitarian Christian visions and movements throughout the centuries. The reality of the discipleship of equals is already and not yet. It is the eschatological project of the "basileia", the intended society and world of God, that must be realized again and again in and through the continuing struggle against dehumanizing kyriarchal powers of oppression which are theologically named as structural sin.

However, one would be ill-advised if one were to tackle the question as to whether scripture supports a democratic ekklesial "round table" and the full citizenship of women in an apologetic fashion. For it is not possible methodologically to "prove" that the scriptures advocate egalitarian democracy rather than kyriarchal monarchy, since both forms of social organization are inscribed in the socio-symbolic universe of biblical writings. Contrary to popular opinion, the Bible does not speak for itself. Rather, interpretations of biblical texts and reconstructions of early Christian history are shaped by the contemporary interests of the biblical historian, theologian or general reader just as much as they are by historical realities. For our experience functions as what the anthropologist

Clifford Geertz calls "a model" of reality.[1] The notions and beliefs we hold today inform how we read the texts of the past.

Without such "analogical" models or "designs" we would have no basis for comprehending the past, which requires interpretation. It is not simply there in the text, waiting for us to discover how things really were or what Jesus really said. In other words, those biblical interpreters who favour a "discipleship-of-equals" model of the church will emphasize the radical democratic elements inscribed in biblical texts, and those who favour a "hierarchical" one will stress the kyriarchal aspects advocated by biblical writers. Interpreters can do so, because variations of both models of church are inscribed in biblical traditions and available as models of reality for today. As far as we can still see, the followers of Jesus did not all conform to the kyriarchal ethos and structures of their own society and religion. But neither did they all conform to a radical democratic ethos, for the texts that transmit this ethos are frequently prescriptive texts indicating that not all the disciples observe such a radical ethos of discipleship.

Reconstructions of the Jesus movements in Palestine have underscored that these movements are best understood as inner-Jewish reform movements which proclaimed the gracious goodness of the Sophia/creator God who wills the well-being of everyone without exception. Well-being and inclusiveness are the hallmarks of the gospel, i.e. good news. Like Israel's prophets, Jesus promised God's renewed society and world not to the rich, the pious or the learned, but to the poor, the destitute and the prostitutes. This inclusive ethos of the Jesus movements allowed women as well as men, poor as well as rich, cultically unclean as well as strict observers of the Torah to become disciples. Women such as Mary of Magdala were among the most prominent and faithful in this discipleship of equals. So-called church "fathers" still acknowledge Mary of Magdala as a key apostolic witness when they call her the "apostle to the apostles".

This ethos of the discipleship of equals was anti-patriarchal insofar as it required the breaking of natural kinship ties and household relationships. Those who have followed the Jesuanic basileia-vision were promised a new familial community in return. This new "family" of equal disciples must not call anyone "father" (Matt. 23:8-11) or accord status on the grounds of motherhood (Luke 11:27-28). Whereas "fathers" are mentioned among those left behind, they are not to be included in the new kinship community which the disciples enter "already now in this time". Insofar as this new familial community has no "fathers" it implicitly rejects patriarchal socio-religious power and status. This ethos expresses what the young Luther would later call the "priesthood of all believers".

This discipleship community of equals was experienced as already present in the inclusive table-sharing, in the healing, making well and liberating practices of the disciples, and in their domination-free kinship affiliation. At least those segments of the Jesus movement which recruited their followers among the poor, the despised people of the land, the outcast and among women, the discipleship community of non-persons, must have attempted to realize this radical ethos of inclusiveness and equality, since we still find historical traces of it.

Rather than reproducing the kyriarchal status relationships of the "household" in antiquity, this ethos of the Jesus movements demands a radical break with them. The child/slave who occupied the lowest place within ancient kyriarchal structures becomes the primary paradigm for true discipleship. Such discipleship is not measured by the honour and respect given to the father/lord/master position but by that of the child/slave. This is stressed in the paradoxical Jesus saying: "Whoever does not receive the basileia of God like a child/slave shall not enter it" (Mark 10:15). This saying is not an invitation to childlike innocence and naiveté, but a challenge to relinquish all claims to the power of domination over others.

The actual political context of the Jesus movements' good news about God's different society and world was the Roman form of imperial domination. Whereas the *pax romana*, the "new world order" of imperial Rome, created opportunities for people in the cities of the empire, it intensified the colonial oppression of the rural population. The colonial situation of 1st-century rural Palestine was characterized by the tension between the urban ruling-elites aligned with the Roman occupation and the 90 percent of the rural population whom they exploited through heavy taxation. The Jesus traditions are best contextualized in a situation of colonial oppression that favoured the Herodian or Roman elites and exploited the bulk of the people.

In this socio-political colonial context the Jesus movements proclaimed a Jewish vision. It is the vision of the basileia, of God's alternative society and world that is free of domination and does not exclude anyone. Submerged fragments of the earliest traditions picture Jesus as standing in a long line of Sophia's prophets and witnesses who were drawing on the prophetic basileia traditions — as well as on the Wisdom traditions — with their elaboration of creation theology. As prophets of divine Wisdom, the Jesuanic discipleship of equals stood on the side of the exploited and poor population of Palestine, and indicted the elites. They sought the renewal and well-being of Israel as the people of God, as a commonwealth of priests and a holy nation, and criticized the high-priestly establishment that abused the temple as an "instrument of imperial legitimization and control of a subjected people". They announced the basileia, the reign of God, as an alternative vision to the imperial utopia of Rome. In distinction to democratic Greco-Roman kyriarchy, the Jesuanic basileia movement did not secure its identity by drawing exclusive boundaries but by welcoming all the people of God, even tax collectors and sinners, as children of the divine creator, Wisdom.

The term "basileia", usually translated as "kingdom" or "rule", belongs to a royal monarchical context of meaning that has as its socio-political referent the Roman empire. But basileia also is an ancestral symbol of second temple Judaism that appeals to the democratic traditions of ancient Israel. These traditions, which are located in the prophetic milieu of the north, assert a democratic counter-meaning to the royal meaning of the term. According to these northern traditions, Yahweh saved the children of Israel from Egypt (Joshua 24:7) and made a covenant with the people (e.g. Ex. 3:9-14) who are called "a basileia of priests and a holy nation" (Ex. 19:4-6). These traditions are critical of kingship and monarchy (cf. the Jotham fable in Judges 9:8-15). Because monarchy engenders militarism, economic exploitation and slavery, they regard it as a rejection of

God's commonweal (1 Sam. 8:1-22). Israel's great sin and wickedness consists in asking for a human king (1 Sam. 12:16-20). For in so doing, the people have rejected God who liberated and delivered them from "all the kingdoms that have oppressed" and "saved [them] from all their misery and distress" (1 Sam. 10:17-27; Hos. 8:4; 9:15). Kingly rule or kyriarchy is not a divine but a human institution.

However, the proclamation of the basileia of God alluded not only to a range of ancestral democratic religious traditions which proclaimed God's liberating power. It also functioned as an anti-imperial political symbol that appealed to the oppositional imagination of Jewish and other peoples victimized by the Roman imperial system. The gospel of the basileia envisioned an alternative world free of hunger, poverty and domination. The Jesuanic "discipleship of equals" promised God's basileia to the common people in the villages and small towns of Israel. This hope for the basileia sustained those who were impoverished, those who were hungry in the present time, and who groaned under oppressive conditions (Luke 6:20-21). It summoned the people in the local villages, the sinners, tax-collectors, debtors, beggars, prostitutes and all those who were exploited and marginalized, the lost "sheep" of the house of Israel (Matt. 15:24; 10:6). Its shalom, i.e. liberation and salvation, was present in the healing and liberating practices of the Jesus movement, in its inclusive table-sharing, as well as in the domination-free kinship relations among the disciples.

These traces of the discipleship of equals that surface as "dangerous memory" in a critical, radical, democratic reading of the Jesus traditions are also inscribed in the Pauline correspondence. Although they are articulated differently here, they still indicate that the ethos of the discipleship of equals was also at work in the ekklesia — the public assembly or congress of the Christ-movements in the Greco-Roman urban centres. The key symbols of their self-understanding were "soma" or body/corporation of Christ and ekklesia. Both terms evoke an emancipatory political symbolic universe and vision. The metaphor of the messianic body is not conceptualized in anthropological terms, but is best contextualized within the popular political discourses of antiquity that understood the polis or city state as a "body politic" in which all members were interdependent. The metaphor of the body describes "being in Christ" with the political language of the day.

For just as the corporation (soma) is one and has many members, and all the members of the corporation, though many, constitute one corporation, so it is with Christ. For by one Spirit we were all baptized into one corporation — Jews or Greeks, slaves or free (both women and men) — and all were made to drink of one Spirit (1 Cor. 12:12-13).

Equality in the Spirit

In the messianic body politic all have equal access to the gifts of the Spirit. This equality in the Spirit does not mean that all are the same. Rather, the gifts of the members vary and their individual functions are irreplaceable. Yet no one can claim to have a superior function, because all functions are necessary and must be equally honoured for the building up of the "corporation". Solidarity and collaboration are the "civic" virtues in the political order (*politeuma*) of Christ, which is best characterized as a pneumatic or charismatic democracy. "In

Christ", i.e. in the body politic, the messianic sphere of power, all socio-religious status inequalities are abolished, including those between priest and laity, between officials and ordinary members of the community, as well as between especially holy or religious people dedicated to the sacred and the common people who are immersed in profane matters of everyday life. Equally, social status distinctions and privileges between Jews and Gentiles, Greeks and barbarians, slave and free — both women and men — are no longer defining those who are "in Christ" (Gal. 3:28).

Those within the Christian, i.e. messianic, movements in Greco-Roman cities understood themselves as equally gifted and called to freedom. God's Spirit was poured out upon all, sons and daughters, old and young, slaves and free, both women and men (cf. Acts 2:17-18). Those who have been "baptized into Christ" live by the Spirit (Gal. 5:25). They are pneumatics, i.e. spirit-filled people (Gal. 6:1). They are a "new creation" (2 Cor. 5:17). Those who have entered into the "force-field" of the Resurrected One have been set free from "the law of sin and death" in order to share "in the glorious freedom of the children of God" (Rom. 8:21).

As siblings, they are all equal because they share in the Spirit as God's power for salvation. They are all called, elect and holy, adopted children of God. All without exception: Jews, pagans, slaves, free, poor, rich, both women and men, those with high status and those who are "nothing" in the eyes of the world. Their equality in the Spirit is expressed in alternating leadership and partnership, in equal access for everyone, Greeks, Jews, barbarians, slaves, free, rich, poor — both women and men. They, therefore, call their assembly with the democratic name ekklesia.

The full decision-making assembly of Christians who were exiles and resident aliens in their societies (1 Pet. 2:11) and constituted a different political order (*politeuma*) (Phil. 3:20), met in private houses. House-churches were crucial factors in the missionary movements insofar as they provided space, and actual leadership in the Spirit. As their name indicates, these house assemblies, however, did not take over the structures of the patriarchal household. Women played a decisive role in the founding, sustaining and shaping of such house ekklesiai. They could do so because the classic division between private and public spheres was transformed in the ekklesia that assembled in the "house". In the Christian ekklesia, the private space of the house is the public sphere of the ekklesia-church.

Christians were neither the first nor the only group who gathered together in house assemblies. Religious cults, voluntary associations, professional clubs, funeral societies, as well as the Jewish synagogue, gathered in private houses. These organizations did not adopt the structures of the patriarchal household, but utilized rules and offices of the democratic assembly, i.e. ekklesia, of the polis. Such assemblies were often socially stratified but conceded an equal share in the life of the association to all their members.

Just like other private associations, the Christian ekklesia was considered with suspicion and as potentially subversive to the dominant kyriarchal imperial order of Rome. Insofar as the Christians' association admitted individual converts as equals independently of their status in the kyriarchal household, membership in the Christian ekklesia often stood in tension with the structures of household and state.

Such hegemonic kyriarchal structures were legitimated in the 1st century, especially through neo-Platonic and Aristotelian political philosophy. These philosophical legitimizations found their way into Christian scriptures in the form of the so-called household code texts, which are kyriarchal injunctions to submission. Whereas, for example, 1 Corinthians 11:2-16 argues on scriptural grounds for women's subordination in terms of the neo-Platonic chain of the hierarchy of beings, the first epistle of Peter utilizes the neo-Aristotelian pattern of kyriarchal submission. The authors of 1 Peter admonish Christians who are servants to be submissive even to brutal masters (2:18-25) and instruct freeborn wives to subordinate themselves to their husbands, even to those who are not Christians (3:1-6). Simultaneously, they entreat all Christians to be subject to and to give honour to the emperor as well as to his governors (2:13-17).

The contradiction between Greco-Roman socio-political structures of domination and the radical democratic vision of the ekklesia as the "alternative discipleship community of equals" and God's "new [social] creation" engendered the need for such apologetic arguments, in the past and still today. The struggle of freeborn women and slaves (women and men) to maintain their authority and freedom in the Christian ekklesia, therefore, is to be seen as an integral part of the struggle between, on the one hand, the emerging Christian movement and its vision of equality and freedom, and on the other hand the kyriarchal ethos of the Greco-Roman world advocated by other Christians. As those with kyriarchal interests gained more power and influence, freeborn women's and slaves' (women and men) leadership in the ekklesia envisioned as a charismatic democracy was partially submerged again, transformed or pushed to the fringes of malestream churches.

In sum, like that of the basileia, the democratic construction of the Christian ekklesia constitutes a partial reality and provides an enduring vision. Such a radical democratic vision of the discipleship of equals is not simply a given fact nor just an ideal. Rather, it is an active process moving towards greater equality, freedom and responsibility, as well as towards communal relations free of domination. All women silenced and marginalized by kyriarchal hierarchic structures of domination are crucial in this ekklesial process of radical democratization that is inspired by the basileia-vision of a society and world free of exploitation, domination and evil.

These radical egalitarian currents of early Christian communities have never been eliminated completely. Liberation struggles in the 4th, 16th and 20th century cannot be understood if one does not take this radical democratic scriptural undercurrent into account. These biblical traces of the radical egalitarian vision of church and society have again and again spawned Christian movements of resistance, reformation and renewal in protest against the hierarchical form of church and the kyriarchal structures of society. In the past these reform movements have appealed to the traditions of freedom, equality and dignity of all the people of God which have shaped the socio-symbolic universes of biblical writings. They could do so — and still do so today — because scripture still allows us to glimpse the "dangerous memory" and vision of a movement and community of radical equality in the power of the Spirit. By using a reconstructive model that reads kyriocentric biblical texts in terms of the early Christian struggles and arguments about both the politics and rhetorics of "equality in the Spirit" and that of "kyriarchal submission", one can identify the cultural roots and effects generated by these early Christian debates and struggles.

This radical egalitarian spiritual vision inscribed in Christian scriptures is at once a new articulation and a reaffirmation of the red, brown and black roots of feminism. For it to become effective, feminist theology must learn from and be reshaped by the different democratic traditions of indigenous peoples around the world. In an article on the "Red Roots of White Feminism", Paula Gunn Allen, one of the foremost Native American literary critics in the USA, has argued that the roots for a radical democratic feminist vision cannot simply be derived from the democratic traditions of ancient Greece or modern America or France because the classic European form of democracy did not allow women and subjected men to participate in decision-making government. Rather, according to Gunn Allen, a feminist spiritual vision of radical democracy must be derived from tribal forms of government in the Americas, such as the Iroquois confederacy, in which the council of matrons was the ceremonial, executive and judicial centre. I quote Gunn Allen:

> The root of oppression is loss of memory. An odd thing occurs in the minds of Americans when Indian civilization is mentioned: little or nothing... How odd then must my contention seem that the gynocratic tribes of the American continent provided the basis for all the dreams of liberation that characterize the modern world... The vision that impels feminists to action was the vision of the grandmothers' society, the society that was captured in the words of the 16th-century explorer Peter Martyr nearly five hundred years ago. It is the same vision repeated over and over by radical thinkers of Europe and America... That vision... is of a country where there are "no soldiers, no gendarmes or police, no nobles, kings, regents, prefects, or judges, no prisons, no lawsuits... All are equal and free."[2]

To European eyes, Native Americans seemed gloriously free. Their willingness to share their goods, their respect for the earth and all living beings, their living in a classless society without personal property rights, all these attitudes led to the impression of a "humanity unrestrained". In contrast, Iroquois observers who travelled to France in the colonial period in turn expressed shock at the great gap between the life-styles of the wealthy and the poor and marvelled that the poor endured such injustice without rebellion.

I join Paula Gunn Allen in arguing that only the "indigenization" of classical notions of democracy and biblical understandings of ekklesia, a merging of the "grandmothers' society" with Western articulations of individual freedoms and equal rights, will result in a Christian vision and practice of radical egalitarianism that can fashion a global societal and religious vision of well-being for all without exception. A feminist theological re-visioning of the biblical past for creating a just society and future for the "global village" must consequently locate itself in such a radical oppositional democratic imagination. The radical democratic imagination of the grandmothers' society, which is still alive among many indigenous peoples today, challenges us to re-vision Christian community, spirituality and theology in such a way that they can contribute to the creation of a Spirit-centre for a radical democratic confederacy of global dimensions.

This radical democratic religious vision is feminist insofar as it continues to insist that equality, freedom and democracy cannot be realized if women's voices are not raised or not heard and heeded in the struggle for justice and liberation for everyone, regardless of sex, class, race, nationality or religion. If our diverse struggles for the radical democratic equality, dignity and well-being of all in society and church continue this feminist tradition of struggle, the discipleship of equals becomes an ever-expanding reality. Struggle is indeed a name for hope.

We are not the first ones to follow this radical democratic vision and to stand up and insist on our Christian birthright, and we are not alone in our struggle. A "great cloud of witnesses" surrounds us and has preceded us throughout the centuries in the discipleship of equals. Divine Wisdom has brought us to this time and place. She has accompanied us in times when we were tempted to give up the struggle in despair. She has sustained us in the face of repression, just as she has succoured the Israelites on their journey through the wilderness and desert:

> Divine Wisdom gave to holy people the reward of their labours; she guided them along a marvellous way, and became a shelter to them by day, and a starry flame through the night. When they were thirsty, they called upon you, and water was given them out of a flinty rock, and from hard stone a remedy for their thirst (Wis. 10:17).

The table of divine Wisdom provides spiritual food and drink in our struggles to transform the oppressive structures of church and society that shackle our spirits and stay our hands. This spiritual struggle for a different world and church of justice, equality and well-being does not turn us into idealistic dreamers, but gathers the ekklesia of women as a movement of those who in the power of Wisdom seek to realize the dream and vision of God's alternative community, society and world, of justice and well-being for everyone.

NOTES

1 "Religion as a Cultural System", in *Anthropological Approaches to the Study of Religion*, M. Banton ed., London, Tavistock, 1966, pp.1-46.
2 "Who Is Your Mother? Red Roots of White Feminism", in *Multicultural Literacy*, pp.18f

2. Vocation and Ministry

EUGENE L. BRAND

One of the most important contributions of Reformation theology was the rediscovery of the biblical concept of vocation (*voco* = call; *vocatus* = calling). It is usually referred to by the code-phrase "the priesthood of all believers". This rediscovery broke the back of mediaeval clericalism and called into question what was arguably the most important institution of the mediaeval church — monasticism. My judgment about breaking the back of clericalism may be questioned, for surely the churches of the Reformation have been plagued with clericalism of their own vintage. But in the Reformation and the post-Reformation periods, though the theological insights did not alter the church's practice sufficiently, they made some difference. More important, they were there waiting like time bombs (seeds) to explode (flower) upon Christian praxis at some future date.

Two mid-century books were benchmarks for the growing impact of the concept of vocation in Protestant circles: Hendrik Kraemer's Hulsean lectures, *A Theology of the Laity* (1958), and Gustav Wingren's *Luther on Vocation* (1942; English 1957). In Roman Catholic circles, the documents of the Second Vatican Council are affected by it in rather dramatic ways. Perhaps the most obvious example is *Lumen Gentium*, the Constitution on the Church (1964), which begins not as one may have expected with a chapter on the papacy of the clergy, but with chapters entitled "The Mystery of the Church" and "The People of God". The Faith and Order document *Baptism, Eucharist and Ministry* (1982) also begins its ministry section with a chapter on "The Calling of the Whole People of God". The impact on the Orthodox churches of the East is discernible,[1] but is only of secondary interest for purpose of the immediate discussion.

The concept of vocation or of priesthood, which I wish to sketch in the first part of this paper, has been responsible — at least in part — for the difficulties Lutherans have had with their concept of the ordained ministry of word and sacrament. And it is interesting to observe how similar difficulties have arisen in the Roman communion following its rediscovery of the concept. For at the same time as the "Western" churches have come to understand ministry in a comprehensive sense as a baptismal vocation, they have continued — at least in their better moments — to insist on the unique nature of the ministry of word and sacrament: the ordained ministry. The question thus becomes how to do justice both to a comprehensive concept of the ministry of the whole people of God *and* to a concept of the ordained ministry which regards it as the essential and central ministry of the church.

The tension between these two concepts of ministry has played a role in the debate about women in ministries. There has seldom been a question about women exercising vocational ministries other than that of word and sacrament. The one exception may be those teaching ministries or administrative ministries which would put women in authority over men. But even in those circles still adamantly opposed to the ordination of women, the question of women teaching mixed-sex classes is seldom heard and even less seldom does it influence actual practice.

Thus if we are successful at integrating the two concepts of ministry, we may have a persuasive argument not just for the ordination of women, but more importantly for removing the question of gender from the discussion of ministry altogether.

That provides the outline of this paper. I use the adjective "Lutheran" in the outline because this conference consists mostly of Lutherans discussing specifically theology and praxis in Lutheran churches. But I hope that this presentation has an ecumenical breadth and would not be contested seriously in other communions of the Western church.

The Lutheran concept of priestly ministry

The priestly concept derives from baptism and thus applies to all Christians. No baptized person may be exempted from inclusion in the priesthood of all believers. Such an inclusive concept of priesthood is unique among the religions, though priesthood is one of the most fundamental parts of the human society almost everywhere. Usually priests form a special caste which functions *within* a society and on its behalf. To extend the priesthood to include the entire group is, from the standpoint of religion in general, a revolutionary idea.

While Old Testament priests formed a special caste within the people of Israel and had access to taboo places, the OT also reveals a concept of the whole people as priestly in character (Ex. 19:6; Isa. 61:6). Thus in the OT we find both the expected traditionally religious view of priesthood, but also the germs of the New Testament concept.

It is often pointed out how seldom the word "priest" occurs in the NT. Already in the Septuagint, the Greek term *hieros* had been avoided wherever possible and less freighted terms had been substituted. Both Hellenistic Jews and early Christians were afraid of the sacred vocabulary of paganism.[2] In Jesus himself we find little use of priestly imagery. Instead he uses images from the common, workaday world. This NT reticence is remarkable in a world very conscious of priesthoods of various sorts and their authoritative position in society.[3] And never is "priest" used for those who later would be considered clergy: disciples, apostles, etc.

In its description of the post-Pentecost situation of the Christian community, the NT abandons a clerical or cultic concept of priesthood in favour of an ethical concept. The whole people is "a holy priesthood" whose vocation it is "to offer spiritual *(pneumatikas)* sacrifices *acceptable to God* through Jesus Christ" (1 Pet. 2:5). Or the people is a "royal priesthood" (1 Pet. 2:9). In Revelation, the term is used of individuals (1:6; 5:10; 20:6), but obviously as a group, not individualistically. To speak of the Christian community as a priesthood, as Peter does, is to extend the OT promise into the people of the new covenant. The absence in the nascent church of any cultic use of the terminology of priesthood, however, removes the ambivalence of OT usage. The major reason for that should be seen in the sacrificial death of Jesus once for all. After the supreme offering of the Great High Priest, no further cultic sacrifice was needed or expected.

It is to St Paul's writing that we turn to find out what acceptable spiritual sacrifices are. In Romans, following eleven chapters of theological development capped off with praise of the greatness of God, comes the resounding Pauline "therefore":

> I appeal to you... by the mercies of God, to present your bodies as a living sacrifice, holy and *acceptable to God* [cf. 1 Pet. 2:5], which is your spiritual [*logikén*] worship [*latreian*].

Romans 12:1 leads us into Paul's development of the ethical implications of the gospel he has articulated.

That the concept of sacrifice in Paul is not cultic is signalled by the adjective *living*. A living sacrifice is a contradiction in the terms of traditional religious discourse. But we need not depend only on one adjective. The remainder of chapter 12 speaks of forms of ministry or service, all of which have love as their chief motivation.

In the NT, therefore, we find a concept of service or ministry which is cast in terms of priesthood and sacrifice — terms which the whole biblical tradition transforms from the realm of cult to the realm of ethics.[4] This is not an arbitrary development, however. It has its focal point in Jesus. The NT sees Jesus as the culmination and crown of the OT sacrificial system. On the cross Jesus is both the victim and the priest: his is the perfect sacrifice. But there is more. In his teaching Jesus stands in the prophetic tradition of the OT which saw in a person's motivation the crux of religion. The prophets hold before the people the futility of religious observance as such. They are not against sacrifice. It is, after all, God's law. But to borrow Paul's language, sacrifice without love is empty and worthless. And the test of love, of course, is one's ethical behaviour.[5] One cannot, therefore, take refuge from love's demands of service in formalistic cultic observance. To use modern labels, for those who are in Christ ethics and liturgics must always be the two sides of one coin. In the early church the combination found expression in the intimate relationship between the offering of service (*diakonia*) and worship. The separation of eucharist from the agape meal weakened the liturgical expression of this linkage, but it continued to be expressed in the offertory of the mass. The bread of the eucharist was bread which had been offered for the relief of the poor. The deacon presided over the distribution of that bread and also selected a portion for purposes of the eucharist.[6] The diaconal ministry, then, becomes a sign of the relationship between liturgy and ethics (worship and service).

At this point we must not fall into the trap of divorcing the cross from the resurrection — the trap of a truncated view of Christ's sacrifice. Cross and resurrection belong together, as they are in Johannine theology. This means that, for purposes of our discussion, the *priestly* view of the Christian community and the cognate *sacrificial* view of Christian ministry bear the stamp of the future. They are eschatologically conditioned.[7] The job description of Christians reflects the life to come; it is a kingdom product. When we speak about priesthood and sacrifice, then, we are speaking the language of faith. We are applying the dynamics of the kingdom to our lives as we go on our pilgrimage towards it. Christians serve others, including those still "in the world", as people who have died to the world and are alive in Christ. We must be careful, therefore, not to apply casually the prevailing cultural concepts of human interaction and social responsibility to the church and its ministry. The possibility that God is teaching us something through external sources is always there. But what we learn from them must be scrutinized in the light of Christ, of faith, of the eschaton.[8]

Before leaving the NT writers, another concept of the Christian community must be registered. The first letter of Peter speaks not only of a holy or royal priesthood, but also of "God's own people" (RSV) or, more accurately, "a people for God's possession" (2:9). And in the following verse this people of God is contrasted with their previous condition as "no people". As before, we find a concept applied to Israel being transferred to the church. Since 1 Peter is a so-called *catholic* epistle, the contrast with "no people" does not refer to the Jewish people per se. The Greek word for people is *laos*, from which the term laity derives. In light of the transformation of meaning this word has undergone, it is important to observe that all Christians belong to the laity, that laity means the people of God. So just as all Christians are members of the priesthood, so all Christians are members of the laity.

The root of "clergy", *kléros*, also appears in the NT, even in 1 Peter. Basically it means "lot" or "portion", i.e. what one receives. While the meaning of *kléros* in 1 Peter 5:2 is still debated by scholars, most seem to agree that it means "the portion allotted to each individual elder", and that it is not used to imply that the elders possess something which other Christians lack.[9] In the NT, then, both *laos* and *kléros* denote the same people, not different people.

The common usage of the Greco-Roman city-state, however, gave these terms opposing meanings: *kléros* was the magistrate and *laos* was the people over whom the magistrates exercised authority. As the church developed clearer and more uniform structures in the centuries following the NT era, it was this concept which prevailed. There were, of course, theological developments which reinforced such change in usage.[10] The clergy came clearly identified out of the multitude of ministries reflected in the NT itself. That increasing uniformity should develop should not surprise us, and we should admit how unlikely the survival of the church would have been without it. But that the offices of bishop and presbyter (and deacon) should become a separate ruling class in the church is clearly in violation of NT teaching.

If this were a book instead of a paper, this would be the time to present an analysis of the development of a separate and superior clerical class in the church. Space and time limitation make that impossible. It is a very complex process about which there is still much to learn. Clearly it is the result both of cultural factors and theological development. Edward Schillebeeckx speaks of a "sacerdotalizing" of the ordained ministry in the period after the council of Nicea, and shows how in the second millennium of the Christian era the notion of church (i.e. community) fades into the background and privatization begins.[11] The result was that by the time of the Reformation the clergy were thought of as an authoritarian sacerdotal caste with only formal ties to a community. Their ordination was absolute (i.e. not tied to a community of believers) and conferred the power of consecration of the eucharist. Indeed, one could question whether the laity — those under the authority of the clergy and the sacramental system — thought of themselves as other than a collection of Christian folk in a given area who happened to perform their religious duty in the same building to which was assigned the requisite number of priests. The church was more a service centre than the house of a Christian fellowship.

The separation between clergy and laity was parallelled by a separation between sacred and profane spheres of existence. Not too much was expected of lay folk who had to engage in mundane work and marriage. The clerical church expected their obedience and participation — minimally — in the sacramental system. Little effort was expended to educate them at all beyond training them for needed skills, and this attitude also prevailed in Christian education. The only exceptions were those of noble birth and the emergent bourgeoisie.

Real Christians — those who lived according to the superior ethic of the gospel — were thought to be the clergy and especially monastics, both women and men. These were people unencumbered by marriage and other profane involvements who were free to involve themselves totally in the sacred sphere of life. If one were really serious about Christianity, one became a monastic and/or a priest. Christian vocation could only be spoken of in connection with such people's lives. In practice the line between the world and Christianity was no longer drawn at baptism, but rather at religious profession.

On the eve of the Reformation Europe was ripe for religious change. People had begun to question the power of the church both on theological and non-theological grounds.

Luther's concepts of vocation and the priesthood of all believers are argued against the prevailing mediaeval Catholicism. The development of Luther's thought is sketched by Wingren in the introduction of his book. Elsewhere Wingren defines Christian vocation broadly as *"everything* that brings me into relation with other people, everything that makes my action events in other people's lives is contained in 'vocation'."[12] The motor driving Luther's thinking is his doctrine of justification. Justification causes him to question the use to which sacraments are put — they have become tools for gaining merit — and to question the concept of ordained ministry which underlies such sacramental piety. In the NT Luther encounters the concept of the Christian life as service; that he sees to be the true exercise of priesthood.

> ... no one remembers that true Christian work is to serve one's neighbour, to counsel and aid even one's enemies and do good to them; instead they think it is to endow masses, build churches, eat neither milk nor meat, and as I have said, keep the pope's laws. So you see that Christ's priesthood has less chance of existing with the pope's pseudo-priesthood than death has with life or heaven with hell (Misuse of the Mass, 1521, *LW* [Luther's Works, American ed.] 36, 203. Cf. *WA* [Luther's Works, Weimar ed.] 8, 482-563).

This statement is not unlike prophetic critiques of worship in the scriptures.

Where Luther goes beyond our sketch of NT teaching is, however, in making *explicit* the *implicit* biblical connection between priestly service and baptism. Keeping within the metaphor of priesthood, he sees baptism as ordination:

> For a priest, especially in the NT, was not made but was born. He was created, not ordained. He was born not indeed of flesh but through a birth of the Spirit, by water and Spirit in the washing of regeneration... Indeed all Christians are priests, and all priests are Christians. Worthy of anathema is any assertion that a priest is anything else than a Christian. For such an assertion has no support

in the word of God and is based only on human opinions, on ancient usage, or on the opinions of the majority... (Concerning the Ministry, 1523, *LW* 40, 19. Cf. *WA* 12, 169-196).

The reasoning is clear. If all Christians constitute a priesthood (1 Pet. 2:5,9), and if God makes people Christian in baptism, then baptism is ordination to the priesthood. Surely Luther's conclusion is compatible with both Peter and Paul.

Two years earlier, Luther had spelled out the christological dimension of Christian priesthood:

> This is a spiritual priesthood held in common by all Christians, through which we are all priests with Christ (The Misuse of the Mass, *loc. cit.*, 138).

This point also lends depth to the connection between baptism and priesthood, since it is in baptism that God incorporates us into Christ's body, the church. But the immediate conclusion reveals a *flaw* in Luther's concept:

> Thus every Christian on his own may pray in Christ and have access to God... Thus every Christian is himself taught and instructed by God...
>
> Through these testimonies of the scriptures the outward priesthood in the New Testament is overthrown; for it makes prayer, access to God and teaching (all of which are fitting and proper to a priest) common to all men. Why does one need a priest, if one does not need a mediator and a preacher? (The Misuse of the Mass, *loc. cit.*, 139).

While Luther's militant tone against sacerdotal clericalism is understandable and excusable, and though his teaching was effective in breaking that hold, the view that "everyone is his or her own priest" contains "a germ of individualism, of egalitarianism, which does not sound wholly consonant with the biblical view of the 'royal priesthood' which belongs to the body of Christian believers as a whole".[13] This emphasis in the concept of priesthood of all believers has unleashed criticism from such theologians as T.F. Torrance, who views it as "unfortunate" because "it carries with it a ruinous individualism".[14] We have noted above the fundamentally corporate character of the NT concept. Fortunately it is possible to adopt the positive features of Luther's position without being obliged to take the individualistic thrust as part of the package. Perhaps the best safeguard against the individualist perversion is the baptismal fountain from which the priesthood concept flows. Were it not so firmly embedded in post-Reformation vocabulary, however, it *would* be clearer to speak either of "the priesthood of all *baptized* believers", or of "the priesthood of the whole church" (Kraemer).

The Reformation concept of priesthood also suggests a sacrificial concept of vocation. In the tradition, priesthood and sacrifice are cognates. Our sacrifice, says St Paul, is ourselves. That makes our priesthood total; it encompasses all of life and extends to every authentic aspect of creation. If our priesthood has its origin in the waters of baptism, then there is no occasion in our lives in which we are not an instrument of Christ's ministry.[15] At this point the contra-monastic character of Luther's concept is very clear. What he has done is to expand the ideals of monastic life to the life of every Christian. Put in the language of cross-bearing: one does not select one's cross by some sort of mortification as mediaeval monks were wont to do (as Luther himself had done), rather the cross is laid on the world, in the context of one's family and social relationships, job obligations, civic responsibilities, etc. It is there that I minister; it is there that authentic cross-bearing occurs; it is there that I live out daily baptismal death and resurrection. To quote Wingren:

> For the interpretation of the world and society as full of "crosses"... is part of his [Luther's] polemic against the *monastic life*... Luther combines... serving one's neighbour and bearing one's cross, and places this combined act in the *world*... But when all this is transferred to this earth, to the world, to purely secular working life, then it is transferred to the very place in which God creates life every day...
>
> The Christian goes about his workaday life surrounded on all sides by God's creation. Round him are his fellow-men whom, according to God's command, he shall serve. The worldly acts which provide my fellow-man his livelihood are acts of Christian love and at the same time they mould me in Christ's image, through death and resurrection to eternal life...[16]

As Atkinson points out, Luther's concept was not a mere changing of church discipline or social practice. Luther's concept of vocation and priestly ministry has roots deep in his theology of justification and thus in his teaching on baptism. That was his route to a view again compatible with primitive Christian conviction and practice.[17]

As Jürgen Moltmann puts it:

> The *vita Christiana*, the Christian life, no longer consists in fleeing the world and in spiritual resignation from it, but is engaged in an attack upon the world and a calling in the world.[18]

But the contextual concept of ministry still holds, even if that context is an assembly line — a job selected with relative freedom.

The LWF 1983 statement, "The Lutheran Understanding of Ministry", attempts to describe the ministries of the baptismal priesthood as follows:

> 13. Ministry is the function of the whole people of God because the foundation of the church's ministry is in the ministry of Christ made present to us in the gospel and the sacraments. Christian ministry cannot be the privilege of a special group or class within the church (priesthood of all believers). To speak of ministry, however, is to use an abstraction. The ministry of the people of God becomes real in particular *ministries* performed either corporately or individually.
>
> 14. From the concept of the priesthood of all believers it follows that individual ministries are determined by the context of one's life — family, job and civic relationships — and by the manifold gifts of the Holy Spirit. An individual will be involved, therefore, in several ministries simultaneously... Each provides the opportunity to minister by one's style of life, concern for others, attitude of service, dedication to justice and equality, and one's explicit gospel witness (cf. *BEM*, 5).
>
> 15. The ministries of most Christians are carried out primarily outside the life and activity of the institutional church. Thus they constitute the front-line of the church's ministry to the world. The most effective ministry of witness occurs most often in the context of personal relationships which frequently provide the initial contact with the community of faith. One reason why no

Christian may delegate his or her ministry to someone else is that no one else stands in precisely the same context of relationships.

16. The corporate life of the people of God is another context for ministries... In some places these ministries are part-time and occasional, in others they are full-time and become part of the regular life of the institutional church, often requiring periods of specialized training.

17. Whether institutional, whether exercised within the Christian community, or whether exercised in the world, all Christian ministries are concrete instances of that one ministry to which God has called the whole church.[19]

The Lutheran concept of pastoral ministry

The Lutheran concept of priestly ministry logically suggests a functional understanding of pastoral ministry. If the church's ministry is seen to involve the whole people so that all participate as priests, and if it is the vocational context which makes one's priestly ministry specific, then pastors would be Christian priests whose vocational context is ordained ministry. In other words, ordained ministry differs from other ministries only in function. Luther lends support to such a view in his polemics:

> It follows from this argument that all are consecrated priests through baptism, that there is no true, basic difference between laymen and priests, princes and bishops, between religious and secular, except for the sake of office and work *(den des ampts odder wercks halben)*, but not for the sake of status. They are all of the spiritual estate, all are truly priests, bishops and popes. But they do not all have the same work to do (To the Christian Nobility of the German Nation, 1520, *LW* 44, 129. Cf. *WA* 6, 497-573).

This view was criticized by the humanist reformer Hieronymus Emser (1478-1527) in his *Quadruplica* (1521). Emser held that the NT, especially 1 Peter 2:9, refers to two kinds of priesthood: the spiritual priesthood common to all Christians and the "outward" priesthood, i.e. the ordained priesthood.[20] Luther replied by reiterating his view of baptismal priesthood and by describing ordination as the way some priests "become the others' priests' workmen, servants and officers..." He accuses cannon law of perverting the clear teaching of scripture in making of the clergy a "spiritual estate", i.e. superior to the estate of the laity.[21] Though the language of the treatise against Emser is sarcastic in the extreme, Luther is nuancing his polemic. He still objects to a clerical class and insists that all baptized priests share the same status. But he makes place for an ordained ministry as a special servanthood. And he sees the call to that ministry as crucial.

> [You, Emser,] lie that I have made all laymen to be bishops and priests and spiritual in such a way that they may at once without a proper call perform the functions of the office. Pious as you are, you suppress my accompanying words, that no one shall undertake what he has no call to do except in case of extreme need (Dr Martin Luther's answer..., *loc. cit.*, p. 345).

What distinguishes pastors from other Christians is that they occupy a specific office *(Amt)*, namely "to preach the word of God and administer the sacraments".[22] People already priests by virtue of their baptism are called to this pastoral office by the church.

The question then becomes, What is the origin of this pastoral office? Given the functional thrust of the concept of priesthood, one might expect the answer to be rather pragmatic. The office is established by the congregation in order that for the sake of good order the ministerial obligation of all can be transferred to the one called as pastor. This line of thinking is not unknown in Lutheran circles, but it is not the line taken by Luther or the confessions. It is the confessions, of course, and not the writings of Luther which together with the Bible and the ecumenical creeds form the doctrinal basis for the Lutheran churches.

But before moving to the substance of the confessions we should remind ourselves of the *polemical* thrust of the writings of Luther which have been quoted. He was determined to break the clericalism of his day and his chief weapon was the biblical concept of baptismal priesthood. Later, in conflict with the Enthusiasts, he placed great stress upon *the call*. But he was not out to destroy or even diminish the pastoral office. Quite the contrary. And as Wilhelm Brunotte has demonstrated, Luther's concept of pastoral ministry shows an inner consistency in basic themes throughout his career.[23] The other, non-polemical face of the Lutheran Reformation was its desire to remain in the church, albeit in a form purified by the gospel. Indeed the Augsburg confession was written to demonstrate their evangelical catholicism.

The Augsburg confession (CA), the principal Lutheran confession, ties the proclamation of the word of God and the pastoral ministry together. CA 4 deals with justifying faith; CA 5 says that the pastoral ministry was instituted so that such faith may be obtained and then seems to equate ministry with the gospel and the sacraments. It is instructive to note that the pastoral ministry precedes the article on the church (CA 7), hardly allowing that ministry to be derived from the church. It is also instructive to note that the Confutation did not contest CA 5. There is, thus, no corresponding article in the Apology. One should, however, note Apology 13,11-13, which deals with ordination, affirming the stance of CA 5. Both the pastoral ministry and the church have a common origin in the apostles (cf. CA 28).[24]

In CA 5 we get a forthright answer to the question about the origin of the pastoral office: "To obtain such justifying faith God instituted the office of the ministry — *solchen Glauben zu erlangen, hat Gott das Predigtamt eingesetzt.*" The tradition is thus affirmed that the pastoral or ordained ministry has its origin in Christ or in God. Since they were eye-witnesses, the office of apostle could not be passed on as such, but the calling and sending of the apostles by Jesus has been seen by the church as the origin of the office of the ministry.[25] Luther takes a similar forthright view:

> God wants to work through tolerable, kind and pleasant means, which we ourselves could not have chosen better. He has, for instance, a godly and kind man speak to us, preach, lay his hands on us, remit sin, baptize, give us bread and wine to eat and drink... God commanded it, ordered it, instituted it and ordained it; he himself is present and will do everything himself (On the Councils and the Church, 1539, *LW* 41, 171. Cf. *WA* 50, 509-653).[26]

Not only is Luther affirming the divine origin of the pastoral ministry, he is also expressing the concept that the pastors perform their ministry of word and sacrament as instruments of Christ (at least akin to the Roman Catholic concept of *in persona Christi*).

It would be impossible to develop this section on the Lutheran concept of pastoral ministry further. That seems unnecessary because the Lutheran concept is basically an affirmation of the traditional concept. It is not, as is true of what we have called the priestly concept, a discovery or rediscovery of the Reformation. It was a matter of dispute only with the Enthusiasts. A further development might point out that the Lutheran insistence on God's working through means or through the external word requires that those who proclaim that word have their office from God and not from the church. It is the church which calls people into the office, but in no sense does the church establish the office. Otherwise the word could be taken captive by the church.

Problem of ministries in the church

The proper balance

The difficulty for Lutherans in arriving at a satisfactory understanding of ministry has lain in finding the proper balance between the "priestly" and "pastoral" aspects. High church Lutherans and those of authoritarian bent have emphasized the pastoral or office line. Pietistic Lutherans and contemporary egalitarians have emphasized the priestly or functional line. And the picture has become more complicated still by the fairly recent but profoundly biblical emphasis of the ministry of the whole people of God.

On the basis of the foregoing discussion, let me try to sort this out in a set of thetical statements which, I believe, reflect the Lutheran understanding and the growing ecumenical consensus:
1. Ministry means carrying forward the work of Christ in the world.
2. Ministry thus comprises proclamation (*martyria*) and loving service (*diakonia*) and, for the church, worship (*leiturgia*).
3. The ministry of the church is the priestly service of the whole people of God to which they are called by the gospel and "ordained" in holy baptism.
4. Since baptism initiates people into an eschatological community, the ethics and standards of the priestly ministry are those not of the "world" but of the kingdom.
5. The ministry of the church is, in practice, carried out in a variety of ministries, some formal and institutional but most informal and more spontaneous.
6. Work performed for the welfare of the human community is included in one's ministry; no distinction is possible for the Christian between ministry and a "secular occupation". Such secular work often partakes of the nature of *diakonia*.
7. Personal ministries of proclamation/witness and service are largely determined by the context of one's life; they are vocational and societally determined.
8. One vocation in the church is unique and necessary to its own life, growth and well being: the pastoral ministry of word and sacrament.
9. This ministry is related to that of the apostles and has its origins in Christ's command. Thus the pastoral ministry is of divine origin.

10. The church has the duty to maintain the pastoral office and to call qualified people into it. But it does not thereby become the church's office. It remains an office of the word which is sovereign over the church.
11. The context of certain Christians' ministry, therefore, is the pastoral office. Ordination does not give them superior status; they retain their baptismal status as priests. But ordination gives them a specific vocation: the ministry of the word and sacraments. To them is entrusted the public or external ministry of the church, and they become symbols of the whole church in that sense.
12. But sovereignty remains with God's word; it does not devolve upon the pastor or the office. The pastoral ministry exists to serve the church by serving the gospel.
13. As servants of the gospel, pastors have a ministry of leadership in the congregations. They serve having the authority of the word, but that authority is always subject to testing by the whole church, which shares responsibility for the authenticity of its public proclamation.

If I have succeeded balancing the two aspects properly, then the traditional concept of pastoral ministry is prevented by the Reformation concept of priestly ministry from becoming autonomously authoritarian and/or a sacerdotal caste within the church. On the other hand, the concept of priestly ministry is protected by pastoral ministry from becoming mere egalitarianism on the model of current concepts of democracy and equal rights.[27]

Women in the ordained ministry

That I turn only at the end of my paper to the theme "women in the ministries of the church" is not to suggest that it is an addendum. It is rather because of my conviction, which I hope you share, that one begins with the concept of ministry, not with the status of women in the church. Whatever the particular ministry being considered, it should be the same ministry whether performed by a woman or a man.[28] Even to assume that some diaconal ministries, for example, are best filled by women because women are more tender and caring — to stereotype talents according to gender — has proved a highly dubious procedure. Some ministries do require persons with specific talents or gifts, but these may be found both in certain women and in certain men.

The question is: On the basis of our investigation, are any ministries of the church closed to women? Canonically, of course, the answer is yes — at least in some LWF member churches. In others, it is only recently that codes of polity have been changed to include women. Ultra-conservative Lutherans will not even allow women to serve in unordained ministries if such service puts them in authority over men. In some churches prohibitions against women are determined by custom rather than by church polity.[29] In general, however, it can be said that Lutherans accept women in the ordained ministry.

The Lutheran concept of baptismal priesthood means that the life of every baptized believer is or should be a ministry. Baptism births a community of priests who are both women and men. The concept of priestly ministry brooks no sexual discrimination in the ministries of the church. Furthermore, since ministries are instances of the one ministry of Christ which is the responsibility of the whole church, and since women and men are equally members of the church by virtue of baptism, a very strong case indeed would be required to prevent women from any ministry. Gifts and talents or their lack may disqualify someone from a particular ministry — not every member of Christ's body has the same function — but not gender.

Women have always, of course, exercised their priestly ministries in the context of their personal lives — in their jobs, in their familial roles, in their community and social responsibilities, etc. And lately most barriers to other ministries have fallen where a generation ago women would seldom have been found: e.g. serving on church councils both local and supra-local, assisting in the leadership of corporate worship as lectors or ministers of communion or acolytes or ushers. Furthermore, women are found teaching at all levels of church life — not just small children, but classes which include adult men.

The problem of women in the priestly ministries, by and large, seems to be that of more equal sharing with men, and not whether or not women may serve. Church councils and other governing groups often have only token female representation. Member churches still tend to send men to international meetings. Much consciousness-raising and advocacy work must still be done, therefore, and I do not mean to suggest that the struggle is over. What is possible in theory may still be most difficult in practice.

It is the question of women in the pastoral or ordained ministry, however, which still proves intractable throughout the majority of the Christian world and even in some member churches of the LWF. Because the pastoral office in all Lutheran churches was, until recently, occupied by men only, the question is often put, May women be ordained? In other words, may women occupy the pastoral office? But I hope to have demonstrated that that form of the question is out of order for Christians. The question must rather be, Is there any reason why women may *not* be ordained? In other words, that they may *not* occupy the pastoral office? On the basis of the participation in the baptismal priesthood, the assumption should be that, of course, the pastoral ministry is open to women just as it is to men.[30]

The objections to women as pastors may be primarily cultural. The pastoral ministry is a ministry of leadership, and women as leaders may be, or seem to be, impossible in some societies. Cultural or social strictures on such a role for women are apparent in the NT itself. On the one hand, the church cannot and should not divorce itself from its social context totally. It may be that, for a time, cultural considerations prohibit the ordination of women, and to act otherwise would seriously impair the witness of the church in that place and that time. But if that is the case, the Christian community itself should be clear on the reasons and not pretend there are *theological* problems. On the other hand, the church is the sign of the kingdom in every cultural context, and must witness to the equality of women and men. To be such a sign, the church may have to ordain women before the time when women leaders are generally tolerated elsewhere. All too often, the churches have followed rather than led. Determining what stance the credibility of the church's witness requires is an arduous task and one which must not be pre-empted by people or agencies outside the cultural context.

The objections most often heard are based on the biblical record itself where women are seen as subordinate to men according to the order of creation and, therefore, where women are admonished to keep silent in the assembled congregation.[31] It is obvious — especially to Lutherans who connect closely the pastoral office with the proclamation of the gospel — that a pastor cannot be silent in the assembly. The scriptures themselves, therefore, are seen to prohibit women from ordination both because they must not be leaders of congregations and because they cannot proclaim.

Some have pushed the former point to the degree that they were prepared to ordain women so long as they served only in such all-women contexts as women's prisons. Such persons have not begun to understand the communion character of the church!

This is not the place to involve ourselves in careful exegesis of the biblical text in question. It is the place to say, however, that all passages in the scriptures which subordinate women to men or which silence women in the assembled church are culturally conditioned and are not part of the gospel itself. To judge otherwise is not to recognize the eschatological nature of baptism and the Christian community it births.

St Paul is crystal clear about the Christian priesthood: "There is neither Jew nor Greek, there is neither slave nor free, there is neither male nor female; for you are all one in Christ Jesus" (Gal. 3:28). The statement is the more powerful because it is the conclusion to Paul's discussion of faith and baptism: "for in Christ Jesus you are all sons [KJV, interestingly, translates 'children' as does Luther] of God, through faith. For as many of you as were baptized into Christ have put on Christ" (Gal. 3:26-27). In other words, in the church the distinctions among persons which the world regards as important no longer apply, any more than they do in God's kingdom. In the face of this pronouncement which, incidentally, comes out of the heart of the Pauline corpus and is totally consistent with Paul's theology of baptism and of the church, we can only interpret the other passages regarding women as being culturally conditioned. It also explains how women *could* function in seemingly forbidden ways in the NT church (e.g. Acts 21:9; Romans 16:1; the roles of Lydia, Priscilla and Thecla). Furthermore, we must regard the orders-of-creation picture of female subordination the same way. It is, of course, true that Paul (Eph. 5:21ff.) upholds the subordination of women in marriage on the analogy of the relationship of Christ (the head) and the church (the body). Whether he means to generalize such subordination for all male-female relationships could be debated. But even if subordination be granted in marriage, that says nothing about it in the church. Marriage belongs to this world, even when the couple are baptized; the church belongs to the kingdom of God where another set of norms applies. Any biblical support for withholding ordination from women evaporates in the glare of the light from God's future. This eschatological argument is dominant in the 1993 LWF statement on the ordained ministry.[32]

Another argument found more often outside Lutheran circles focusses on the representational aspect of the pastoral ministry. Though Lutherans have questioned Roman Catholic expositions of the idea that the pastor acts *in persona Christi* (or *alter Christus*), especially in presiding at the eucharist, the concept is there also in our own tradition.[33] Women may not be ordained, the argument states, because Jesus was a man. No woman can function as the sign of a man. Yes, Jesus was a man, but that is hardly the point of the incarnation. St John says, "the Word became *sarx* (flesh)...", not "the divine Logos became male"

(1:14). It is the *humanity* of Christ, not the *maleness* of Jesus, which is important.[34] Furthermore, post-Pentecost, it is of great theological significance that the concept under discussion is *alter **Christus***, not *alter **Jesus***. Presiding at the church's eucharist is not playing the role of Jesus in the upper room scene of a passion play. In the church's eucharist, the body of *Christ* receives the body of *Christ*. This Christ whose body we are and whose body we receive is the exalted Lord of heaven and earth. Christ cannot simply be equated with the male person Jesus of Nazareth. Also to the point is the eschatological reality of the eucharist.

Taking all that into account, it would follow that any baptized person may be ordained and, as pastor in a community of believers, may act *in persona Christi* in that community's worship.[35] One should also remember that the intimate linkage between ordination and eucharistic presidency which has played such a prominent role in Roman ordination theology since Lateran IV (1215) is now revealed as a second millennium development in the Western Church.[36]

My conclusion must be that nothing theological prevents women from occupying either priestly or pastoral ministries in the church of Christ. Furthermore, where cultural factors prevent it, the church must ask in what manner the clear witness of the kingdom regarding gender may be borne. While the cultural problem must be addressed with the seriousness our incarnational theology requires, it must not merely be acquiesced in, for it mutes an aspect of the church's witness as eschatological sign in human society.

Indeed our whole view of ministry in the church would be enhanced if we shifted our focus from the *persons* of ministers (in terms of gender, race and social class) to the needs of the church in its mission in our world. It may well be that traditional structures of ministry, if they can be opened to all Christians, may provide the best answer. At least they should not be cast aside brashly. At no point in its history is the church *tabula rasa*. Still it is the needs which call forth the ministries, and the only question should be whether a candidate has the requisite talents, skills and spiritual maturity. Above all, de facto leaders of Christian communities should be ordained so that their ministry may be complete and may be recognized by the whole church. As Schillebeeckx notes, if there seems to be a chronic shortage of ordained ministers somewhere, something is wrong and standards must be changed. Standards which are not "intrinsically necessary" must give way to "the original, NT right of the community to leaders". In that case this apostolic right has priority over the church order which has in fact grown up which in other circumstances may have been useful and healthy.[37]

NOTES

1 E.g. Alexander Schmemann, *The World as Sacrament*, London, 1966, pp.115ff.

2 Cf. Gottlob Schrenk, "hieros..." ThDNT 3, Grand Rapids, 1965, p.229.

3 *Hierus* and its cognates occur only 33 times in the entire NT; 19 references are to the OT priesthood. Jesus is called priest eight times. The remaining five applications are to the Christian community.

4 A.G. Herbert demonstrates the importance of the theme of sacrifice in the Pauline corpus as embracing liturgy and life: "A Root of Difference and of Unity", *Intercommunion*, Baille

and Marsh, eds, London, 1952, 241. Cf. Konrad Weiss, "Paulus — Priester der christlichen Kultgemeinde", *ThLZ*, 79, 1954, pp.358f.

5 One can even see in the prophetic tradition the germinal idea that righteous behaviour can stand as sacrifice. Romans 12:1, thus, is a culmination of that trend. Cf. Hans-Jürgen Hermission, *Sprache und Ritus im altisraelitischen Kult*, Neukirchen, 1965, pp.118f.

6 See G.W.H. Lampe, "Diakonia in the Early Church", *Service in Christ*, McCord and Parker, eds, London, 1966, pp.49-61. On the offertory see Gregory Dix, "The Idea of the 'Church' in the Primitive Liturgies", *The Parish Communion*, Herbert, ed., London, 1937, pp.113f. On the Agape and its gradual disappearance see Bo Reicke, "Diakonie, Festfreude und Zelos in Verbindung mit der Altchristlichen Agapenfeier", *Uppsala Universitets Arsskrift*, Uppsala/Wiesbaden, 1951.

7 "The horizon of expectation within which a Christian doctrine of conduct must be developed is the eschatological horizon of expectation of the kingdom of God." Jürgen Moltmann, *Theology of Hope*, New York, 1967, p.334.

8 On the eschatological implications of Romans 12:1, see Ernst Käsemann, "Paulus und der Frühkatholizismus", *Exegetische Versuche und Besinnungen 2*, Göttingen, 1964, pp.200ff. English: *New Testament Questions Today*, Philadelphia and London, 1969, pp.236-51.

9 Werner Foerster, ThDNT 3, Grand Rapids, 1965, p.764. Cf. Hendrik Kraemer, *A Theology of the Laity*, London, 1958, p.52.

10 Kraemer, *op. cit.*, p.51. Cf. Edward Schillebeeckx, *Ministry, a Case for Change*, London, 1981, p.71.

11 Schillebeeckx, *op. cit.*, pp.48ff.,52ff. Cf. another recent work on ministry, the massive study by Bernard Cooke, *Ministry to Word and Sacraments*, Philadelphia, 1977. However, it must be read with discernment.

12 Gustav Wingren, "The Concept of Vocation — Its Basis and Its Problems", *Lutheran World*, 15, 1968, p.94.

13 Kraemer, *op. cit.*, p.62.

14 T.F. Torrance, *Royal Priesthood*, Edinburgh, 1955, p.35 n.1.

15 Cf. Robert A. Brungs, *A Priestly People*, New York, 1968, pp.150ff.

16 Wingren, "The Concept of Vocation", pp.89f.

17 *Lutheran World*, 15, 1968, p. 81.

18 Moltmann, *op. cit.*, p.331.

19 M.W.B., pp.41f.

20 Cf. Luther, *Misuse of the Mass, loc. cit.*, 141.

21 *Dr Martin Luther's Answer to the Superchristian, Superspiritual, and Superlearned Book of Goat Emser of Leipzig*, 1521, Luther's Works, Philadelphia ed., 3, 326.

22 Misuse of the Mass, *loc. cit.*, 159. For a complete systematic treatment of Luther's concept of pastoral ministry, see W. Brunotte, *Das Geistliche Amt bei Luther*, Berlin, 1959.

23 Brunotte, *op. cit.*, pp.112ff.

24 Cf. E.W. Gritsch and R.W. Jenson, *Lutheranism*, Philadelphia, 1976, pp.110ff.,116ff.

25 See Leonard Goppelt, "The Ministry in the Lutheran Confession and in the NT", *Lutheran World*, 1964, p.418 and, especially, pp.421ff. Cf. Arnold Hultgren, "Forms of Ministry in the NT — and Reflections Thereon", *Dialog*, 18, 1979, p.209, n.6. The recent *Baptism, Eucharist and Ministry* espouses this view: "As Christ chose and sent the apostles, Christ continues to choose and call persons into the ordained ministry..." (Part 3).

26 For further documentation on Luther, see Brunotte, *op. cit.*, pp.118ff.

27 Perhaps today the judgment of Hendrik Kraemer applies beyond the USA: "Since the 19th century American Christianity has been by far the most lay-centred form of Christianity in the world. This has, however, pragmatic reasons, not theological..." *Op. cit.*, p.36.

28 Another observation is pertinent: "... with both men and women functioning in full sacramental fashion, we will have a fuller and more balanced reflection of the church's faith, and therefore an integral expression of the community's sacramental existence... by opening up the possibilities of men and women interacting creatively at every level of the church's existence, the ordaining of women to full sacramental ministry will help humanity realize its revealing role as the image of God." Cooke, *op. cit.*, pp.655-56.

29 See para. 18 in the ministry section of *Baptism, Eucharist and Ministry*
30 Cf. Cooke, *op. cit.*, p.654: "From a theological point of view [whether women may be ordained] is really a non-question. There is no apparent reason why the ability and right of women to function in this manner should even be questioned... The positive arguments for women's sharing in ministry are, really, the arguments for any Christian participating in ministry."
31 Luther himself argued this way. See Brunotte, *op. cit.,* pp.193ff. Brunotte summarizes Luther's views as follows: "Die Frau verfügt Kraft des allgemeinen Priestertums über die Fähigkeit, das Wort Gottes in jeder möglichen Form zu verkündigen und bringt damit die notwendige geistliche Qualitas für das geistliche Amt mit. Ins geistliche Amt darf sie aber wegen der Gen. 3,16 niedergelegten göttlichen Ordnung dort nicht berufen werden, wo Männer zur christlichen Gemeinde gehören. Die göttliche Ordnung wird bestätigt durch die Erfahrung, dass eine Frau in jener Zeit nicht fähig war, ein öffentliches Amt zu bekleiden. In Gemeinden, die allein aus Frauen zusammengesetzt sind, kann sie dagegen zur Ausübung des geistlichen Amtes berufen werden; wobei zu beachten ist, dass Luther den Auftrag zur Predigt und den Auftrag zur Spendung der Sakramente nicht auseinanderreisst" (p.199).
32 *LWF Studies*, "Ministry. Women. Bishops", 1993.
33 *Presbyterorum Ordinis*, 1965, from Vatican II, states it thus: "12. By the sacrament of order priests are configured to Christ the priest as servants of the Head... They are consecrated to God in a new way in their ordination and are made the living instruments of Christ the eternal priest, and so are enabled to accomplish throughout all time that wonderful work of his which with supernatural efficacy restored the whole human race. Since every priest in his own way assumes the person of Christ he is endowed with a special grace... 13... Priests as ministers of the sacred ministries, especially in the sacrifice of the mass, act in a special way in the person of Christ who gave himself as a victim to sanctify men..." (English text from Flannery, pp.885,887).
34 "... if to call Christ humanity is to call him by too abstract a term, to limit him to an individual is equally to fail to do justice to the facts. For his individuality is somehow inclusive: he is representative man; he includes mankind and in fact fulfills the destiny of man." C.F.D. Moule, *The Sacrifice of Christ*, London, 1956, p.38.
35 In view of the weight placed on this argument in the so-called historic churches, one would expect to find evidence of it in classic ordination prayers. A perusal of them yields no instance. The imagery is rather of Levitical priesthood. Cf. H.B. Porter, Jr, *The Ordination Prayers of the Ancient Western Churches*, London, 1967; cf. Schillebeeckx, *op. cit.*, pp.48ff. In the present Roman rite for the ordination of priests (1972), there is also no instance. If the form of address were changed, the rite could be used with women. The one exception might be the portion of the prayer of consecration which connects with the OT priesthood. But that alone is not a convincing negative point.
36 Schillebeeckx, *op. cit.*, II, esp. pp.54ff.
37 *Ibid.*, p.37.

3. In Search of a Round Table

CHRISTINE GRUMM

The first step is to get through the door and find a place at the table. We have begun with the election and appointment of women for church governance and staffing, the ordination of women in many of our member churches, the election of women bishops, and the appearance on churches' agendas of issues relating to women. As we look towards the future, it is no longer enough that we have a place at the table: now we need to be involved in actually reshaping that table to accommodate our presence. Recently, I discovered a poem that speaks directly to this very issue. With this poem as a guide, let us begin our search for the perfectly shaped table from which to carry out God's mission and ministry in the world.

In search of a roundtable

Concerning the why and how and what and
who of ministry,
One image keeps surfacing:
A table that is round.
It will take some sawing
to be roundtabled,
some redefining, some redesigning.
Some redoing and rebirthing
of narrowlong churching
can painful be for people and tables.
It would mean no daising and throning,
for but one king is there,
and he was a footwasher, at table no less.
And what of narrowlong ministers
when they confront a roundtable people,
after years of working up the table
to finally sit at its head, only to discover
that the table has been turned round?
They must be loved into roundness,
for God has called a people,
not "them and us".
"Them and us" are unable to gather round
for at a roundtable, there are no sides,
and all are invited
to wholeness and to food.
At one time
our narrowlong churches
were built to resemble the cross
but it does no good
for buildings to do so,

if lives do not.
Roundtabling means no preferred seating,
no first and last, no better and no corners
for the "least of these".
Roundtabling means
being with, a part of
together, and one.
It means room for the Spirit
and gifts
and disturbing profound peace for all.
We can no longer prepare for the past.
We will and must and are called
to be church,
and if [God] calls for other than
roundtable
we are bound to follow.
Leaving the sawdust
and chips, designs and redesigns behind
in search of and in the presence of the
[kingdom]
that is [God's] and not ours.
Amen.

Chuck Lathrop

A round table is certainly a fitting image for us to use as our symbol. It is an image that may assist us in describing to our brothers and sisters in the church some of the changes we believe are necessary in order to be truly an open and inviting community. However, before we start redesigning the table we must begin with a concept or a picture. And that conceptualization should be articulated to reflect better the kind of space that is needed to accommodate the whole community.

Why redefining, redesigning, redoing and rebirthing?

One of the key understandings about being an inclusive community is that when marginalized people join, the community will begin to look different. A sure sign that women's participation is only tolerated rather than welcomed is when some women are scattered throughout an organization, but the organization continues to act and function just as it always has done. In her presentation to the International Consultation of Women in Mexico City in 1989, the late director for the LWF Department of Studies, Erika Reichle, had this to say:

As far as LWF staff in Geneva are concerned, it will not suffice to have the correct percentage of women in charge of projects and in leading positions; rather it will be much more important that such women be given sufficient scope and time to be able to develop their own style and truly contribute new points of view to the whole of the LWF's tasks. It is still a daily experience of many women not to be listened to, to be ignored where power is involved, unless they are prepared to give up their identity and to accept that their gifts are used as instruments for the interest of others. Thus, women either stop trying to be heard, or they adjust, or they look for another arena. It will be illusory to think that real progress can be made within the LWF until the number of women in important positions is considerably higher. Dear sisters, let us encourage women to take up positions in Geneva in various bodies of the LWF. And let us make sure that they will not have to fight their battles single-handedly.[1]

Erika's words still speak to us today, not only in regard to the LWF secretariat but to all our churches. For if we are not attentive to the situation in our own settings, we may find, instead of women changing structures, structures changing women. Leadership styles are frequently modelled only on those who are already inside. The gifts that women or other marginalized groups bring to the table are often neither acknowledged nor fully utilized.

There is a classic example of how structures can change women. Fifteen to twenty years ago in the USA, when women were moving into the business world in large numbers, the business clothes worn by women were modelled on men's business suits. Women were told to wear only blue or black, certainly nothing bright and with flowers or "feminine". It was almost as if women feared being discovered in a place of business. If they dressed the same as men, then maybe they could continue to work undetected, as if they otherwise did not belong. One sometimes hears the complaint about a female boss that "she is worse than a man". One has to dig a little deeper to understand what impact an institution has had on such a woman and her particular style of leadership.

In order for women to survive, their individual styles often have to be discarded or else are rejected once women have become part of an institution. In other words, the table remains in its original form, regardless of who is present. While the shape of the table was of use to the previous group, it has limited use for the new constituency and in reality still belongs to the people historically in power. Just in case we think this is a problem faced only by women, we need to remember that many who have been selectively invited to the table, in order to make it appear more representative, find themselves in hostile territory. So, while the table is expanded to mirror better the community, the shape of the table, unfortunately, no longer reflects the experience of those seated around it. And at some point no one around the table feels comfortable any more, because for those who are new "the shoe does not fit" and those who have always been there live in the uncomfortable recognition that "things are just not what they use to be". So everyone is angry, dissatisfied, and unable to break the impasse and move forward. It is often at this point that a backlash begins, but I will come to that issue later.

First, I should like to think about what women have contributed to this situation and, second, how we can change the dynamics to bring about some movement. As women, we have done an excellent job of articulating what we want when we are outside the institution, banging on the door trying to get inside. We have organized our statistics and our arguments for why more women should be invited in, we have spoken eloquently about the injustice of keeping us out, and through much of that hard work we have begun to open doors and some women have been admitted. However, a problem arises once we are through the door and have been invited to the table, for we have just not developed the appropriate analysis and strategies required to redefine and redesign the table. We know something is wrong, but we often have difficulty identifying the exact problem. Consequently, women frequently find themselves alone, unable to articulate and therefore unable to put into practice alternative styles of work and leadership. For it is clear from either direct or more subtle messages that in order to survive, one must follow the rules. We are reminded in a hundred different ways that trying to change the rules will brand us as trouble-makers and poor team-players. I recall talking to a group of US ordained women who were calling for new models of parish ministry because they believed that the traditional style of ministry, which promoted the concept of a seven-day working week and the parish as one's first and only priority, was not a healthy model for the appropriate integration of work and family. The more these women pushed for change, the more they were labelled "problem" clergy who were considered hard to place in congregations because of their "special" requirements.

From another part of the world, we hear about a situation where women as women are ignored. This is a story from a woman pastor in Brazil:

> I am a little annoyed with my church, because we women are very well accepted and everything is okay when we are male-woman pastors. When we talk about women, as specific things, there we have problems. Legally, as a woman pastor I have the right to a maternity leave for 120 days, but in fact this doesn't work. I am ready to give birth and until now nobody worried about looking for a substitute. I think I will have an ecclesiastical delivery, because I will have to carry on with work until the birth and still after, too.

So while women make their way to the table, searching for a seat, they find that very little has changed in order to accommodate their presence. The table is still long and narrow. The consequence of this is the creation of an unhealthy environment for women with the following results:
— women find that they cannot work for the church and have a home life as well, and therefore have to make a choice between the two;
— women leave because they are burned-out and unable to take the daily abuse of a system that does not fully recognize them, but insists that they perform with above-average results;
— some women have a place at the table but have forgotten how to support the participation of other women;
— some women support the traditional shape of the table because they have found a way to benefit as individuals from the system, but they have lost sight of the fact that many other women are not beneficiaries.

It is for these reasons that tokenism is so detrimental to women. One or two women cannot do all the work: if change is to take place it must be done in the context of community, so no one person can become a single target or carry the burden alone. For when women are left standing alone in such situations, they can be put into a position where they begin first to question their judgment and finally their sanity: "Did I hear it correctly?" "Am I being overly sensitive?" "Maybe I am just being paranoid." Alternatively, they give up working for change and become an integral part of an unchanged system. When fewer women are present, mistakes made by women are less tolerated and can be held up as examples of why women should not be in those positions. More women decision-makers are needed so that this situation can be rectified. One has to begin, therefore, with the rounding of the table in order to attract and maintain a higher percentage of women. The environment of an institution must be made a healthy place for all those who participate. Yet when the number of women in an institution such as the church reaches what is called "critical mass" (moving beyond tokenism to over 20-30 percent representation), an interesting phenomenon can occur within the organization. It is called a backlash.

Let's go back for a moment to the poem I read at the beginning:

> And what of narrowlong ministers
> when they confront a roundtable people,
> after years of working up the table
> to finally sit at its head,
> only to discover
> that the table has been turned round?

For those who have always benefited from the system, it may seem as if the system has betrayed them; and therefore they lash out in anger at those whom they feel are responsible for their lack of success. Examples of attitudes and situations which are the result of this backlash include:

— men who have supported the first wave of women into an organization now feel threatened and back away from that support;

— men in organizations develop the attitude that enough time has been spent on women: "Let's move to another issue";

— with women present in real numbers in an organization, men perceive themselves as discriminated against: in other words, they dismiss the claim of an oppressed group by making it everyone's claim and therefore no one's claim;

— it is asserted that unqualified women are hired and promoted and that "we need to get qualified people back on the job";

— some professions become more identified as female, thereby losing their status;

— organizations on a downhill slide — with a loss of funds or power, etc. — often employ women in key decision-making positions only to set them up for failure;

— women are employed in departments that have (1) smaller budgets, (2) less status, and (3) which are service-oriented rather than programmatic: yet these positions are used to showcase the increasing number of women in leadership positions.

All of these situations point to an unchanged environment. The old patterns remain the same. Yet as in the poem ("for God has called a people, not 'them and us'"), God has called us to develop new patterns that encompass the whole community. And we are called to this task, not because we are special and have all the answers, but rather because we have spent so much time on the outside that we have both felt and observed the abuses of the system. We have observed how the system works hard to be exclusive rather than inclusive. We have watched the system not always work very well because it is built on the concept of task completion rather than relationship-building. Not that either one or the other should be dismissed, but without both something is missing — it becomes a one-sided process. Yet somehow, once we are in the system itself, we lose some of that outsider insight. We need to recapture what it felt like to be outside the door and build on that understanding as we begin to reshape the table.

We can no longer just accept the opportunity to participate in the process, but rather we need to be a part of its redefining and redesigning, understanding very clearly that what we are calling for is radical change. This understanding was clearly defined in the report of women's work in the Evangelical Church in Württemberg, when they wrote:

> The task of the women's department is to change structures in such a way that women will no longer be at a disadvantage... Therefore, establishing a women's desk is a fundamental challenge to an organization because its task is precisely to change this very organization and its way of working. For this reason it was important for us from the beginning to adopt confidence-building measures. In about seventy introductory conversations with the church board and church agencies, bodies and institutions, it became clear where the shoe pinches, what the fears are and where allies are to be found.

We need not shy away from the fact that the process of change "can be painful for people and tables". Like the women from Württemberg, this does not mean that we cease our activities, but rather that we are aware of the environment and act accordingly. We do not accept being dismissed, but rather we listen even more carefully and speak more articulately. We do not accept our gifts being minimalized, but rather we lift up all the gifts of the people of God. We do not accept that power can only be shared with a few, but rather we work with the belief that power is only increased when it is shared. We do not accept responsibility for the anger of men, but rather we understand it and push for a continuous dialogue between men and women. We do not accept that what we bring to the table is unworthy of the churches' time and energy, but rather that the death and resurrection of Jesus Christ have made time for all of us at the table. We are worthy participants at the table and are called to act like we belong. As the poem says, "We respond by loving people into roundness." We can be angry and frustrated and should in general expect to experience all the other emotions that are a part of loving another human being, but always remembering that the community which Christ has set before us is one that is filled with the gospel spirit, a spirit that generates hope out of the passion in compassion, rather than the attainment of a position in the composition of the community.

God's call moves us towards the future

"We can no longer prepare for the past, we will and must and are called to be church", but believing that a round table might be a better design and articulating that to the broader community can be two very different things. We must learn to articulate our belief about what the shape of the future church ought to be in order for it to be an inclusive rather than an exclusive community, thereby reflecting God's call to us as the "one body of Christ". What changes might remove the "them and us" syndrome or the "preferred seating" arrangement and bring the "least of these" to the table? Here is the beginning of a list which I hope will soon multiply tenfold:

— leadership drawn from an understanding of communion;

— power not seen as a limited commodity, but one which when shared only expands;
— process being as important as function;
— breaking the pattern of secrecy in organizations;
— understanding and practising the concept of "shared wisdom";
— taking the power to name the agenda;
— making change for the sake of the community rather than just for oneself;
— changing the dynamics of relationships as an approach to conflict resolution;
— creating the space for differences.

One could write a paper on each of these points. Instead, I shall deal specifically with only three of them: breaking the secrecy pattern, practising "shared wisdom", and taking the power to name the agenda.

Secrecy: how to rid ourselves of the disease

Just as we have fought against the secrecy surrounding wife-battering, rape and sexual abuse, we need to do battle in order to eradicate the pattern of secrecy in the church. Whether we hold on to the secret pain in our lives because of an atmosphere of unacceptance, or the institution itself fosters secrecy by withholding information, the dynamics of secrecy are very damaging to women and men in the community. However, for women the secrecy cycle has damaged so many lives that it becomes imperative that it be broken in order for us to attain wholeness. Be aware, however, that breaking the cycle of secrecy in an institution such as the church is as difficult and painful as the sharing of our stories of sexual abuse and rape. The church needs to be a nurturing community where members are not forced to live secret lives in order to meet some unreasonable standard of human behaviour. We are a grace-filled church which at times has forgotten that we are all in need of God's gift of grace.

We all participate to some degree in the process of institutional secrecy and therefore we need to examine our own patterns as well as those of the institution. Whether in the spreading of rumours about others or accepting the privilege of being "one of the select few" who has access to the working information of an institution, we contribute to creating an unhealthy atmosphere of "them and us". This is not to suggest that there is no need to keep certain information confidential, but we must speak against the withholding of institutional information that comes with the amassing of power for a few rather than facilitation of empowerment for the whole community. The rounding of the table, because of its equalizing effect, may help us to break the cycle. Here are just a few of the strategies that could assist us in moving closer to that rounded table:
— creating an atmosphere that is safe for people to share concerns;
— developing more open agendas;
— being transparent about decision-making processes;
— decreasing the need to make all information confidential;
— encouraging all agendas to be out on the table, rather than hidden;
— encouraging people to solve conflicts between themselves;
— people taking responsibility for their own words and actions;
— asking people to participate at the beginning of a process rather than after it is underway;
— transparency in money matters;

— not allowing oneself to be drawn into a web of information sharing that leaves some people informed while others remain ignorant, and thereby unable to fully participate in the process.

None of these factors alone will guarantee a different atmosphere, but practised together they can affect great change in an institution — change that is healthy for all involved.

Shared wisdom: a practical approach to decision-making

Mary Berate McKinley coined this phrase in her book of the same title. She describes the wisdom that God gives us as "shared wisdom". "The Spirit, in order to share with us the very wisdom of God, promises to each of us a piece of wisdom... No one can contain all the wisdom of God, for that would be to be God." So, therefore, it is the collective wisdom of the community that should define the vision. Of course, for the Christian community that vision is always set under the umbrella of God's mission to the world. Leaders of round-tabled communities listen to the shared wisdom of those in and outside of the institution and then are able to articulate a vision which mirrors people's hopes and dreams. In this way it becomes the vision of the community, implemented by the same. All are given credit, and the power of this visioning approach is that it speaks to the whole rather than just a select few.

This is a much different approach from that taken in the context of a more traditional leadership style which depends only on the wisdom of a few to create the vision and solve the subsequent problems. Just think how many skills and God-given gifts have been missed or dismissed in this process! "Round-tabling means being with, a part of together, and one... It means room for the Spirit and gifts and disturbing profound peace for all."

The power to name the agenda

Access to the naming of the agenda is key to changing the shape of our church, for the issues named on the agenda determine the scope of the vision. However, before we move too far into this subject we need to be quite clear about the ownership of the issues. There is a tendency to allow our concerns to be defined as "women's issues" rather than as belonging to the whole community. By allowing the phrase "women's issues" constantly to be used, we perpetuate the view that these concerns belong only on the agenda of women and not on the broader church agenda. For illiteracy, poverty, lack of access to health care, violence, and under-representation in decision-making circles are societal problems, not women's problems. So the first action in taking the power to name the agenda is to speak in terms of issues that drastically affect the lives of women and therefore need to be addressed by the larger community. In addition, the agenda for the church should reflect the concerns of the community at large. With that in mind, it is well to review some of the recommendations of the UN's fourth world conference on women in Beijing in 1995 and see how they might fit into the agendas of our churches.

The following are a selection of declarations and actions found in the Beijing declaration and platform of action:

Declaration: Acknowledge the voices of all women everywhere and take note of the diversity of women and their roles and circumstances, honouring the women who paved the way.

To truly acknowledge the voices of women everywhere, the church would need to shift dramatically its agenda priorities. For example, the inclusion of numerous women in our theological institutions would be automatic, because without them these places of higher learning would never be considered as having met the standards set by the church. When reviewing a speakers' list for a church meeting or conference the question should no longer be "Are there women on the list?" but rather "Which women are listed?" Theological reflection as seen through the eyes of women would be considered the norm rather than categorically marginalized with the label "feminist theology". Taking note of women's diversity would mean that the stereotyping of women and their work would no longer be tolerated in the church. Church dinners in congregations across the globe would not only have the imprint of women's hands, but alongside them would be the volunteered contributions of men. Honouring those women who paved the way would not only occur at an LWF women's consultation, but also at the LWF assembly.

Declaration: Recognize that the status of women has advanced in some important respects in the past decade, but that progress has been uneven, inequalities between women and men have persisted and major obstacles remain, with serious consequences for the well-being of all people.

While churches around the world have celebrated the ordination of women and the election of female bishops, there is often a less than full acknowledgment in terms of programmes and funds that there remains a long road to travel. More important in this discussion is the need for the church to accept that just adding numbers will not be change enough, but rather one of the major obstacles in the advancement of women is the very structure of the institutional church itself. This must change.

Declaration: Prevent and eliminate all forms of violence against women and girls.

While the churches in our communion have made some progress in this field, we have a long way to go. In most of our churches it continues to be very difficult for a woman to charge a pastor or church worker with sexual abuse or rape. Sexual harassment continues to be misunderstood, and in many countries the church has not taken the lead against this type of violence. There are many who still laugh it off and say, "Oh, he was just joking, and women should not take those advances so seriously." While violence against women in society has been publicly denounced by the church, very little funding and programmatic efforts are coming out of the churches. In many cases it is "good" churchgoing men who are the perpetuators of that violence. I am aware of an ordained pastor who as a counsellor was found to be guilty of sexual misconduct in his client relationships. The evidence was overwhelming and he was removed from the clergy roster by his bishop, but many of his male clergy friends continued to refer women clients to him, because they thought he had been unjustly accused. And to make matters worse, the female counsellor who exposed him was boycotted by this same group of clergy. Only when the church makes it clear throughout its structures that it is unwilling to accept any violence against women will it be taken seriously by secular institutions when it calls for changes in society.

> *Action*: All sectors of the community are called upon to take strategic action against the inequalities and inadequacies in and unequal access to education and training.

Education has been emphasized by Lutheran churches throughout the world, yet if one were to review all the churches' educational institutions in the light of this action, how would they fare? What percentage of women are in key administration and teaching roles? What educational models are being used to reflect the needs of women who are now part of the system? Is the inclusion of more women in institutions of education and training a serious agenda item for your church?

> *Action*: All sectors of the community are called upon to take strategic action against the inequality between men and women in the sharing of power and decision-making at all levels.

If one were to analyze church structures on a scale of one to ten, with ten being the highest and one being the lowest level of impact, how much decision-making power would women truly wield in those structures? The question here is not one of women in executive positions, but rather women in key executive positions whose decision-making power radiates throughout an organization. I would surmise that this question would be answered very differently in churches throughout the world, but even in those institutions where women are more visible in decision-making roles, it would be interesting to analyze the effects of those decisions throughout the church.

> *Action*: Develop conceptual and practical methodologies for incorporating gender perspectives into all aspects of economic policy-making.

This is an area where the church has done the least work in regard to gender sensitivity and yet this action could have some of the greatest impact on the life and work of women, both in the church and outside. When allocating church budgets, how often do we speak about gender perspectives and how they might affect the role of women in the church? How much money is actually going towards women in development? Where are the large sums of money being spent in the churches? Before we can suggest strategies for change we need to have information about the current situation. If one were to do a full analysis of church budgets would we be surprised where the money is being spent?

> *Action*: Introduce and promote training in peaceful conflict resolution.

This should certainly be a key role for the church to play in our societies. If one were to single out one major factor that prevents women from escaping poverty and a basic existence, then it would be violent conflicts throughout the world. Women are more frequently messengers of peace than war; yet how often are they utilized by the church or secular community to settle disputes? The role of women as peace-makers in their own homes needs to be recognized by the church, but how can we expect the church to lift up this role when we as women have done very little to promote it? Again, we need to study this domestic peace-making role and present our findings to the church. I do not mean to imply that only women have a corner on the peace and hope market, but as Denise Ackermann of South Africa writes:

> I draw from women's experiences, not because we have a copyright on hope, but rather because at this time my dominant images are of men at war and of women weeping. Pictures of men with guns, of men triumphantly waving arms astride vehicles of war, of men refusing to speak to one another, contrast painfully with images of starving women and children, women at graves, women scratching in the dry earth for food, women praying.

Women need to be more actively involved in the solving of conflicts that radically affect their lives. We need to insist that more energy and funds are targeted for peace-making efforts.

To summarize, we have to be aware of what we want on the agenda and then find the channels through which it will happen within the church — not an easy task, but certainly one that needs to be done. If we do not take action now, the church agenda in the 21st century will not reflect our needs. The table will stay narrow and its rounded edges will disappear.

We can make a difference

In the face of what seems like an almost impossible task, how do we keep from getting discouraged, how do we get energized and how do we keep hope alive? How do we make a difference in a world where for every problem solved, five more seem to surface? First and foremost we must remember that we are not alone, that God has provided more than enough of the Holy Spirit to go round, that we have been given the gift of community from which we can act. As agents of change in the world, we need to practise the same patience that is required in the rearing of a child. We do not expect a child to walk, talk and take on adult responsibilities in its first year of life. Rather, we take one day at a time, good days and bad, never giving up, but accompanying that child day by day, knowing that our presence will make a difference one day. I am reminded of a story which I think is a wonderful illustration of how one simple act can make all the difference.

> One day a young girl walking on a beach came across a strip of sand where the tide had gone out and had left in its wake a beach with thousands of starfish stranded and struggling for their lives. The girl began to quickly pick up one starfish after another and throw them back into the sea. As the girl made her way down the beach, an old man stopped her and said, "Why do you bother? There are thousands of starfish on this beach, and you will never be able to save them all? What difference can you make?" The young girl looked up at the old man and, holding up in her hand a starfish on the verge of being flung back into the water, responded by saying quietly but firmly: "I may not save them all, but for this starfish I will make a difference."

The ordained women of the Church of England are making a difference. The following article appeared in the magazine of the Lutheran church in Alsace-Lorraine, France:

> Approximately a year ago, 32 women were ordained in the Church of England. Today, they total more than 1400, constituting one-tenth of clergy in that church. The Anglicans have observed an increase in religious practice in parishes where a woman priest officiates... the number of parishioners increased by between 10 and 30 percent following the calling of a woman to serve as parish priest.

We can make a difference, but only if the journey we set out to walk is one that is defined by God's own journey. For if we take seriously God's call as described in the poem — "If God calls for other than roundtable, we are bound to follow. Leaving the sawdust and chips, designs and redesigns behind in search of and in the presence of the [kingdom] that is [God's] and not ours" — then we need to stay alert and not let our agendas take over when God's agenda points in a different direction. We do not have all the answers, but then in the presence of God's gift of grace we are not required to have all the answers in order to ask the questions.

NOTE

1 *Women*, 1989, 33, p.4.

4. Re-reading Scripture: A Hermeneutical Approach

NIRMALA VASANTHAKUMAR

I should like to introduce this topic by describing two events from my own life. I am an ordained presbyter of the Church of South India (CSI).

Like my male colleagues in the ministry, I met all the necessary requirements to be ordained as a deacon. My male colleagues who were ordained with me as deacons in 1976 were ordained as presbyters in the following year, but I was not, the reason being that the CSI was still involved in discussions about accepting women into the ordained ministry. These discussions went on at all levels. It was interesting to note that both the proponents and opponents of the ordination of women to the presbyterate based their arguments mainly on the Bible. By the time the church had agreed to ordain women and had removed the constitutional barriers to implement the decision, several years had gone by; I was ordained as presbyter in 1984, along with another sister. When the diocese posted me as full-time presbyter, I felt that it was worth the wait.

While I was in this frame of mind — thanking God for the opportunity to serve as a presbyter — my aunt (a pious and devout woman) told me: "Nirmala, you have gone against the word of God, since the Bible says that women should keep silent in public." I was upset, not just because my own aunt did not appreciate my commitment to pastoral ministry, but because a woman could not understand another woman's feelings. I replied to her in the same vein: "My dear aunty, the resurrected Lord told Mary, 'Go and tell my brothers that I am risen'. So the mandate to proclaim the message of resurrection was given first to women and only afterwards to men."

Biblical authority

It is not my intention to describe my own agony — that is another story. Rather, I wish to draw attention to the fact that in both events the Bible was an important document to justify mutually exclusive positions: the authority for both springs from the Bible.

We all know that before the Reformation the authority of the Bible was hardly questioned. The authority of the Bible and the tradition of the church went hand in hand. For Martin Luther and other reformers the scriptures contained the word of God whereas tradition was man-made. Therefore tradition could not be counted as equal to the scriptures. For Luther, a Christian derives authority only from the scriptures, and all other authorities should be subject to them — hence, Luther's *sola scriptura*. He further liberated the scriptures from the hands of the professionals, saying that everyone should have free access to them so that they may confront the individual directly. As a result, the authority of the Bible was taken seriously, although of course it has been interpreted differently by different theologians and denominations within the Christian church.

Robert Bryant defines authority as that which "is acknowledged as rightly and worthily commending loyalty and obedience".[1] Authority, therefore, contains a sense of identity, the feeling of hope, the standard for belief and norms for behaviour. Christians look for all these things in the Bible. The very fact that the proponents and opponents of the ordination of women to the presbyterate use the same texts to justify their stand demonstrates that the authority and interpretation of the Bible go hand in hand; they are very much linked with hermeneutics.

It is necessary at this juncture to identify some different views about the scriptures. Broadly speaking, they can be classified as follows:
1) the Bible *is* the word of God;
2) the Bible *contains* the word of God;
3) the Bible *becomes* the word of God.

A note of caution: these categories are not absolute in themselves and they are very broad. Within each of them there are divergent viewpoints, which are not discussed here as they do not have a direct bearing on the topic in hand.

The Bible *is* the word of God

The proponents of this theory believe that the Bible is the word of God because it is inspired by God. The Bible is a record of events and truths describing the eternal communication of God to God's people through the mediation of prophets and apostles.

God chose the writers in different generations and inspired them through the Holy Spirit to record God's words for their contemporaries as well as for future generations. Hence, God is the principal author of biblical texts and the "writers" are only the instruments of God. The proponents of this theory quote passages like 2 Timothy 3:16, 2 Peter 1:20-1 and John 10:35 in their support. They conclude that since God is perfect, God's words in the Bible are also perfect. As such, the words of the Bible are absolute and eternal truths for all generations. The Bible, therefore, is perfect and inerrant in its entirety and in all its details.

The strength of this position is very clear: the Bible in its entirety is an authoritative document. Christian life, witness, theology and faith must spring from that authority. But the weaknesses of this position are many. When it is said that the Bible in its entirety is the word of God, it is not clear whether this refers to the original languages or to translations. It is also not clear as to which of the texts is inspired when there are textual variations. Further, it looks as though this position confuses inspiration with authority. Inspiration means solely that the authors were divinely inspired; that does not explain how an ancient book can become an authoritative document for the modern age.

Finally, even though the advocates of this position say that the whole Bible is authoritative, it ultimately boils down to the selective use of texts. For example, when a person asks a question like, "Are you saved?" there is an underlying concept of "saving" as a one-time event and as a past event. They quote from the Bible to justify the belief that one needs to be "born again" in order to be a true Christian, but they fail to recognize that the New Testament speaks of saving in all three tenses, past, present and future, indicating that saving is a continuous process. This inadequacy in the understanding of the authority of the Bible has led to another misunderstanding.

The Bible *contains* the word of God

The advocates of this position believe that the writers were divinely inspired and that they were writing the word of God for the people of their time. Therefore, the Bible is a product of its own socio-cultural and political context. They also believe that, although the message of the Bible is divinely inspired, it is given to human beings. In as much as human beings were recipients of the message, they understood and communicated God's message in their own language and culture. Hence, the message of the Bible is hidden in the socio-cultural and political context of their time. Furthermore, the Bible might even contain some errors simply because its recipients were human beings. So in order to get at the true message it is necessary to place the text in its socio-cultural and political context. The word of God, therefore, has to be discovered in its own context. Hence, the Bible contains the word of God and becomes authoritative only when that word is discovered in its own context.

The strength of this position is also very clear: the Bible is the product of its own period, and as such it was easily understood by the people to whom it was addressed. A person in this modern age needs to discover the word of God. Hence he or she has to go back to its original context. This explains why different views are expressed in different passages in the Bible. It also explains why some errors have crept into manuscripts.

It is correct to say that the Bible should be understood in its own context and that it is necessary to read it with the socio-cultural and political situation of the time in mind. But then the question arises as to how an ancient text taken out of its archaeological confines becomes relevant to modern times. This is not explained.

The Bible *becomes* the word of God

The proponents of this theory believe that the Bible is not identified with the word of God because the source of the Bible *is* God. The Bible is only an instrument to disclose the revelation of God, and as such it witnesses to the word of God. When readers encounter Christ by reading the Bible they discover the word of God in their own existential situation. Hence, the authority of the Bible does not lie in its intrinsic value but in its capacity to address human beings in their own existential situations.

The strength of this position is very clear: the Bible becomes the word of God when a person meets Christ in his or her existential situation. The scriptures become authoritative because they provide an opportunity for a divine-human encounter. The impact of the Bible upon theology, teaching and faith is taken seriously in this position, but its main weakness is that it does not take into consideration the context in which the scriptures were written — to the extent that the reader is tempted to interpret the scriptures to suit his or her existential situation regardless of the principles of hermeneutics.

Hermeneutics

But what is hermeneutics? According to Georges Casalis, hermeneutics is the science of Hermes. Hermes was the Greek god who was entrusted with transmitting to human beings the results of the confused and stormy deliberations of Olympus. Hermes was also responsible for getting that commodity across the border from one culture to another. He was the protector of physicians who were trained to restore the fullness of life to those threatened by death. From this description, Casalis concludes that hermeneutics has four dimensions:

1) it translates a divine message into human words;
2) it transposes what was said "at that time" into contemporary categories;
3) it reclaims possession of the text and its meaning from those who have unwarrantedly locked them away;
4) it revives the past in order to retain its value for the present.[2]

Hermeneutics, therefore, is a principle by which the biblical text is interpreted to make the message relevant to the modern situation. It takes into consideration the text and its context, as well as the reader and his or her context. If the former is taken seriously without the latter then we end up with an ancient text without any relevance for the present. If the latter is taken seriously without the former then we are in danger of advocating subjective interpretation.

The text and its historical context

The Bible is not a collection of metaphysical ideas. It contains events in history. It has geographical names, names which can be verified in history. It demonstrates how a community of faith expressed the salvific activities of God in their own lives and how generations of faith communities appropriated this experience in their historical praxis. To put it in the words of Croatto, "the whole Bible as we have it today is the result-product of a long hermeneutical process".[3]

Before the text came to be written, God's word was experienced and lived by successive generations, and finally a witness put that experience into literary form. Hence, the word is an event, a creative act and not just a written word. As the result of the discovery of various manuscripts, archaeological excavations and scientific criticism, we can conclude that the biblical witness itself is bound by time and place. To understand this witness we have to understand the economic, political, social and cultural factors within which the biblical texts first saw the light of day. The text is therefore not free of the conflicts of the milieu in which it arose. Hence, it is necessary to identify the theological framework implicit in a given situation. As Casalis says: "To understand the text we must not only decode, translate and analyze what is written but also reconstruct the situation and the role that the witness played in it."

For this reason, the word of God cannot be identified with the written word. Hence, the fundamentalist's interpretation that the whole Bible is inspired and inerrant cannot stand the test of hermeneutical principles. One needs to go beyond that position to discover the word of God for Christian obedience.

The reader and his or her context

No reading is neutral. The fact that the proponents and opponents of the ordination of women to the presbyterate quote the same text to justify their stand demonstrates that every reading is done from an ideological position. Such ideological positions are sometimes openly acknowledged but often they are not. Yet always the ideological bias of the reader determines his or her reading of the Bible.

When a woman reads the Bible, the context in which she finds herself is always at the back of her mind; it shapes ideological bias. For example, in the context of the subjugation of women in India for some 4000 years of its history a woman will either be very submissive, accepting her role as God-given, or she will rebel against her subjugation as something man-made. Thus, her ideological bias determines her reading of the scriptures.

Liberation is one of the dominant themes in the Bible, particularly so in the context of women's struggle for humanhood. There are few references to the involvement of women affirming their human dignity and establishing equal partnership in the ministry. The fact that the books of the Bible are a product of their own historical context — in which subjugation of women was a reality — further worsens the situation. Women's struggle has not been faithfully recorded. However, in the few places where references are found a liberating process is depicted and the message is conveyed very effectively if the passages are read in their own historical context.

In other words, the scriptures have to be re-read in the context of the struggle of women to affirm their human dignity and humanhood. Only then is the message of the Bible recreated and reactivated and not just updated. It becomes contextualized, made relevant and not allegorized.

The task of hermeneutics in this situation is to find a correct interplay between the text and its historical context and what it says to us in our current context. The historical and scriptural contexts are thus held in tension with each other in order to find the word of God for our context. This process is named the "hermeneutic circle" by Casalis or the "hermeneutical circulation" as José Míguez Bonino prefers to call it. In the words of Míguez, the hermeneutical circulation

> creates an ongoing circulation from the text to the praxis and to the text again or from the past historical context to the present context and back again... Thus a hermeneutical circulation is between the text and its historicity and our historical reading of it in obedience.[4]

Re-reading the scriptures

Let us apply this hermeneutic principle to the struggle of women to affirm their humanhood. We will begin with the context in which the struggle is taking place and then proceed to look at the scriptures within that context. Pauline writings provide a reference point.

The struggle of women to affirm their humanhood

I will limit my observations to the Indian context, but I am sure the description will find similarities in other countries of Asia.

The situation in India is paradoxical. Religiously speaking, at one level women are held in high esteem. Many gods are female. The universe is created out of the *Shakti* or power of woman. The goddess of education/learning is Saraswathi; the goddess who destroys evil in the world is Chamundeshwari/Durga. Hence, women can attain the highest possible recognition; that is, to become gods themselves.

The most powerful and dynamic leader in independent India was a woman, Indira Gandhi. She was so powerful that Hussein, a famous Indian artist, depicted her as Durga in one of his paintings.

Yet in spite of this the socio-cultural conditions prevalent in India are appalling. Historically, women have been subjugated to the authority of men. As a child, a girl comes under the authority of the father; as a married woman, of her husband; and as an old woman, of her son. At no time in her life is she independent of a man.

Women from the middle and lower classes have to work to maintain their families. After work, they have to attend to household chores while men normally have only their professional jobs to fulfill. The daily newspapers describe incidents such as dowry harassment, dowry deaths, assault, rape and other crimes against women. Even though in some temples female deities are installed, around the temple the *devadasi* system is encouraged whereby women are "married" to one of the male gods in the temple and as such they are available for high-caste men to be used as prostitutes.

It is in this context that the women's struggle takes place in India. Women who are conscious of their human dignity are now raising their voices against such atrocities. They are educating other women to stand firm against the evil forces that perpetuate such demeaning practices. This movement is gaining momentum. Of course, there are many women who believe in their traditional role, and one can understand such feelings for the oppression of thousands of years has made such women so docile that they cannot see a way out of their predicament. Therefore, any movement to bring about changes in outlook and attitudes will have the difficult task of conscientizing people, especially women themselves. The authority of the scriptures has a lasting impact in this context. So it is necessary to interpret Bible texts correctly.

Paul and women

It is generally agreed that Paul firmly advocates the subjugation of women to men. Passages like Ephesians 5:22, Colossians 3:18, and 1 Corinthians 14:33-36 are quoted to justify this understanding. The hermeneutical principle holds that Paul should be understood in his own context. Before we analyze some of these passages we should be aware of the socio-cultural context in which Paul was operating.

Women did not have a positive role to play in the Judaism of Paul's time. They were considered inferior and their role was limited to their families. Though the New Testament presupposes monogamy, polygamy was legally permitted. Women could attend synagogue but they had to be seated apart from men and they were not allowed to speak. The minimum number of people required for worship in the synagogue was ten, but however great the number of women present it is possible that they would not have been counted. Above all, women were not allowed to read the Torah.

In the Hellenistic world there was more freedom. Women were involved in public life; wives could take part in symposia and they could accompany their husbands to parties and other public functions; women participated in sports, except in the Olympics; priestesses played a very important role in cult worship.

It is against this background of traditionalism and conservatism propagated by Judaism and the liberalism advocated by Hellenism that Paul needs to be studied.

I shall not analyze those Pauline passages where women's roles are described, but concentrate only on the undisputed letters of Paul. The majority of New Testament scholars agree that there are only seven undisputed letters of Paul: 1 and 2 Corinthians, Romans, Galatians, Philippians, Philemon and 1 Thessalonians. On the basis of their style, content and theology some New Testament scholars believe that Ephesians and Colossians are not directly from the pen of Paul but from that of a close friend or disciple. I shall simply accept these findings as true for the time being. This means that the injunction that a wife should be subject to the authority of her husband — found in Ephesians and Colossians — should be regarded as a Deutero-Pauline injunction and not as written by Paul himself.

Paul advocates two basic concepts. They are the equality of men and women "in Christ" and the bestowal of charismata on all members of the community.

For Paul, Galatians 3:28 is a basic text. Once a person is in Christ, all man-made distinctions become peripheral. As a result, all members of the community will have equal rights. As against the practice prevalent in the synagogues, Paul advocates equal partnership of men and women in the ministry. So he uses words like "when the whole church comes together" (1 Cor. 14:23) to indicate that he is addressing men and women.

According to Paul, all believers have been endowed with charismata (1 Cor. 12 and 14 and Rom. 12). The concept of charismata occurs throughout Paul's epistles. There is a multiplicity of charismata in the body of Christ, given for the edification of the community. Each person has his or her role in the church; men and women exercise ministry according to the charismata given to them; so there is no silent partner in the Pauline community. It should be pointed out that Paul advocates such a positive role for women against the background of Judaism, where women's role was passive. So for Paul, all normal categories like Jews and gentiles, male and female, slave and master, are broken down in Christ. Spiritual virtues are applicable in the realm of social and religious life as well. Because of this understanding, Paul goes one step further and advocates collective leadership in his community. Out of forty fellow workers, ten are female; that is, one quarter of the Pauline missionary team consisted of females. The efforts of women in missionary work are described in Romans 16.

Because of this new-found freedom in Christ and the bestowal of charismata on all believers, men and women were allowed to prophesy in church assemblies (1 Cor. 11:5,6). Here we must take into consideration 1 Corinthians 14:33-36, where it is said that women should keep silent in church. Many recent scholars believe that this passage is an interpolation, the reason being that the text is not contextual; it contradicts the idea propagated in 1 Corinthians 11 and is in tension with the views about marriage expressed in 1 Corinthians 7. The New Revised Standard Version of the Bible puts this passage in brackets to indicate that it is a later interpolation. If this explanation is accepted, then it is abundantly clear that Paul gives a prominent role to women in the church.

It is in this context that one has to look at Paul's injunction to women to cover their heads in public worship. This should be treated not as a theological dictum but as an affirmation of the social practice of that time in the interest of maintaining decorum in the church. Paul says not only that women should cover their heads, but also that men should cut their hair. Thus it is a social custom that Paul is addressing and not a theological doctrine.

Even if one interprets this passage from the point of view of the subordination of women to men, one can discern in Paul that the equality of men and women and the exercise of charismata by all in the community predominate over the other view. In other words, the liberatory motif is more pronounced in the Pauline epistles than the subjugation of women to men. When we re-read the Pauline epistles in their own context and in the light of the basic concepts that he advocates, we are bound to discover in them a positive role for women. It is this liberatory motif which becomes the word of God for those involved in the struggle of women to affirm their humanhood.

Conclusion

From the above description of Paul's treatment of the role of women in his community, it is clear that the interpretation and authority of the Bible go hand in hand. When the reader in his or her present context re-reads the Bible in its own context, the word of God is discovered. When the text of the Bible in its own context and a reader in his or her present context confront each other, the word of God comes out vividly. That is the way to understand the authority and interpretation of the Bible. Thus, the authority and interpretation of the scriptures in the context of women's struggle to affirm humanhood are intrinsically linked with the re-reading of the scriptures: it is a hermeneutical process.

NOTES

1 R. Bryant, *Bible's Authority Today*, Minneapolis, Augsburg, 1968.
2 G. Casalis, *Correct Ideas Don't Fall from the Skies*, Maryknoll, Orbis, 1984.
3 S. Croatto, "Biblical Hermeneutics in the Theologies of Liberation", in V. Fabella and S. Torres, eds, *Irruption of the Third World*, Maryknoll, Orbis, 1985.
4 J.M. Bonino, *Doing Theology in a Revolutionary Context*, New York, Fortress, 1975.

5. Power, Authority and the Bible

WANDA DEIFELT

A conflictive appropriation

Among feminist scholars interested in the issue of hermeneutics, perhaps the strongest contribution and criticism to traditional, androcentric scholarship has been the notion that the authority of the scriptures cannot be taken for granted. There is a consensus even among non-feminists that it is necessary to evaluate and interpret biblical texts critically, to analyze a text's context and our own context in order to affirm authority of the scriptures as the word of God. The critical reading of the Bible is not specific to feminist interpretation. There are other methods that critically evaluate the formation of the Bible: how it changed from an oral to a written tradition, how Hebrew culture relates to other Middle Eastern cultures, and so on.

In its own research, feminist scholarship has been deeply influenced by the historical critical method. My suspicion is that feminist hermeneutics, when it appropriated this method, also carried over some of its not-so-obvious agenda.

First, one of the main thrusts of the historical critical method is against a fundamentalist, literalist reading of the Bible. The archaeological and redactional history of the text emphasizes that the formation of the Bible was not a once-and-for-all type of event but that it was a slow, sometimes conflictive process. With its emphasis on "what really happened" from a historical perspective, the historical critical method wants to show the historicity of the exodus event, of Jesus, of the early Christian church, etc. The hermeneutical principle seems to be that of St James: it is necessary to see in order to believe. For something to be true it has to be proved historically. In attempting to recover women's history, however, we learn how difficult it is to prove women's existence.

The notion of history which the historical critical method uses cannot see beyond official historiography. Although this method exercises the principle of suspicion towards the formation of biblical texts and how these texts continued to be used, it does not immediately suspect the existence of an unofficial history — the history of those who are not heroes and heroines. In Latin America, one of the first discoveries among liberation theologians was the fact that the Bible is one of the few written sources that speaks from the perspective of the poor and oppressed. But if this is true (I believe that it is in part), how does that relate to the fact that it includes so few women? If it is a book written to translate faith in God using everyday experiences, why does it describe so few women's experiences? In many cases, we cannot prove women's presence historically, but we can assume it, even if that means going against "historical" records.

The second problem which feminist hermeneutics inherited from the historical critical method is related to its critical aspect. Here I refer primarily to the rationalist approach to texts, the attempt to demythologize and sub-estimate the subjective or mystic aspect of biblical society. The historical critical method is clearly an attempt to wrap biblical faith into a rational and reasonable package, to make it more acceptable for a modern audience. This critical aspect is evident in feminist hermeneutics, with the suspicion that the divine authority of texts ought not to be taken for granted. Again, it becomes clear that the issue at stake is a reading of the Bible which does not take into account the historical setting in which the text was elaborated, its oral and written tradition and/or its own historical context.

Feminist hermeneutics

What is specific to a feminist reading is its freedom to deal with scripture. We start with the assumption that the authority of the Bible is not the direct inspiration of the word of God. We start by saying, in feminist theology and hermeneutics, that the biblical text is deeply influenced by its own social, political, economic, cultural, geographical and religious setting. This means recognizing that the text also carries within it a heavy load imposed by an androcentric and patriarchal society. The word of God is, therefore, mediated through that setting. It is important for us to make clear that each new generation of believers has to appropriate religious teachings and the biblical faith and translate them into their specific context. This becomes obvious when we notice how the same text is used differently not only in its own context, but also within the context of the Bible itself.

What makes feminist hermeneutics more critical of the formation and interpretation processes of the Bible is the fact that its content has a direct impact on the way women are perceived and what is expected from us in contemporary society. It is impossible for women to interpret a text from an analytical, value-neutral perspective because of the strong impact the Bible has had on our own lives. The message of the book seems to affect women more than men when it comes to defining religious (and social) roles for human beings in general. It seems that when we come to the way human beings should behave, women are expected to act according to certain norms, defined beforehand by another culture in another time. Thus, whether we agree with it or not, the Bible has had a very strong influence on Western Christian culture. Therefore, the way the Bible has been used and misused to keep women bound to a certain type of submissive, subordinate behaviour is the starting point of many feminist hermeneutics.

Analyzing some of the current feminist hermeneutics, it is possible to describe three methodological steps. The first is to become aware of women's absence from the biblical tradition. At this stage we become aware of women's non-normative status in the body of traditional literature and criticize the stereotypical portrait of women. The second step is the discovery of women's presence in the biblical literature: that women have a literature of their own, with themes and approaches that differ from those of men. This literature, however, has been buried by the patriarchal establishment. The third step is a demand not only for the recognition of women's experiences and writings as belonging to the normative body of literature, but also a demand for a radical rethinking of the traditional mode by which literature is evaluated (up to this point, evaluated entirely on male experience).

Feminist hermeneutics begins by acknowledging that women have been excluded from the mainstream of history and literature. Women have been silenced, marginalized and perceived as inessential to the making of civilization. Their deeds have been left almost entirely unrecorded, leading to their historical and literary invisibility. Traditional male scholarship perpetuates the exclusion of women by making men the normative and dominant representation of humankind and by placing women as subordinate and secondary to men. Feminists point out that the record of the past is only a partial record since it omits the past of half of the human species, and it is distorted since it tells the story from the viewpoint of the male half of humanity only.

Re-vision

The task undertaken by feminist hermeneutics unfolds in two stages: it starts by pointing out androcentric social constructs, but it moves on to show that reconstruction is necessary. The first stage, however, is to acknowledge the historical exclusion of women from social and religious leadership. Feminist hermeneutics critically evaluates the body of literature taken as normative and accepted by religious and educational establishments. It begins by pointing out the patriarchal content of the scriptures and by denouncing misogynist texts such as 1 Timothy 2:12. It questions the process of canonization, which reflects a patriarchal selection of texts with the intent of preventing women from exercising their deserved leadership. And it proposes re-vision.

Re-vision — the act of looking back, of seeing with fresh eyes, of entering an old text from a new critical direction — is for women more than a chapter in cultural history: it is an act of survival. Until we can understand the assumptions in which we are drenched we cannot know ourselves. We need to know the writing of the past, and know it differently from the way we have ever known it: not to pass on a tradition but to break its hold over us.

Feminist hermeneutics questions the universalization of male experiences as normative, the consequent diminishing of women's perspectives to a secondary rank, and the view that over half of humanity is not relevant insofar as their participation in history is concerned. As a result, feminist hermeneutics questions the authority of a body of literature, such as the Bible, which aims to speak to the whole of humanity when only one half is truly represented. In addition, it also challenges the way women are portrayed by scripture, church fathers and theology in general. Second in creation but first in sin, women are described as physically deficient, lacking the capacity for rational activity and incapable of moral self-control.

The history of woman is ignored, hushed up, censored in the most literal sense of the term. This method of eliminating the social and political destiny of half of humanity is the most effective form of supremacy. For a long time the lower class, the poorest social strata — whether the plebeians in Rome, the serfs or the proletarians at the beginning of the 19th century — also had little place in history, but it was still not possible to write history without going into class differences. This has led to enormous conflicts in historical interpretation. However, the history of women is different. Their resistance can be silenced, snuffed out as if it had never existed, because the battle of the sexes is considered a basic fact of nature.

Feminist hermeneutics does not limit itself to a description of women's oppression. It also searches for its causes and the arguments for its perpetuation. Feminist scholars refer to the fixed social destiny dictated by a principle of distinct male and female natures, which deems women inferior because of their reproductive capability. For centuries, the basis for such discrimination was women's alleged physical, mental or moral weakness. Women were generally placed on the side of irrationality, nature, silence, privacy and the body. Men, on the other hand, were identified with reason, culture, discourse, public and the mind.

In other words, woman's body seems to doom her to mere reproduction of life; the male, in contrast, lacking natural creative functions, must (or has the opportunity to) assert his creativity externally and "artificially" through the medium of technology and symbols. In doing so, he creates relatively lasting, eternal, transcendent objects, while the woman creates only perishables — human beings.

Feminist scholarship starts with the assumption that the inequality between men and women is a social and cultural construct as opposed to a biological or divine mandate. Feminist theorists point out that the discriminatory arrangement of women is rooted in a dualistic comprehension of the world and humanity. Rationality and passion, mind and body, culture and nature, and discourse and silence are all categories that establish a hierarchy in which the first is superior to the second.

Because our culture is so deeply rooted in such notions, to challenge these dichotomies means to attack the foundations of authority, which takes the dichotomies for granted. To question women's exclusion from the mainstream of history is to question women's exclusion from the literature as well. Feminist hermeneutics points out the need for deconstructing patriarchy in its social, cultural, political and ideological aspects through the literary expressions that patriarchy engenders.

Biblical as well as secular texts reflect the androcentric culture in which they were born and bred. Feminist hermeneutics challenges the notion of biblical canonization as a finished process. It shifts the authority from the text onto the readers, who decide whether or not to ascribe authority to the scriptures. Thus, canonization is an ongoing process, "a fluid as well as stabilizing concept, subject to the continuing authority of believing communities". Feminist hermeneutics seeks a more holistic approach so as to include as many perspectives as possible in the making of theology. In relation to the Bible it proposes revision, continuous reading, and interpretation to bring to the biblical canon the experiences of women.

Alternative histories

When women cease to be consumers of male-produced literature and start questioning the validity of this body of literature, biblical texts can no longer be acclaimed as universal and prescriptive. They become one among many representations of reality. But to challenge their authority is not enough. Only when women are capable of producing textual meaning, and thus becoming active participants in history, is it possible to achieve a holistic world-view. Feminists, therefore, look within the Bible, history and literature for fragments of women's active participation. The second stage of feminist studies, then, is the search for an alternative history and tradition to support the inclusion of women as full historical human beings. This stage of feminist hermeneutics starts by acknowledging that although women have been basically written out of history and excluded from texts, without recognition of their acts and deeds, they are indeed participants in the processes of culture and society. Furthermore, studies show that the exclusion of women from leadership roles is not the whole picture. There is growing evidence that within Judaism and Christianity women were not uniformly excluded from religious studies and practices. Rather, the body of literature taken as normative is only one side of the argument. While feminists begin by pointing out women's historical victimization and secondary status, they also point out that victimization is not sufficient to describe the dynamics of women in history.

Women are essential and central to creating society: they are and always have been actors and agents in history. Women have "made history", yet they have been kept from knowing their history and from interpreting history, either their own or that of men. Women have been systematically excluded from the enterprise of creating symbol systems, philosophies, science and law. Women have not only been educationally deprived throughout historical time in every known society, they have been excluded from theory-formation.

There is a tension between being "essential and central to creating society", on the one hand, and being systematically excluded from decision-making processes, on the other. Gerda Lerner calls this tension "the dialectic of women's history", for it represents the contradiction between being an agent of history without being one of history's interpreters.[1] The awareness of this contradiction is essential to the consciousness-raising that characterizes the feminist movement. The consciousness of exclusion, in turn, becomes a force that leads women to challenge the institutions that justify their exclusion. In the process of recognizing that women are historical beings, the question of the untold history of women comes up. Based on the understanding that women could not be completely erased from texts, and that even the most misogynistic text has to refer to women, feminists continue in their search for the female tradition.

Feminist scholarship, then, has two concerns: it revises concepts previously thought universal, but now seen as originating in particular cultures and serving particular purposes; and it restores a female perspective by extending knowledge about women's experience and contributions to culture.

To recognize women's participation in history is to reject the position of "other" attributed to women. Thus, feminist theory proposes that women cease to remain always the other, the defined, the object, the victim, believing that there is a unique quality of validation, affirmation, challenge, support that one woman can offer another. Within the Judaeo-Christian setting, new discoveries on the prominent role of women in the scriptures have led to a hermeneutics of women's affirmation. Feminist scholars such as Elisabeth Schüssler Fiorenza and Phyllis Trible have found an alternative tradition in the Bible, which presents women in prominent roles. But the quest for alternative traditions is not exclusive to the Bible. Also within church history there are examples of many prominent women who have helped to shape religion. Outside the church, feminist scholars find other sources of empowerment, ranging from goddess worship and witchcraft to the participation of women in secular movements that seek equality for women.

Recognizing alternative traditions

In an interdisciplinary fashion, feminists have also drawn on the tradition of feminist foremothers, who have left a legacy of scholarship produced from women's perspectives. Among these figures, Mary Wollstonecraft (1759-97), Elizabeth Cady Stanton (1815-1902) and Virginia Woolf (1882-1941) represent almost two centuries of women's writings. In the 18th century, Wollstonecraft criticized women's blind submission to authority, and she proposed that women have access to education so that they may become equal to men. Stanton struggled with other suffragettes to obtain legal equality through the right to vote. In the tradition of Margareth Fell, who in the 17th century wrote *Women's Speaking Justified*, Stanton wrote a series of commentaries to the Bible, condemning the use of religion to keep women submissive.[2]

Virginia Woolf not only discussed women's secondary status in culture and society, but she also advocated a feminist mode of writing, based on the experiences of exclusion and the search for equality.[3] From different fields of research, feminist scholarship is unveiling a wealth of female role models, both inside and outside the religious arena. The ultimate goal is to foster a tradition which belongs to women.

The discovery of such an alternative tradition, however, does not mean that feminists merely supplement patriarchal history by adding women to it. What it means is that feminists are attempting to construct a new form of the interpretation of the tradition. The stories of women can be found buried under layers of patriarchal practices and ideologies. In spite of patriarchy's attempt to keep women's participation concealed and forgotten, feminist scholarship has been able to catch glimpses of a tradition of women as full persons — as subjects of history, actors in their own right, and agents of God in their ministries.

It seems that every generation of female scholars needs to address the same questions as the previous generation. Like Sisyphus rolling his stone up the hill, they continue to address the questions that define women's existence today. Although some female scholars insist on repeating the pattern previously established by male scholars, others have discovered that this pattern does not fit women. Unlike Sisyphus, these female scholars would rather let the stones roll down the hill onto the plains, where they could be used for building something new. This new tactic comes primarily from the discovery that the exclusion of women cannot be overcome by "adding" women to texts and traditions. Instead, a major change is in order in the way tradition and interpretation are perceived.

The third stage of feminist criticism is, in Cheri Register's words, the attempt to formulate a "prescriptive" criticism to "set the standards for literature that is God's from a feminist viewpoint".[4] Although feminists agree on the need to implement such standards, the development of criteria to deal with literature is ongoing. The need for guidelines in relation to feminism both for writing and for the analysis of texts is one of the major theoretical springboards in contemporary feminist theory. The shift from women as readers to women as writers represents, in Elaine Showalter's view, a dramatic change in the way women relate to the canon, tradition and culture in general.[5]

This is the stage in which women restate the norms and methods of theology in light of the critique of tradition and the search for alternative feminist models. In this third stage, feminist theology functions not only as a critique of the past and a quest for lost stories of women. It is also a reconstructive theology, re-creating and re-visioning theological categories by using as its starting point women's experiences of oppression and struggles for liberation. The basis for such reconstructive theology does not necessarily lie within the institutional church, its tradition and the scriptures, but in the conviction that women are human beings created in the image of God living within a community of faith engaged in exodus from patriarchy. Alternative understandings of the scriptures, the redefinition of traditional theological terms such as *sin* and *salvation*, and the ascribing of new roles for the church may lead to conflict with patriarchal establishments.

The patriarchal distortion of all tradition, including scripture, throws feminist theology back upon the primary intuitions of religious experience itself, namely, the belief in a divine foundation of reality which is ultimately good, which does not wish for nor create evil, but affirms and upholds our autonomous personhood as women, in whose image we are made. It is engaged in a primal re-encounter with divine reality and, in its re-encounter, new stories will grow and be told as new foundations of our identity.

In the field of theology, much of the reconstructive work has been done in relation to language. Feminists recognize that language, as a means to pass on tradition and culture, does not belong to women, because it is "the oppressor's language". Language is not always adequate for expressing women's experience, since it is the same language that has kept women silenced. To repeat the language is to perpetuate the tradition, instead of changing it. As Audre Lorde says, "The master's tools will never dismantle the master's house. They may allow us temporarily to beat him at his own game, but they will never enable us to bring about genuine change."[6] In religious terms, the scarcity of female imagery for God means a lower self-image for women in the Judaeo-Christian tradition, since female experiences are non-normative and therefore have less ownership over that tradition. Feminists point out that whoever names the world owns the world, and because women are not part of the naming process they have no direct claims over it. In order to overcome this, feminist theologians have translated the Bible using inclusive language, searched for new metaphors for the divine, and drawn on sources other than the scriptures as references.

The question is, how can women make use of the language and tradition in alternative ways without perpetuating patriarchal culture? Some feminists give up on the Judaeo-Christian heritage because they see it as unredeemable. Others realize that solely emphasizing women's silence within the patriarchal establishment is no alternative. The task of feminist criticism is to expose the collusion of language, tradition and canon with male ideology and androcentric values. It is the task of feminism to find new ways of expressing ideas that begin with the experiences of women. The task is to write women back into history and theology and to reinterpret traditional theological terms from the perspective and the experiences of women.

Woman must write herself, because this is the invention of a *new insurgent* writing which, when the moment of her liberation has come, will allow her to carry out the indispensable ruptures and transformations in her history, first at two levels that cannot be separated.

> By writing herself, woman will return to the body which has been confiscated from her, which has been turned into the uncanny stranger on display — the ailing or dead figure, which so often turns out to be the nasty companion, the cause and location of inhibitions. Censor the body and you censor breath and speech at the same time.
>
> This is an act that will also be marked by woman's *seizing* the occasion to *speak*, hence her shattering into history, which has always been based on *her suppression*. To write and thus to forge for herself the anti-logos weapon. To become *at will* the taker and initiator, for her own right, in every symbolic system, in every political process.[7]

Foundations

Feminist writing focusses on the specificity of women, questioning hierarchies and absolutisms and searching for a feminist tradition. This tradition also proposes new forms of expression that do not rely only on exegesis of past traditions for the definition of female experiences with the divine. New religious expressions need to be created and incorporated as normative and part of the religious canon. Thus, feminist hermeneutics proposes the revaluation of social, political, philosophical and theological values. It proposes the revision of concepts and traditions, searching for women's stories in past and present. Finally, it points to the present contributions of women, towards the need to find new expressions and new ways of bringing theological meaning to the lives of women.

Feminist hermeneutics attempts to find women's voices in texts. In breaking the silence, naming women's oppression, and recovering lost traditions, feminist hermeneutics affirms women's presence in the past and encourages women's active participation in the present. Each stage of feminist theory asks the following questions: how to combine the theoretical and the personal; how to include one's own experience in the reading of texts; and, in turn, how to connect the content of the text with one's life. These questions determine the foundation of feminist hermeneutics. Feminist hermeneutics is aware of women's exclusion in past and present, suspecting that women's voices were not completely silenced, and it is confident that it can write women into history. Drawing on women's experiences, feminist hermeneutics attempts to formulate a method of interpretation to which women can relate.

NOTES

1 *The Creation of Patriarchy*, New York, Oxford UP, 1986, p.5.
2 *The Woman's Bible*, Seattle, Coalition Task Force on Women and Religion, 1974.
3 *A Room of One's Own*, San Diego, Harvest, 1957. Woolf's feminist writing introduces the notion that the personal is political. Frequently accused of being apolitical for her interest in issues other than the right to vote, she tried to point out the intricacy of patriarchy and how women have to know about the power and social structure. "For Virginia Woolf, feminism

meant more than the vote, and more also than sisterhood, shared grievances, mutual support, and independent achievement. It meant, specifically, the beliefs that make up social feminism." From Naomi Black, "Virginia Woolf. The Life of Natural Happiness", in *Feminist Theorists: Three Centuries of Key Women Thinkers*, Dale Spender ed., New York, Phantom Books, 1983, p.299.

4 "American Feminist Literacy Criticism: A Bibliographical Introduction", in *Feminist Literary Criticism: Explorations in Theory*, Josephine Donovan ed., Lexington, Univ. Press of Kentucky, 1975, p.2.

5 "Toward a Feminist Poetic", in *The New Feminist Criticism: Essays on Women, Literature and Theory*, New York, Phantom Books, 1985, p.128.

6 *Sister Outsider: Essays and Speeches*, Trumansburg, NY, Crossing Press, 1984, p.112.

7 Helene Cixous, "Utopias", in *The New French Feminisms*, E. Marks and I. De Courtivron eds, New York, Schocken, 1981, p.250.

6. Reading the Bible as Equals

ELISABETH SCHÜSSLER FIORENZA

Definitions

I should like to explore a reading of the Bible in terms of the radical vision of church as a discipleship of equals. I will elaborate the frameworks, practices and goals for such a critical reading of the Bible as I have developed them in my own work. A critical feminist interpretation for liberation is part of the development of feminist biblical studies which has been pioneered as a new area of biblical scholarship in the past two decades.

Since for many audiences "feminist" is still a negative label and a "dirty word", I hasten to explain how I understand it. If this expression generally evokes negative reactions, emotions and prejudices, and includes a variety of theoretical perspectives, it is necessary first to delineate how I use the term in my own work. To my mind, the political notion of feminism is best expressed by a popular bumper-sticker which — tongue-in-cheek — defines feminism as "the radical notion that women are people". Women are not beasts of burden, temptresses, goddesses, incarnations of the ideal feminine or "eternal woman", but fully responsible citizens in society and church, made in the image and likeness of God and therefore God's representatives. Women are the people of God, the church.

This definition of "feminism" positions feminist theology within emancipatory discourses and movements which assert the power and interests of all the people. Its contextualization evokes centuries of radical democratic struggles for liberation, emancipation and equal citizenship of women in society and church, who fought for dignity, respect, well-being and self-determination. As a radical democratic feminist notion, the expression "ekklesia of wo/men" — and I use the term "wo/men" always in an inclusive sense to linguistically encompass men — asserts that wo/men are both equal citizens in society and "equal disciples" in the church. At the same time, it seeks to interconnect global emancipatory movements for freedom and equality with women's struggles in Christianity and biblical religions.

In short, feminism as I understand it connotes not only a world-view or body of theory, but also describes a movement of those who seek not just to understand biblical texts but to transform kyriarchal structures of domination. As one of the oldest maxims of the women's liberation movement states: as long as not every woman is free, no woman is free. There are no liberated women. In short, a critical feminist interpretation for liberation reads the Bible in the context of feminist movements that seek to eliminate the exploitation and dehumanization of all wo/men without exception.

The diverse theoretical articulations of feminism generally agree in their critique of elite male supremacy and hold that gender roles are socially constructed rather than innate or ordained by God. The "root-experience" of feminism makes one realize that cultural "common sense", dominant perspectives, sacred writings, scientific theories and historical knowledge are not only androcentric, i.e. male-biased, but they are also kyriocentric: master/lord/father/husband-centred. In so far as feminist discourses have restricted themselves to a gender analysis and have conceptualized Woman in analogy and opposition to universal Elite Man, they have valorized the category of Woman as opposite or superior to that of Man. Therefore, they have tended to reproduce the symbolic construction of male-female polarity and compulsory heterosexuality which — as we have seen — are constitutive of the kyriarchal order. This Western kyriarchal regime of wo/men's subordination has been enforced and legitimized ideologically also by biblical texts and Christian traditions. Hence, a feminist reading of scripture must always be both critical and constructive. In the following, I shall first discuss the critical theoretical frames of such a reading and then illustrate the process of such a reading with reference to the interpretation of a biblical text, the story of the Syrophoenician woman.

Feminist hermeneutical frameworks

In conjunction with feminist literary criticism, critical theory and historiography, feminist biblical studies originated within the women's studies movement of the 1970s. They have adopted various scientific methods and developed particular reading strategies. All the different forms of feminist biblical enquiry acknowledge two seemingly contradictory insights: on one hand, the Bible is written in androcentric, or better, kyriocentric language, has its origin in the patri-kyriarchal cultures of antiquity, and has functioned throughout its history to inculcate misogynist values. On the other hand, the Bible has served as inspiration and authorization for wo/men and other non-persons — to use an expression of Gustavo Gutiérrez — in their struggles against kyriarchal dehumanization and oppression.

Over and against those who use the Bible against women and powerless men struggling for emancipation, feminist scholars have begun first by examining what biblical texts actually teach about wo/men in order to prove wrong the opponents of freeborn wo/men's emancipation and slave wo/men's liberation. This approach has generally focussed on "key" passages about women, such as Genesis 1-3; on biblical laws with regard to women, slaves and homosexuals; or on the Pauline and post-Pauline injunctions for freeborn and slave women's subordination. It has done so in order to show that these biblical texts have been misunderstood or misused by the conservative political Right. The selective cutting-up and cutting-out method of this approach isolates passages about wo/men from their literary and historical contexts and interprets them "out of context" for apologetic purposes. Such an apologetic approach, which often justifies Christian at the cost of Jewish traditions, has engendered anti-Jewish attitudes and interpretations, although its apologetic intent is to reclaim the Bible as a positive support for wo/men's emancipation.

In short, in response to those who quote the Bible in support of the socio-symbolic patriarchal order, feminist apologists assert that the Bible correctly understood does not prohibit but rather authorizes the equal rights and emancipation of wo/men. Consequently, they have concentrated on the question of scriptural authority and argued that a feminist biblical interpretation must "depatriarchalize" the Bible and provide correct biblical readings of the passages on women. However, such defensive feminist discourses have remained caught up not only in an apologetic but also in an andro- and kyriocentric cultural framework.

Euro-American feminist discourses generally have used categories such as androcentrism, patriarchy or gender dualism as synonymous and overlapping concepts. In this use, the term "androcentrism" refers to a linguistic structure and theoretical perspective in which "man" or "male" stands for human. Biblical languages, such as Hebrew and Greek, and their English translations are grammatically masculine classificatory language systems. They function as so-called generic languages whenever they use male terms as inclusive of women and the pronoun "he" as inclusive of "she". When, for instance, we speak of Africans, Europeans, the poor or minorities, these terms can be understood as inclusive of women. However, when we speak of Africans, Americans, the poor and women, we speak as if only men, but not women, belong to those social ethnic groups. In addition, such grammatical linguistic androcentrism obscures the fact that the category "wo/men" includes not just white, elite, Western, middle- or upper-class women, as conventional masculine generic language suggests, but that it means all humans born female.

According to the Western cultural androcentric framework, masculine and feminine are the two opposite or complementary poles in a socio-symbolic sex/gender system. This system is asymmetric insofar as masculine is the primary and positive pole. Dualistic oppositions such as man/woman, subject/object, culture/nature, law/chaos and orthodoxy/heresy legitimate masculine supremacy and feminine inferiority. This androcentric conceptualization of the Western socio-symbolic cultural order, however, is not just androcentric but kyriocentric, insofar as it positions elite Euro-American Man as the transcendent, universal subject having privileged access to truth and knowledge. European understandings of reason, rationality, philosophy or theology have been conceived within the binary structure of male dominance as transcendence of the female. Linguistic kyriocentrism not only "naturalizes" cultural asymmetric gender dualism, in which femininity is constituted as an exclusion and repression by identifying grammatical gender with natural gender. It also represents race and ethnic characteristics as biological "givens" or facts of creation.

Feminist liberation theorists around the globe have unmasked this universalizing and essentializing Western discourse on gender and race as reproducing kyriarchal relations of domination. Their analyses have pointed out that not only the nature of elite women but also that of subordinated and colonized peoples has been construed as the devalued and deficient opposite of that of elite Western Man. Western philosophy has defined the "nature" of the colonized "others" as analogous to that of "woman" and the "feminine" in order to rationalize the exclusion of the subordinated "others" from the institutions of knowledge, culture and religion. Women are not only defined by gender but also by race, class, culture, religion or ethnicity.

Liberationist feminists, therefore, have consistently maintained that an analysis of wo/men's situation only in terms of gender does not suffice. The general understanding of patriarchy as gender dualism or as the domination and control of man over woman does not comprehend the complex systemic interstructuring of gender, race, class and ethnicity which determines women's lives. Although much of Western feminist scholarship has become skilled in detecting the androcentric-gender contextualization of malestream biblical interpretation — they argue — it has not paid sufficient attention to its own internalization of gender stereotypes, white supremacy, class prejudice and theological confession-alism. For instance, African American feminist scholars have pointed out that a reading of the story of Sarah and Hagar in Genesis 16:1-16 and 21:1-21 just in terms of gender does not suffice. Rather, it must be read as the story of the Hebrew slave-holding mistress Sarah and that of the Egyptian bondwoman Hagar. It is a story not only of socio-economic disparity but also of rivalry and hostility between women. As Renata Weems points out, the story of Sarah and Hagar is the story of a "slaveholding woman's complicity with her husband in the sexual molestation of a female slave woman".

In short, if feminist biblical interpretation should not reproduce its own internalized structures of oppression, it needs to reconceptualize its categories of analysis. As I have argued, one must distinguish between the categories of linguistic kyriocentrism and ideological gender dualism on one hand, and kyri-archy understood as a complex overarching social-religious system of elite male domination on the other. The kyriarchal pyramid of domination and subordina-tion is structured by the overlapping systems of racism, sexism, classism and colonialist imperialism. Western cultural discourses are not just androcentric, i.e. male-centred, but also kyriocentric, i.e. master-centred. Although cultural and religious kyriarchy as a "master-centred" socio-political discursive system has been modified throughout the centuries, its basic structures of domination and ideological legitimization are still operative today.

Hence, feminist biblical readings which are committed to the struggle for changing patriarchal structures of domination cannot primarily seek for identifica-tion with biblical texts and their wo/men characters. Rather, they must critically track the ideological functions of biblical texts in inculcating and legitimating the kyriarchal order. From its inception, feminist biblical interpretation, therefore, has had not just a religious but also a public political goal. Such a political intent was already articulated by Elizabeth Cady Stanton in the last century, who insisted that feminists — whether they believe in the Bible or not — must engage in biblical interpretation. As long as scripture is not only used against women struggling for emancipation and in support of kyriarchy, but also influ-ences women's self-understandings and lives, feminist biblical interpretation must pay attention not only to the kyriocentric text but also to women as reading subjects. Recognizing the kyriocentric dynamics of biblical texts, a critical feminist theological reading therefore abandons the quest for a liberating canoni-cal text, biblical figure or scriptural principle, and shifts its focus to a discussion of the process of a biblical reading that can grapple with the oppressive as well as the liberating imprints and functions of particular biblical texts in the lives and struggles of wo/men.

Feminist literary critics have pointed out that readers do not engage texts in "themselves". Rather, in so far as readers have been taught how to read they activate reading paradigms. Both professional and non-professional readers draw on the "frame of meaning" or contextualization provided by shared symbolic religious constructions of social worlds. In light of this insight, a critical feminist biblical interpretation must first of all become conscious of and explicate its own reading paradigm or reading formation in relation to the hegemonic symbolic world constructions which it engages.

Reading paradigms consist of a set of discursive determinations which organize the practice of reading in so far as they relate texts, readers and contexts to one another in specific ways. For instance, whereas the dogmatic reading paradigm relates biblical texts, readers and contexts in terms of church doctrine, the historical reading paradigm seeks the text's "original" meaning, and the literary analytic paradigm traces the kyriocentric narrative strategies and symbolic world constructions of biblical texts. For instance, a dogmatic reading of the story of the Syrophoenician woman will insist that Jesus could not be prejudiced, whereas a historical reading paradigm will try to ascertain whether Jesus really said the offending prejudicial statement, and a literary analysis will trace the different narrative or rhetorical strategies of the story in the gospels of Matthew and Mark. In short, biblical texts, readers and contexts are not fixed once and for all in their relations to each other, but they function differently within different reading paradigms.

If reading paradigms establish different relations between texts, readers and contexts, then such different rhetorical readings cannot be adjudicated in terms of "the true meaning of the text itself"; rather, they must be assessed ethically and politically in terms of their implications and consequences for the struggle to transform patriarchal relations of oppression. However, such a political ethics of interpretation and its claim that wo/men have the authority to assess and evaluate scholarly interpretations and biblical texts stands in tension with the dominant historical/literary or doctrinal reading paradigms of biblical scholarship. If the literary canonization of texts in general places a work outside of any further need to establish its merits, the canonization of sacred scriptures in particular brings even more sympathy and uncritical acceptance.

Early on, readers of biblical texts learn to develop strategies of textual valorization and validation rather than hermeneutical skills to interrogate and assess critically scriptural interpretations and texts along with their visions, values and prescriptions. Canonization compels readers to offer increasingly more ingenious interpretations, not only in order to establish "the truth of the text itself" or "a single-sense" correct meaning of the text, but also to sustain the acceptance and affirmation of the whole Bible, either as sacred scripture or as cultural classic. By taking the experience and analysis articulated in feminist struggles for transforming kyriarchy as its point of departure, feminist biblical interpretation seeks to develop methods and strategies that can question and contest the patriarchal authority claims and values encoded in scripture.

Feminist critical readings no longer can construe biblical texts in an archetypal fashion as having a fixed timeless normativity and universal validity. Instead, they seek to understand the Bible as prototype, as a formative root-model of religious and cultural identity that informs Christian readings but requires critical discussion, deliberation, evaluation and transformation rather than simple acceptance and obedience. A critical hermeneutics and rhetorics of liberation attends, first, to how hegemonic biblical interpretations reinscribe kyriarchal legitimizations; second, to the ways in which kyriarchal power is encoded in biblical texts; third, to the consequences of these kyriocentric inscriptions for wo/men as biblical characters, readers or critics; and finally, to the implications of these inscriptions, not just for a feminist reconstruction of the past, but also for the transformation of the kyriarchal present and for engendering a different vision for the future.

Consequently, a critical feminist interpretation pays special attention to the "frame of meaning" determining its readings. By making conscious the dominant kyriocentric symbolic "frame of meaning" it can empower women to participate as reading subjects in the construction of meaning, while at the same time becoming conscious of such a process of construction. By showing how gender, race or class affect the way we read, it underlines the importance of the reader's particular socio-cultural location. Reading and thinking in a kyriocentric, i.e. master/lord/father/husband-centred, symbol-system entices readers to identify not only with what is culturally "male" but also with what is "elite" male. Thus, reading intensifies women's internalization of a cultural system whose misogynist, racist and Western supremacist values alienate us both from ourselves and from each other.

However, a feminist interpretation for liberation is not only critical but also constructive. It seeks to make a difference by empowering wo/men for reading kyriocentric biblical texts differently. It makes conscious that the kyriocentric biblical text derives its seductive as well as its critical "power" from its generic "inclusive" aspirations. For instance, in a context of liberation struggles women may read stories about Jesus without giving any significance to the maleness of Jesus. Yet, reading such stories in a cultural ecclesial contextualization that places emphasis on the maleness and Lordship of Jesus reinforces women's cultural male identification and subordinate subject-location. Such readings found Christian identity not only as elite male identity but also as an identity shaped by domination and exclusion. Focusing in Bible readings on the figure of Jesus, the Son of the Father, and Lord of the Universe, internalizes wo/men's multiplicative oppressions. In the act of reading, wo/men not only suffer from the alienating division of self against self but also from the realization that to be female is to be excluded from "divine power as that of the master/lord/father/husband" and never to be "a son of God".

However, such cultural religious elite male identification is not total because of wo/men's conflicting position within two contradictory discourses offered by society and biblical religions. Wo/men participate at one and the same time in the specifically "feminine" cultural discourses of submission, inadequacy, inferiority, dependency and irrational intuition on the one hand, and in the generic "masculine-human" discourse of subjectivity, self-determination, freedom, justice and equality on the other hand. Similarly, Christian wo/men participate at one and the same time in the biblical discourse of subordination and in that of the discipleship of equals. If this cultural and religious location and reading-participation becomes conscious, it allows the feminist/womanist interpreter to become a reader resisting the persuasive power of the kyriocentric biblical text.

When wo/men recognize our contradictory ideological position in a generic kyriocentric language system, we can become readers resisting the master-identification of the androcentric, racist, classist or colonialist text. However, if this contradiction is not brought into consciousness, it cannot be exploited for change but leads to further self-alienation. For change to take place, subordinated people must concretely and explicitly claim as their very own the human values and democratic visions that the kyriocentric text reserves solely for elite man. Yet, insofar as modern "democratic" discourses have been constituted as elite Euro-American "male" discourse, the equality, justice and freedom to which they point are only partially realized but still incipient reality. The emancipatory reality to which they point has to be imagined differently. Such "imagination" is not pure fantasy but historical imagination, because it refers to a reality that has been already accomplished not only in discourse but also in the practices and struggles of "the subjugated others".

To that end, a critical feminist reading of the Bible for liberation insists not only on a hermeneutics of evaluation, imagination and reconstruction, but first of all on a hermeneutics of suspicion that is capable of unmasking the ideological functions of androcentric biblical texts and commentary. It does not assume a kyriarchal conspiracy of the biblical writers and their contemporary interpreters. Rather, it insists on a hermeneutics of suspicion first of all for linguistic reasons, *because women do not, in fact, know whether they are meant or not when reading grammatically masculine supposedly generic texts.* Kyriocentric biblical language and texts, literary classics and visual art, works of science, anthropology, sociology or theology do not adequately describe and comprehend reality. Rather, they are ideological constructs that produce the invisibility and marginality of women.

Thus, a hermeneutics of suspicion reveals that wo/men — like men — are both kyriarchally "scripted" and at the same time historical subjects who can evade or alter the kyriarchal script. To that end, feminist readers who are privileged by race, class and education must cultivate the habit of ideological suspicion, not only with respect to the Bible's androcentric deformations but also with respect to its kyriocentric, i.e. master-centred, deformations. African-American feminist scholars have pointed out that white biblical interpretation is suffused with racism, Jewish feminists have highlighted the anti-Jewish tendencies of Christian feminist biblical interpretation, and Latin American feminists have pointed to the elite character of academic biblical interpretation. Consequently, a critical feminist biblical interpretation seeks to dislodge the masculine/feminine dualism inscribed in the kyriocentric text in order to unmask the kyriocentric strategies of biblical texts. It does so by focussing on the biblical text as a rhetorical historical practice.

To that end, a critical feminist reading does not subscribe to one single reading strategy and method, but employs a variety of theoretical insights and methods for interpreting the Bible. Hence, it does not understand biblical interpretation and texts in positivist but rather in rhetorical terms. For instance, whereas malestream biblical scholarship takes the kyriarchal injunctions of the pastoral letters as descriptions of the actual historical situation of the churches at the turn of the 1st century, a rhetorical analysis reads them as arguments that point to a quite different situation in the communities of Asia Minor which were inspired by the discipleship of equals. Such a critical rhetorical understanding of text and interpretation investigates and reconstructs the discursive arguments of a text, its socio-religious location, and its diverse interpretations in order to underscore the text's oppressive as well as liberative performative actions, values and possibilities in ever-changing historical situations. The second part of this essay seeks to read the story of the Syrophoenician in terms of such a critical feminist hermeneutics of liberation.

The Syrophoenician woman

A cursory re-reading of the story of the Syrophoenician woman and its diverse interpretations may serve as an example for such a feminist hermeneutic rhetorical process of critical disruption, proliferation, and re-vision. This text can be read as an ideo-story, which according to Mike Bal is a story whose "characters are strongly opposed so that dichotomies can be established".[1] The story's "representational make-up promotes concreteness and visualization" for rhetorical ends. Since the narrative of an ideo-story is not closed but open, it allows readers to elaborate the main characters in an imaginative and typological fashion.

Whether one situates this story's rhetorical practice in the life of Jesus, or in that of the early church, or limits its present narrative context in Mark's or Matthew's gospel, Jesus is seen in it as engaging in an argument that discloses religious prejudice and exclusivist identity because he is quoted as saying: "It is not right to take the children's bread and throw it to the dogs." The woman, in turn, is characterized ethnically and culturally as a religious outsider, who enters a kyriocentric theological argument, turns it against itself, overcomes the prejudice of Jesus, and achieves the well-being of her little daughter.

Different forms of this story are found in the gospels of Mark and Matthew. It is absent in the gospel of Luke, even though Luke is generally praised in malestream exegesis for favouring stories about women. So the story is told in two different versions which have different rhetorical aims. In Mark 7:24-30 the woman's identity is marked through linguistic/cultural (Greek) as well as national/racial (of Syrophoenician origin) characterizations. The text does not recognize the woman either by her own name or by that of her father or husband. Rather, she is characterized by her cultural, religious and ethnic location as an outsider who enters the house into which Jesus has withdrawn. Her disruptive entrance is fuelled by her interest in the well-being of her daughter. Yet, the story does not centre on the telling of the miracle but on the argument of Jesus rejecting her petition because she is a cultural, religious and national outsider. Nevertheless, the woman does not give in but takes up Jesus' insulting saying and uses it to argue against him. She wins the controversy because Jesus, convinced by her argument *(dia touton ton logon)*, announces her daughter's well-being.

A form-critical reading which traces the transmission of this story in the pre-Markan tradition makes it possible to see how rhetorical arguments may have shaped the genesis of this narrative. The story could have begun as a simple Galilean miracle story which was told about a woman asking Jesus to exorcise her daughter, with Jesus granting her request. In the process of the retelling of this miracle story at a second stage, the opposition between Syrophoenician Greek female on the one hand and Jewish Galilean male on the other was probably introduced. Moreover, the parabolic saying about food-children-table-dogs now plays on an "ironic" double meaning, in which Jesus speaks of street dogs and the woman of house dogs. The addition of this saying not only inscribes the opposition between Jew and Gentile. It also ascribes an offensive, exclusivist attitude to Jesus, an attitude which the argument of the Syrophoenician woman challenges and overcomes. Probably at a third stage of transmission, this story was taken over by Mark and tied into the gospel narrative through the introduction in verse 24 and the qualifying addition of "first" in verse 27.

Another version of this story is found in Matthew 15:21-28. In this version, the two protagonists remain embroiled in the argument about food-children-master's-table-house-dogs but both the characterization of the protagonists and the plot of the story change. The woman is consistently rebuffed, not only by Jesus but also by his disciples. She is characterized with the archaic term "Canaanite", which reminds the reader not only of Rahab who facilitated Israel's entry into Canaan, but also of Israel's long struggle with Canaan's cultic heritage. The woman not only enters the public domain, but she does so speaking loudly. The Greek word for her public outcry *(krazein)* also carries cultic overtones.

Matthew's text concludes with Jesus praising the woman's "great faith" and Mark's with announcing that her daughter is freed from the demon because of her word or because of her teaching. Although this is one of the few gospel stories in which a woman character is accorded "voice", the final promise gives in both versions to Jesus the last word and underscores that the authority of the text rests with the "master" voice of Jesus. The woman's argument serves to enhance its discursive resonance. Standard scholarly commentaries also tend to engage in an apologetic defence of the master Jesus if they comment at all on the woman and her significance. Thus, they amplify the marginalizing tendencies not only of the biblical text but also reinscribe it into critical scholarship.

Read in a kyriocentric, i.e. master-centred frame, the story functions as one more variation of woman as outsider in the symbolic worlds and social constructions of male discourse. A substantial part of the Markan manuscript tradition seeks to portray the woman as an example of humble submissiveness by inserting "yes" into the text, to play down the "but" of the woman so that the text now reads: "But the woman answered and said, 'Yes Lord...'" (Mark 7:28). Moreover, both gospel texts contrast the woman outsider with the master figure of Jesus who, according to Mark, has withdrawn inside the house, while in Matthew he is surrounded by his disciples. Whereas Matthew calls her by the antiquated scriptural name Canaanite, Mark elaborately characterizes the woman as a Greek who was a Syrophoenician by birth. Not only by virtue of her gender, but also because of her ethnicity and cultural religious affiliation, the woman enters the site of canonical male discourse as a "triple" outsider.

History of interpretation

This story is theologically difficult because of the saying attributed to Jesus: "Let the children be fed, for it is not right to take the children's bread and throw it to the dogs." The history of interpretation of this saying indicates several rhetorical attempts to change the prejudicial tenor of the story. As I have pointed out already, Mark seems to have sought to soften this Jesus saying of the pre-gospel story by adding "first" *(proton)*: "Let the children be fed first." Matthew's gospel also changed the story's theological dynamics in significant ways by both adding the saying, "I was only sent to the lost sheep of Israel", and introducing the disciples as those who want to get rid of the woman.

To my knowledge the first retelling of the story in the early church emerges in a lesser-known Jewish Christian extra-canonical writing called the *Pseudo-Clementine Homilies*. These are thought to have been composed during the 3rd and 4th centuries, but have probably incorporated older traditions. They tell the story of Clement of Rome who accompanied Peter on his missionary journeys. In their retelling of the Syrophoenician woman's story,[2] the woman for the first time receives a name. She is called in Latin "Justa", which means the "just one" and is characterized as a well-educated upper-class woman. In this version of the story, Justa is joined by the disciples in asking Jesus to heal her daughter. But Jesus replies in the negative: "It is not permitted to heal the gentiles who are similar to dogs in that they use all kinds of food and do all kinds of things, since the table in the *basileia* is given to the sons of Israel." And the woman responds positively: "But hearing this she wanted to participate in the table like a dog, namely in the crumbs from the table, abandoned her previous customs, in that she ate in the same manner as the sons of the kingdom and achieved, as she desired, the healing of her daughter." Although Justa does not persuade Jesus to change his prejudice, she is persuaded by Jesus to change her life-style. Justa converts to Judaism. She becomes the righteous one.

In the subsequent history of interpretation two rhetorical strategies compete with each other. The salvation-historical approach employs the allegorical method of interpretation and carries anti-Jewish overtones. The healing from a distance according to this approach corresponds to the situation of the pagans, the dogs under the table are analogous to the gentiles, the children stand for Israel, the bread of the children signifies the gospel, and the table sacred scripture. Such allegorical interpretations spiritualize and theologize the story in such a way that it can be read in a salvation-historical sense. The woman is seen as a proselyte interceding for the salvation of the gentiles who are saved not through the encounter with the historical Jesus but through his word. Whereas the Jews were the children and the gentiles were the dogs in the days of Christ, now in the time of the church the opposite is the case. Thus, the salvation-historical interpretation is closely intertwined with an anti-Jewish reading.

While the salvation-historical reading is anti-Jewish, the exhortative reading approach focusses on the paradigmatic behaviour of the woman, especially on her exemplary faith, which is differently understood in different confessional histori-cal contextualization. Interpretations of the early church, in mediaeval times, and in the Catholic Counter-Reformation understand faith as a virtue that is expressed as modesty, perseverance, reverence, prudence, trust and especially as meekness and humility. According to this interpretative strategy, the woman's faith comes to the fore as humbleness, especially in Mark 7:27, where she does not reject Jesus' calling her a dog, but accepts it saying, "Yes, Lord." Yet, whereas mediaeval exegetes thought that her behaviour expressed a "masculine" stance, modern exegesis stresses that her humble acceptance of grace expressed her "feminine soul".

The interpretation of the Reformation in turn emphasizes the woman's faith and understands it as feminine surrender rather than as humility. In this way the story becomes a doctrinal discourse on the topic of submissive faith. Faith consists in the unconditional surrender to the Lord, which expresses itself in repeated intercessions and persevering prayer. It consists in the recognition that the self is nothing except for its trust in Jesus, the Lord. Finally, colonialist discourses underscore her subservient behaviour as an example to be imitated. In her book *Discovering the Bible in the Non-Biblical World*, the Chinese scholar Kwok Pui-Lan points to the use of this story for colonialist ends.[3] She highlights that, just like the gentile woman, so also colonialized peoples were expected to be as subservient, obedient and loyal as a "devoted dog" would be. The Western construction of the alien "other" in feminine terms resorts to biblical women and "feminine" virtues in order to inculcate Western values of domination. Moreover, Kwok argues, such a colonialist interpretation contrasts Jesus' attitude towards women with the understanding of womanhood in non-Christian inferior cultures in order to prove the superiority of Christianity. The colonialist use of biblical women's stories parallels the anti-Jewish deployment of such stories in Christian apologetic feminist discourses.

Contemporary interpretations

Most contemporary commentators are troubled by the response of Jesus in Mark, a response that reveals his biased partiality. As a result, exegetes either declare this Markan Jesus saying as historically inauthentic, or they explain away its religious ethnic prejudice and exclusivity by resorting to features of the Matthean version or to anti-Jewish or folklorist considerations. They argue, for instance, that Jesus does not intend an insult to the woman but only wants to test her faith, that he rebukes her because he needed his meal and rest, that he was instructing his disciples and not the woman, that he muttered this harsh word under his breath, or even that it was the woman who first mentioned dogs, since she knew how Jews regarded her people, so that Jesus merely responded to her word. Others suggest that the saying might have roots in rabbinic oral teachings or reflect a Jewish proverb ordering who eats first in a Jewish household. Some in turn explicate that Jesus used the diminutive of "dog" (*kynarion*) in order to soften this allegedly widely known Jewish label for gentiles. All these arguments seek to diminish the insult of the saying on the lips of Jesus by giving good reasons for Jesus' prejudicial words. In short, rather than critically assessing and ethically evaluating the patriarchal politics of the text for Christian identity formation, they try to explain away its cultural religious bias.

In *In Memory of Her* I proposed that the story's controversy is best situated historically in Galilean missionary beginnings.[4] Although the Syrophoenician respects the primacy of the children of Israel, she nevertheless makes a theological argument against limiting the Jesuanic inclusive table-community and discipleship of equals to Israel alone. That such an historical argument is placed in the mouth of a woman gives us a clue to the historical leadership of women in opening up the Jesus movement to gentiles. Thus, the story of the Syrophoenician makes women's contributions to one of the most crucial transitions in early Christian beginnings historically visible. Although I still believe that such an historical reconstruction of an inner-Christian debate about the mission to gentiles is plausible, I also need to point out that it has been construed in an anti-Jewish fashion in Christian apologetic discourses. This interpretation also has been used for deflecting a critical theological discussion and ethical evaluation of the prejudice and discriminatory stance ascribed to Jesus.

The Japanese interpreter Hisako Kinukawa contextualizes the story of the Syrophoenician not within debates on the equal participation of gentiles in early Christian beginnings, but within Israelite purity regulations. She does so in order to draw out parallels between the understanding of ethnic exclusivism and national integrity in 1st-century Judaism and in Japan today. Kinukawa rejects other feminist interpretations that emphasize the audacity of the woman and instead stresses her alien status. She points out that the Israelites

> excluded foreigners from their ethnic borders in order to retain their purity of blood... Geographically they were defenceless against foreign invasions and were invaded by one foreign power after another. Thus it seems natural for Jesus as a Jew to defend his people and not to want to dilute their ethnic integrity.[5]

Yet, by drawing out the structural socio-religious parallel between the situation in early Judaism and contemporary Japan, the danger exists that at least for Western readers the Christian prejudice against Jewish purity laws is re-inscribed. In Western contexts this interpretative strategy may serve, albeit unintentionally, the interest of theological apologetics.

The socio-historical reading which the German scholar Gerd Theissen has developed in turn contextualizes the story of the Syrophoenician not in terms of early Christian theological debates or Jewish purity laws, but rather in terms of inner-Jewish ethnic and class conflicts. This socio-critical reading emphasizes that the story's first teller and audience were familiar with the tensions between Jews and gentiles in the villages of the Tyrian Galilean border regions. The description of the Syrophoenician as Greek characterizes her as an educated upper-class woman who asks Jesus for help. This characterization underlines the "social" clash between her and Jesus, who is portrayed by contrast as an itinerant preacher and exorcist from the backwaters of Galilee.

In the context of such socio-cultural status difference, Jesus' retort must have been heard, Theissen argues, as follows: Let the poor people in the Galilean backwaters be satisfied. For it is unjust to take away food from the poor people in the Galilean villages and to give it to rich gentiles in the cities. This reading situates the story of the Syrophoenician within an inner-Jewish debate, the conflict between poor Galilean villagers and rich gentile citizens. It does not exculpate Jesus because he is seen as expressing the resentment of the underprivileged population. Yet again, this reading does not confront ethically and theologically the prejudicial saying ascribed to Jesus, but ascribes it to the resentment of the underprivileged.

Whereas this socio-cultural contextualization stresses the contrast between poor villagers and rich city folk, the gender reading of Sharon Ringe focusses on the woman as widow, divorcee or never married, as totally alone and isolated from family support. When we meet her she is left with only a daughter who is a further liability in her society's terms. Nevertheless, for the sake of her daughter, the Syrophoenician breaks custom and stands up to the visiting rabbi and miracle-worker. Such a single-minded focus on gender relations rejects the interpretation of the original story in terms of either cultural, class or early Christian missionary conflicts. Instead, Ringe argues that the story's significance is christological. The story could not have been invented by the church because of its shocking portrait of the man Jesus. Rather than inventing such a story, it is more likely that the early church tried to make the best out of a bizarre tradition which must have preserved the memory of an incident in the life of Jesus "when he was caught with his compassion down". Only in the Markan retelling, according to Ringe, does the story become a story about Jews and gentiles.[6]

Ethical evaluation

When trying to assess whether the story of the Syrophoenician advocates kyriarchal values and visions, students in my classes and workshops usually disagree. Those arguing that the narrative is not kyriarchal point to the fact that the woman is the major protagonist in this story, that her argument convinces Jesus, and that her daughter was healed. But at what cost? other students ask. The woman does not challenge the ethnic religious prejudice of Jesus but confirms it with "Yes, Lord." She does not argue for equal access; she begs for crumbs. Thus she accepts second-class citizenship, which she herself has internalized. She acts like a dog who is grateful even when kicked. Hence, it is not surprising that commentators praise her for her humble submission. This is indeed a sacred text that advocates and reinscribes kyriarchal power-relations, anti-Jewish prejudices, and women's feminine identity and submissive behaviour.

In one of these debates, when we came to this impasse in the discussion, Renee, an African-American Baptist student, chided us for not taking seriously the woman's situation of powerlessness and the ironic cast of her words. Maria, a Hispanic student, countered that according to Theissen the woman was upper class, urban and well-educated. Nevertheless, the first student persisted: even as a privileged educated woman she remains a religious outsider, a despised foreigner, and a female who dares to disrupt the discourse of men. If she wants to achieve what she has come for, she needs to "play the game". Readers miss the irony of the story, she argued, if they do not see that the woman humours the great religious man in order to get what she wants. The woman from Syrophoenicia wins the argument; her daughter is liberated. The stress on the "great faith" of the woman in Matthew's gospel must not be read to reinscribe submissive feminine behaviour, but rather in terms of Mark's contestatory discourse.

To sum up my exercise: I hope that I have succeeded in showing how a critical feminist interpretation for liberation explores, problematizes and assesses different reading paradigms and hegemonic interpretations. Its goal is to unmask biblical texts and readings that foster an elite "feminine", racist, exclusivist, dehumanizing, colonialist or Christian anti-Jewish inscription of cultural religious identity. It seeks to re-vision biblical interpretation as an argumentative, persuasive and emancipatory praxis that destabilizes, proliferates and energizes critical readings for liberation in particular socio-historical religious contexts. In so doing, it seeks to undermine a literalist positivist mode of biblical reading that claims to be the only correct or true one. It thereby attempts to overcome a fundamentalist identity formation which invokes the authority of God for biblical texts that reinscribe prejudice and dehumanization. In a socio-economic and cultural political situation of increasing globalization and repressive reaction that provoke insecurities and engender the languages of hate against wo/men and other disenfranchised people, feminist biblical interpretation seeks to empower Christian wo/men to articulate an emancipatory biblical vision and liberatory politics of meaning that does not vilify and block access to the table. Once again, the Syrophoenician challenges us to set liberating readings and arguments against the word that dehumanizes and excludes.

NOTES

1 *Death and Disymmetry: The Politics of Coherence in the Book of Judges*, Bloomington, Indiana UP, 1987, p.11.
2 *Ps. Clem. Hom.*, II, 19, 1-3.
3 Maryknoll, NY, Orbis, 1995, pp.71-83.
4 *In Memory of Her: A Feminist Theological Reconstruction of Christian Beginnings*, 10th ed., New York, Crossroad, 1994.
5 *Women and Jesus in Mark*, Maryknoll, NY, Orbis, 1994, p.61.
6 "A Gentile Woman's Story", in L. Russell, ed., *Feminist Interpretation of the Bible*, Philadelphia, Westminster, 1985, p.68.

7. Naming and Reclaiming Power

MARTHA E. STORTZ

The word "power" defies definition. Perhaps it is like happiness: we can identify its presence and its absence more easily than we can say what it is. We can say what power *does* more easily that we can say what power *is*. The problem of definition is compounded when Christians talk about power because we worship a God "whose weakness is stronger than human strength" (1 Cor. 1:25). Translating Paul into the parlance of power, Christians could say that they worship a God "whose power was made perfect in powerlessness". It is no wonder that talk of power confounds and confuses Christians.

Christian women talking about power face an additional problem of definition. Too often, women have experienced only the absence and abuse of power. Women are not used to having and exercising power. Moreover, because they have so often experienced its abuse, women do not have many good models of how to use power justly and faithfully. What would a just and faithful exercise of power look like?

At the outset, I should like to make three assumptions about power itself: definitional, communal and theological. I should then like to offer three models for using power — power-over, power-within, and power-with — suggesting uses and abuses of each. Then I shall show how a theological understanding of power might form, inform and transform each one of them.

Three assumptions: definitional, communal and theological

A definitional assumption

What is power? Power has been variously interpreted as commodity, as capacity, and as relationship.

As *commodity*, power is external to the individual, a good that one accumulates, like land, money, knowledge, possessions, or people in one's debt. Because there are finite quantities of all of these commodities, power is seen as a commodity in potentially diminishing supply. Thus, the more power someone possesses, the less is available to everyone else. The powerful have; the powerless have not. Power plays like a zero-sum game, regulated by the rules of the market-place: competition, supply and demand, whatever counts as "fair and equitable" exchange.

The church often exercises power as a commodity. Even among the priesthood of all believers, "some priests are more equal than others", if power is measured in terms of ecclesiastical status (clergy/lay, teacher/student, catechist/catechumen, etc.), education, wealth, eloquence or influence. Meetings configure themselves around such figures and people measure their own worth in terms of distance or proximity to them.

As *capacity*, power is seen to be an individual ability that can be used to dominate or to empower, to educate or to brainwash, to inspire or to manipulate.

A justification for this understanding of power in the West lies in its etymological roots. "Power" is derived from the Latin verb *posse*, "to be able to". In this interpretation, the powerful are those who are able to do something important: the strong. The powerless are those who are unable to do anything: the weak. Here, power is played like a cockfight or a schoolyard scuffle and is regulated at best by conscience, at worst by the conviction that "might makes right".

Nor is this understanding of power as capacity alien to church circles. Power as capacity determines leadership in ministry. Training assesses and develops skills and abilities for the practice of ministry. How often do we hear of someone: "If you really want to get something done, ask her." Capacity confers leadership.

But there is a third and final understanding of power: power as *relationship*. In this understanding, power describes the kind and quality of interaction between people, animals, institutions and environments. Seeing power as relationship recognizes that power does not exist in a vacuum, without others with or over whom to exert itself. We attend not to what an individual has (power as commodity), nor to what an individual can do (power as capacity); rather, we attend to how a community interacts and to how someone interacts with the world around her. Michel Foucault elaborates this understanding:

> Power must be analyzed as something which circulates, or rather as something which only functions in the form of a chain. It is never localized here or there, never in anybody's hands, never appropriated as a commodity or piece of wealth. Power is employed and exercised through a net-like organization. And not only do individuals circulate between its threads; they are always in the position of simultaneously undergoing and exercising power.[1]

For Foucault, power is a relationship within a community between the ones who lead and the ones who authorize their leadership. He points to the "powerlessness" of those who lead, as well as the "power" of those who are led.

Philosopher Hannah Arendt further develops the notion of power as characterizing a community. She goes so far as to say that power actually circulates "from below":

> Power belongs to a group and remains in existence only so long as the group keeps together. When we say of somebody that he is "in power" we actually refer to his being empowered by a certain number of people to act in their name. The moment the group, from which the power originated to begin with (*potestas in populo*, "without a people or group there is no power"), disappears, "his power" also vanishes.[2]

Violence is the only recourse a leader has when his or her power has been removed, and violence establishes tyranny. Arendt presents power as a uniquely relational phenomenon.

Examples of power operating as relationship abound in the churches. Many students, possessed of rich and diverse gifts for ministry (power as capacity) and ordained into the ministry of word and sacrament (power as commodity), return to seminary demanding to know where the course in "congregational dynamics" was. Having experienced how power circulates in their congregation and having felt both powerful and powerless, they seek some ways of tracking how power works.

A communal assumption

A second assumption undergirding this work is that every community is an argument for a certain kind of power relationship. Every community proposes a certain style of relationship — and therein a certain theory of power.

A friend teaches in a small institution that has experienced a change in its leadership. The former president had been quite accessible to his faculty: he favoured face-to-face encounters and invited people to share their concerns directly with him. People in the community addressed one another informally; often disagreements were personal differences in disguise. Differing parties addressed each other quite personally.

In contrast, the new president practised a much different style of leadership. He presented a more managerial style: he retreated behind a secretary and an appointment book, advising faculty to schedule to see him or, better, send him a written memorandum about their concerns. He preferred encounters through paper and eventually insisted that people address each other by their academic title. Differences became more impersonal and were formally expressed. The community under each style of presidential leadership presented very different arguments about power.

Philosopher Nancy Hartsock argues that "theories of power are implicitly theories of community".[3] Concretely, this means that communities embody arrangements about power, which can be analyzed, critiqued and structured in more liberatory ways. My synod is investigating a pastor in a local church against whom charges of sexual misconduct have been brought. Sexual misconduct certainly represents an abuse of personal pastoral power, but the incident exposes a lot about power arrangements within a particular congregation. Part of the synod's work investigates the power arrangements between the pastor and the congregation: congregational expectations of the pastor, pastoral expectations of the congregation, decision-making practices within the community. These inquiries acknowledge that power is a communal arrangement.

A theological assumption

A final assumption follows from the prior assumption: every community embodies a certain portrait of God. Different images of God define and direct different religious communities. James M. Gustafson suggests that imaging God as a shepherd engenders a sense of dependence in communities, imaging God as creator engenders a sense of responsibility, imaging God as redeemer and liberator engenders a community of gratitude, imaging God as judge engenders a community of obligation, and imaging God as hope engenders a community of possibility. These five senses of dependence, responsibility, gratitude, obligation and possibility need not be an exhaustive list, but they certainly define very different kinds of communities and very different sorts of power arrangements within them. For example, a community that worshipped God as judge might well expect its leaders to render judgment on God's behalf! Power relations could conceivably be rather hierarchical, directed towards ultimate rectification of the judged before God. A community that worshipped God as a mother might practise different virtues: nurturance, caring, maturity. Power relations might be equally hierarchical, but be directed towards maturity, rather than rectification of one's relationship before God. Both implicitly and explicitly every Christian community embodies a certain image of God, which informs how people within it relate to one another.

Teaching students about the history of the earliest Christian communities, I often invite them to imagine the portraits of God or Jesus that inform the strange theologies they read. They enjoy trying to match up communities and their arrangements of power with images of God. The most important question, of course, is not, "What is Athanasius' image of God and how does it contrast with Arius's?" Rather, the most important question is, "What is the image of God lived out in the community in which *you* worship?"

In summary, then, these three assumptions govern the argument presented here:
1) power is a relationship;
2) every community is an argument about power;
3) every community embodies a certain image of God.

Bearing these assumptions in mind, I propose to examine three different relationships of power — power-over, power-within and power-with — the uses and abuses of each relationship, and finally the images of God that might form, inform and transform them. I ask of each relationship, how is power to be used justly and faithfully? And I suggest that each relationship has its abuses and its appropriate place within church life.

Power-over

Most traditional discussions of power have been conducted from this vantage point, with a resultant definition of power as domination, coercion, influence and manipulation. Law, violence, tradition and even consent undergird this kind of power; and examples of its abuse abound: the power of apartheid and segregation, the power of husband over wife assumed in all too many marriages and buttressed by certain religious and political philosophies, the power of dominion over the earth, creating oil spills and a fast-disappearing ozone layer. As is desperately apparent, this form of power has its abuses. In so far as power-over assumes the posture of absolutist domination and totalitarian rule, it oppresses and destroys.

But I do not want to judge this form of power by its flagrant abuses, for it seems to have an important place in certain areas of our lives. The relationship of power-over characterizes the power parents exercise in caring for their children. Certainly, this power can be — and often is — coercive, but at its best it functions to protect a helpless infant against threat and death. Power-over characterizes some forms of pedagogy which acknowledge the expertise of a teacher, a mentor, a sage. No student would want to learn from someone who knew as little as she did! Power-over characterizes a doctor-patient relationship, as a sick person seeks out the specific expertise of a trained professional. Finally, power-over grounds many aspects of the pastoral office, as a troubled parishioner seeks counselling and confession from her pastor. People come to a pastor for everything from a quick fix to a miracle, and I am not sure that all pastors are —

or should be! — comfortable with the power invested in them. The question is not whether or not it is there but how to use it.

I would argue that this form of power is not intrinsically evil; indeed, to deny its place in our most ordinary relationships would be to deny the real differences that bind us to one another and to buttress our illusions of self-sufficiency. The question to put to this form of power is the question of its use: in a parent-child relationship, is power-over used to protect and to nurture or to abuse? In a teacher-student relationship does it serve to educate or to overwhelm and intimidate? In a doctor-patient relationship does power-over heal or disempower? In a pastor-parishioner relationship is it used to enspirit or to control? The question to put to this form of power is the question of its use.

Three models of power-over surface immediately: a warrior model, a parental model and a bureaucratic model. Each warrants further discussion.

Power-over in its warrior mode is most familiar. The general image of community here is a community under siege, a community threatened by outsiders or enemies. In such a situation, the mood is eternal vigilance or outright war. The warrior community encourages certain values: strength, competition, rationality and physical prowess are admired and cultivated. Finally, because death and extinction threaten, some means of achieving immortality must be present. Songs, stories and poems construct a community of memory and promise continuity.

We still sing hymns that depict the church as a community of warriors, because across the centuries and around the globe the church fights for its very survival: "Rise up, O saints of God... Give her strength equal to her task / Rise up and make her great." "Soldiers of the cross" climb Jacob's ladder. Perhaps the power-over emerges in a warrior mode whenever the church is threatened or under siege.

A second model of power-over is the parental model. The distinction between this mode and the previous one may not be immediately clear to those who are parents, particularly those who are parents of teenagers. I suspect that most parents of teenagers feel themselves to be in a community that is under terminal siege. But ideally the parental model presents community as an organic whole, with each part contributing to the functioning of the whole. Dysfunction threatens this organic community, and dysfunction occurs when any part ceases to function or to fulfill its stated role. It creates a void which must either be filled in by the other parts, worked around or, if possible, ignored. The power of stronger over weaker members focusses on maturation and integration into the whole, which is itself accomplished by imitation and example, instruction and discipline. Each member of the community functions as an important part of a larger whole; interdependence defines the mood. As in the warrior model, various values are here practised and encouraged: individuation and connection, flexibility, harmony and caring. The key virtue is fittingness of that wonderful virtue that Annie Dillard writes about so carefully: attending to the whole.[4] The parental model is another way of constructing power-over.

Think of hymns and songs that present the church as a family: "This is my Father's world"; Christians call themselves "children of the Heavenly Father / safely in his bosom gather", and the church itself has been called the "holy mother church". Liturgy documents this model of power as well.

A final model of power-over is the bureaucratic model, a power which often operates impersonally and anonymously. Here defined roles and stations dictate community life. One receives ministry or bread from the one whose role is to offer a particular kind of ministry or to bake a certain kind of bread, without having to like or even get along with that person. Role, not personal feelings, defines interactions within the community. Accordingly, the danger in bureaucratic communities is depersonalization: a person either gets equated with or lost in his/her role. One of my students fought the depersonalization of her first year at seminary by chanting a mantra before a particularly vexing class: "I am not my Greek grade. I am not my Greek grade. I am not my Greek grade." She refused to become the role of the Greek student.

Disorder, inefficiency and incompetence threaten the bureaucratic community because they disrupt the smooth functioning of the whole. Accordingly, the bureaucratic community encourages and practises certain values: order, efficiency and competence in fulfilling one's designated role. Like the parental community, this community articulates a key virtue: fittingness, the sense of parts working together in a whole.

Liturgical documentation of a bureaucratic community has not yet emerged: it would indeed be hard to pen a hymn of praise to God the prime minister or chief executive officer! But the practices of our communities betray us: all too often churches function not as the *communio sanctorum* but as a *corporatio sanctorum*.

Ministry conducted as a power-over relationship offers both problems and possibilities. Certain images of God can be used to form and inform a ministry of power-over. These images, accordingly, fall into three categories. God as a sovereign, master, lord or judge emerges in warrior communities; images of God as parent, whether father or mother, surface in parental communities; God as judge reappears in bureaucratic communities. These images of God awaken us to the inherent otherness of God and confront us with the side of God that is sometimes hidden from view.

What would a community that worshipped God as sovereign, parent or judge be like? Sovereign images of God engender a community that practises obedience and censures disobedience; parental images of God engender a community that practises honour and censures dishonour; bureaucratic images of God engender a community that stresses competent fulfillment of one's role and censures sloth.

A leader in each of these communities would be acutely aware of the expertise provided by his/her training to do ministry and to equip others to do it. This awareness necessarily separates the leader from the group and the minister from the congregation. It forces the community to deal with the differences which really are present within the group. To pretend away such differences would be an act of denial. The strength of a power-over model of ministry is to present honestly differences that really exist between leaders and groups, as well as to emphasize a leader's responsibility to guide, nurture and, when necessary, discipline the group of individuals therein.

At the same time, too much traffic with this power-over mode feeds three caricatures of ministry. The first caricature calls to mind the warrior and bureaucratic models of exercising power in a congregation: the portrait of the *Herr Pastor* or the *Frau / Fräulein Pastorin*. This is the rather grim portrait of a leader exercising absolute and blind power over a group. The caricature points to the danger of absolutism, domination and oppression inherent in a power-over model of leadership. The second caricature calls to mind the parental model of exercising power in a congregation: the portrait of the pastor as Eternal Earth Mother or Benign Father, a parent encouraging childlike and even childish behaviour in a group through long-suffering patience. This caricature points to the danger of infantilization in the power-over mode of leadership.

A final caricature, again from the parental mode of power-over, is the portrait of the pastor as Compulsive Co-Dependent, dangerously out-of-touch with his/her own feelings, therefore captive to the feelings of the group and vigilantly seeking to control and/or manipulate them. The co-dependent leader is unable to provide coherent and prophetic leadership to the group and only encourages continuing dependence of the group upon its leader. The caricature points to the lure of control and the seduction of indispensability lurking within the power-over model of leadership. So these three caricatures point to real problems with the very real possibilities latent in the same model.

An understanding of God's power acts as an antidote to domination, dysfunction and depersonalization. Understanding of God's power avoids caricatures of pastoral leadership in all of these models. Understanding of God's power instructs us in several ways.

First, God does not hoard power; God pours it out. Christ empties himself and becomes human. The sovereign becomes a servant; the judge, subject to judgment. Kenosis characterizes the way that God exercises power-over: God possesses power precisely in order to pour it out. This is the curb — the only curb — to domination.

Second, God does not hoard power; God pours it out — and God pours it out on us. God empowers God's creatures, a movement that bears both enablement and requirement. The pouring out of divine power on us not only enables us to reach our full potential, but carries with it a requirement: that we "go and make disciples of all nations" (Matt. 28:19). Thus, the one in power *empowers*. This cuts against both domination and dysfunction.

Third, God suffers. This is the revelation of Good Friday. Jesus cries abandonment, but still there is no attempt to control or manipulate events so that things turn out a little less messy. God does not display omnipotence but omni-compassion. God shows that God is able to withstand a mess, not of God's own creation — but absolutely incapable of taking it without utter and absolute compassion: literally, a "suffering with". Compassion cuts against the potential for dysfunction in parental communities, for dysfunction inevitably occurs when a parent moves in to accept final responsibility and to control the pain, humiliation and disaster that befall a child.

Power-within

A second form of power, power-within or charismatic power, is similar to and different from power-over. Like the first relationship of power, charismatic power exerts a power over others which may either oppress or inspire them. But unlike the first relationship of power, charismatic power has very different means of legitimation. External authority buttresses power-over, in the form of law, custom, tradition, coercion or violence. Charismatic power authorizes and authenticates itself. What validates it is nothing more and nothing less than the personal magnetism of the person possessing it. As such, power-within manifests itself as a charism or gift: the sum total of one's spiritual, emotional and psychological resources. Power-within or charismatic power is creative and dynamic, often iconoclastic. Eager to challenge old ways of being or to infuse them with new meaning, charismatic leaders seize new opportunities.

Not surprisingly, power-within often operates in antithesis to power-over. In the early centuries of Christianity, the role of the prophets diminished as the role of the bishops and teachers increased. At stake were relationships of power: the charismatic power of the prophets threatened emerging structures within the church; the charismatic power of prophets attracted people to a person; the bureaucratic power of bishops and teachers gathered people into an institution that was hunkering down for the long haul. Bishops and teachers embodied a power-over, gradually reserving for themselves the right to decide who "true" and "false" prophets were, then finally editing out these representatives of a power-within entirely.

Yet lest these counter-institutional folks appear too attractive, I must caution that power-within runs its own obstacle course. Charismatic power is a gift that can poison; it needs constantly to be tested and tried. Jim Jones was such a charismatic leader, possessed perhaps more by his own demons than by any clear vision or by his followers. They followed him blindly — even to their own deaths. Charismatic power appears to be a prerequisite for television evangelists, and they preach at length with great popularity and efficacy, but also manipulatively. Power-within needs to be disciplined and tested. At the same time, it is difficult to test — too often, the bedazzled masses will be too mesmerized to ask for authenticity. The testing must come from the charismatic leader herself.

So it seems that this form of power, too, has the potential for abuse. Two forms of charismatic leadership emerge as one examines this relationship of power more closely: the hypnotic charismatic leader and the inspirational charismatic leader. Both are possessed of incredible power-within, but the hypnotic leader uses her power to dominate, while the inspirational leader uses her power to educate, energize and empower others. The effect of hypnotic leadership is slavery; the effect of inspirational leadership is freedom that empowers followers to work constructively on their own.

The kind of community formed by hypnotic leadership resembles the kind of community formed by power-over leadership in the basic warrior mode: blind obedience is obligatory. The kind of community formed by inspirational leadership is characterized by a combination of loyalty and critique, loyalty inspired by the charismatic leader herself and critique encouraged by the same. We must note that the line between hypnotic and inspirational leadership is often very fine. Concluding her study of charismatic leadership, philosopher Dorothy Emmet observes that "without self-knowledge, and indeed a sense of humour on the part of the charismatic leader, there is always a danger that his leadership may turn to enslavement".[5] It seems that humour, humility and generosity mark charismatic leadership in its inspirational mode and curb the potential for abuse.

Ministry that emerges from this relationship of power has unique problems and possibilities. Surely the charismatic leadership of specific people has touched each of us and invited us into leadership within the church. As I read through admission files to my seminary, I see the work and support of a cloud of witnesses behind a single decision to enter into one of the leadership ministries in the church. Each of us can trace the impact of charismatic leadership in our lives and our ministries. Probably each of us is herself a charismatic figure for others. Again, the charismatic leadership that does not oppress or overwhelm effectively combines humour, generosity and humility — and when true humility is not an option, wry self-deprecation will do. But again, inspirational charismatic leaders have consciously assessed their "CQ" — charisma quotient — and its effect on others; they possess a keen sense of how to inspire for the sake of ministry.

Certain images of God form and inform a ministry of power-within. God as Spirit infuses this relationship of power, and here the power of God's Spirit connects closely with — and is sometimes even mistaken for! — the spirit of the believer. Christian hymns praise the work of the Spirit: "Spirit of God, descend upon my heart," or "Breathe on me, breath of God".

Worshipping God as Spirit engenders a community counselled to be open to and discerning of the gifts of God's Spirit and cautioned against rigidity and closed-mindedness. It configures a community that practises, in the deepest sense, hospitality towards the stranger, for the stranger always comes bearing gifts. The danger of such a style of leadership would be instability and lack of boundaries.

A leader operating in this kind of power-within mode would be acutely aware of her CQ, her personal power of charisma within a group. Such knowledge would, it is hoped, make the charismatic leader cautious in regard to use and abuse of that power, but also bold in calling out and naming the dormant powers within the group and its members. The power of the leader would initially attract and then graciously empower the group. This describes inspirational charismatic leadership at its best.

At the same time, problems beset this relationship of power, resulting in certain caricatures of leadership: pastor as guru. Too often the charismatic leader wants to be the only person in the group with the goods. Rather than empowering the group, the leader then disempowers the group, rendering the leader indispensable and the group dependent. The leader's exercise of charismatic power affects the group as an oppressive form of power-over. Here, however, the unique form of oppression is impression: dazzled by its charismatic leader, a group unquestioningly conforms to whatever the leader wills, even to the point of blindly following a command to die, as was the case in Jonestown. The caricature of the pastor as guru surfaces the problems of this relationship of power, which must then be held in tension with its real possibilities.

An understanding of God's power acts as an antidote against the problems inherent in this model:

1. God's power calls for discernment, which is appropriate and necessary in any setting where people are trying to decide where the Spirit is leading them. Discernment actively, prayerfully and publicly searches for the guidance of the Spirit; it leads a group to distinguish between God's Spirit and the spirits of various charismatic individuals in its midst.

2. God's power calls for distinction: finding the line between what our own spirit would bid us do and what God's Spirit would bid us do. This sort of discernment is hard enough to do in a group, but it is almost impossible to do

alone. Discernment and the distinction it accomplishes always occur "where two or three are gathered". The isolation that charisma bestows on the one who possesses it often cuts her off from the mutual conversation and consolation of her brothers and sisters, precisely when she most needs their counsel. Discerning and distinguishing the spirits demands a community of prayer and conversation.

3. Finally, God's power reminds the charismatic leader of the real source of her power. As Christ pointed to God, so the leader points finally to the source of her power. Gratitude for the gift and humility in possessing it curb the abuses of charismatic power.

Power-with

A final relationship of power is power-with, also known as co-active power or friendship. Power-with emerges in the strength and solidarity of a grassroots movement. It surfaces whenever a group dares to articulate a common purpose and a common good. Often charismatic leaders galvanize this form of power, and the best inspirational charismatic leaders create power-with in the groups following them, as they call out and name the power which all share in common.

Examples of power-with emerge throughout the history of Christianity. Jesus drew this out of that rowdy crowd known as his disciples — except that each of them kept vying with the others for a special seat of honour next to their Lord! It is the power of monastic communities that strive to live under a rule and according to vows of poverty, chastity and obedience. Lest these vows sound quaint, let us be reminded of how quickly wealth or romantic affections fragment a community and how detrimental such dynamics are to the fabric of a common life. The contemporary feminist movement and the US civil rights movements are organized as power-with movements. Each was graced by the leadership of such charismatic figures as Martin Luther King or Mary Daly, but each tried to articulate a common goal and empower others for its attainment.

So it seems that power-with is a very real realm and important force within our lives. Yet, lest we embrace too enthusiastically this form of power, there are pitfalls here as well. C.S. Lewis, in his delightful and insightful book *The Four Loves*,[6] reminds us of the exclusionary tendencies of power-with for all those who might be on the outside looking in. There is an Olympian elitism in such groupings, he remarks. Feminist Nancy Hartsock, in her book *Money, Sex, and Power*,[7] identifies the fall-out of a movement that stubbornly resisted all forms of power-over, most forms of power-within, and focussed exclusively on power-with: (1) a kind of personal, structureless politics; (2) a widespread opposition to leadership; (3) an insistence on working collectively; and (4) an emphasis on process, often to the exclusion of getting things done.

My own work on the board of the Graduate Theological Union's Center for Women and Religion corroborates these observations. For a long time the Center had three co-directors, which seemed a good idea given its unique needs and three very talented women's diverse gifts. And yet, what we realized was that these three very talented women were spending most of their time in meetings with each other as they tried desperately to figure out what the other was doing and whether and/or how they might work together. So it seems that power-with has its own problems and possibilities, to which one must be attentive.

Ministry conducted in this mode accordingly has unique problems and possibilities. A certain image of God forms and informs a ministry of power-with: the image of God as friend. This image of God alerts us to the mutuality we have with God in God's kingdom and calls us to an active responsibility in working towards that kingdom. We are thus relieved of the passive obedience that a power-over relationship in the warrior mode would demand. We are equally eased away from the idolatry of creating our own kingdom in God's name, the predicament present in a power-within mode of operating. Friendship images of God engender a community that is counselled to be loyal and cautioned against betrayal. Hymns like "What a friend we have in Jesus" document the importance of this relationship in Christian communities.

A leader operating in this kind of power-with mode would be living out a calling to be "first among equals". The task would be one of fidelity to a common goal and active work towards that goal. Rather than being at the top of a pyramid of power as in the power-over model, or at the hub of a centrifuge as in the power-within model, the leader would be the head of the body, directing movement that she would not be able to complete on her own. An organic metaphor for community best describes the mutuality present in a community organized around friendship.

Yet power-with has its own problems, perhaps best illustrated in the caricatures of the pastor as a buddy or terminal facilitator. These caricatures surface when a group loses sight of its common purpose and all that remains is cloying intimacy or terminal process with no product apparent and no end in sight. As buddy, the leader is merely "one of the folks", close and amiable, but because of that proximity unable to empower, direct or chasten any one of the group. As facilitator, a leader is good at getting out the possibilities that lie within the group. But mere facilitation neither challenges nor empowers the group to transcend itself and seek possibilities beyond it. Often, this relationship of power constitutes a denial of differences in power between leader and group; it also denies responsibilities that rest — and rest only — with the leader. The caricatures of pastor as buddy or terminal facilitator point to real problems in the power-with mode of leadership, and these must be held in tension with the equally real possibilities latent in the same model.

An understanding of God's power curbs the emergence of such caricatures.

NOTES

1 "Two Lectures", in *Power / Knowledge: Interviews and Other Writings 1972-1977*, Colin Gordon ed., New York, Pantheon, 1980, p.98.
2 *On Violence*, New York, Harcourt, Brace & World, 1970, p. 44.
3 *Money, Sex and Power: Towards a Feminist Historical Materialism*, Boston, Northeastern UP, 1983, p.3.
4 *Pilgrim at Tinker Creek*, New York, Bantam, 1974, pp. 15–35.
5 *Function, Purpose, and Powers*, Philadelphia, Temple UP, 1972, p. 238.
6 New York, Harcourt Brace Jovanovich, 1960, p. 122.
7 *Op. cit.*, p.3.

8. Power in a Discipleship of Equals

RANJINI REBERA

The prevailing model of leadership

A few years ago I was privileged to direct and teach a young women's leadership training workshop organized by two ecumenical organizations. The participants were 35 women from a variety of ethnic backgrounds and church denominations. The organizing committee was a small group of women church leaders from national church organizations and representatives from different denominations. All of them had different ethnic roots.

As I worked with the organizing committee I realized that beneath the energy expended in the day-to-day running of the workshop, all was not right. There seemed to be a deep sense of mistrust and anger, and a struggle for power, superiority and control. Many times the working meetings of the steering committee were paralyzed as disengaged body-language, innuendo and flashes of power-as-control emerged. As I probed deeper into why this group of dedicated, committed women leaders was being held captive within such a destructive process, I was once again confronted with the dominant model of power within society and church government. It became clear that these women were reflecting the struggle for dominance and power, ethnic and racial superiority, and the denominational arrogance so often visible in church government and within national and local church organizations.

The objective of the organizing committee was to train the next generation of young women leaders, to enable them to discover new and different styles of leadership, and to guide them into becoming equal partners with men and other women. However, these senior women leaders were unconsciously role-modelling a style of leadership that was patriarchal, dominant and sometimes destructive. They were also demonstrating the difficulties surrounding the exercise of power and authority as more women move into decision-making positions within our churches. The model before them was one that accepted leadership styles based on power as dominance and control. Therefore, to be accepted as leaders they had learned to use the rules of this model. For women socialized to accept power as the norm for men and powerlessness as the norm for women, leadership based on dominant power and authority can become both traumatic and destructive to themselves and others. This organizing committee bore all the evidence of such a struggle. Sadly, the process and workshop schedule left no room or safe spaces for these wonderful women to explore why we, as women, find power and authority such difficult issues, or why we often become unsupportive of each other when assuming positions of leadership. It also left no space to explore the reality that being different should not provoke a battle for power and superiority.

I often look back at that workshop as I continue to explore concepts of power, especially within the community of faith. Many issues relating to the use and abuse of power are relevant as they impinge upon the establishing of a community of equals as our response to discipleship. I shall focus here on two issues: power and *difference* and power and *identity* and their relevance to establishing a discipleship of equals.

Power and difference

Why does difference create unequal positions of power, especially within a community of faith? Perhaps the first step in addressing this question is to define the nature of power. The most predominant and visible expression of power within the human community is dominant power. This is at the root of political oppression, economic exploitation, militarism, violence against women and children, racial and religious conflict, and sexism. The abuse of power in these situations is self-evident. It is through such uses of power that one is able to define its nature. Kyle Pasewark, a theologian in search of a theology of power, makes the claim, "Power itself is neutral and formal, almost indifferent. It becomes good, bad, necessary, excessive or abusive only through the object to which it is applied."[1]

For instance, at the moment of birth a baby experiences life as energizing power that enables her to live outside the security of her mother's body. She learns to use power as crying, as claiming attention, as need for food, and as the right to loving relationships. Her ownership of power, used in this manner, is not linked to gender, race, religious affiliations or economic circumstance. It is a human acknowledgment of power as energy — as a life-force. In later years this baby will learn to use and apply power in other ways. She will internalize the social rules that define the use and ownership of power. James Poling, a counsellor and professor of pastoral theology, maintains that:

> Power is a complex term with personal, social and religious connotations. At a personal level all persons have some power by virtue of being alive, along with an inner drive to use power to become all they can be... Society dictates how power is distributed. Institutions and ideologies determine who has privilege to be dominant and who must defer.[2]

As Poling continues to explore ways in which power is distributed within society, he uses the metaphor of a web. He claims it as a "relational web" that becomes the pathway for the distribution of power:

> Power is actually organized by the relational webs of which we are a part. Our ability to act in effective ways depends on our connections with other persons, and with institutions and ideas that form the basis of our experience. Power is gauged by the complexity of the relationships that can be contained in an interaction.[3]

However, within the relational webs that constitute human society there lies the reality of difference. When one of the objects of the application of power is the element of difference, we then create barriers that make a community of equals difficult to attain.

The human community consists of a vast range of differences, from race and ethnic identity, through gender and culture, to ideological and theological differences. At the heart of the creation of humanity lies the concept of difference. This motif runs through the creation story as we observe difference between night and day, water, earth and air, fauna and flora, and male and female. Danna Nolan Fewell and David Gunn, in exploring issues of gender and power in the creation story in Genesis, write:

> God divides up the world in clear categories: light and dark, day and night, wet and dry, plants and animals, heaven and earth. We see a desire to divide, differentiate, categorize and, in a word, name. Of course differentiation could be said to be indispensable to creation. Certainly separation, division, difference is indispensable to meaning. Meaning is difference. A world that is no longer simply *tohu vabohu* ("a formless void": NEB) is a world of difference.[4]

Into such difference we have injected control and power. For Christians, the dualism visible in the creation story has reinforced theories of power, dominance and control. There seems to be an implicit understanding that difference must result in hierarchy. Hierarchy is not confined to male-female relations alone. It was one of the destructive elements that controlled the group of women leaders organizing the leadership training workshop mentioned above. It was evident as different women claimed their right to control, based on their racial origins, or their husband's position of authority in church or society, or their own position of authority within the women's movement. Differences in status, education, economic resources, even denominational heritage, become rungs in the ladder of hierarchy. Within the community of faith these elements continue to contribute to the assumption of power as dominance and continue to place God as head, followed by male, then female, and so on through the different categories of creation. Such interpretations continue to be used when issues of gender cause destabilization or conflict within the Christian community. Margaret Koch, a historian and member of an interdisciplinary team that has researched challenges facing gender reconciliation as we move into the next stage of the debate, writes: "Difference and equality were never intended to be at opposite poles."[5] By placing them in opposing positions we have created a separation between every element of creation. We see the greatest evidence of separation when we address issues of gender. Within the Christian church that has as its centrepiece a gospel of love and peace with justice, we often superimpose the pain of difference and separation in order to dominate and control. Julie Hopkins, a researcher and lecturer in feminist theology, makes the observation:

> The story of how a good prophet who proclaimed that God is a loving destabilizing force for human wholeness and justice came to be crucified as a blasphemer and state criminal is a shocking reminder of the tragic and alienated dimension of human power relations.[6]

The crucifixion of Christ confronts us with the consequence of the abuse of dominant power based on difference and the pain of separation. The power of state and religious establishments, threatened by power in Christ's identity and integrity, perpetrated the violence of the cross. It dealt with difference by claiming religious superiority. It legitimized control by separating authority as power from authority as identity and integrity. The pain in the violence of the crucifixion is the pain of difference and separation. It is this crucifixion pain that is experienced when ethnic and religious differences create rape camps in Bosnia, Rwanda and Sri Lanka, when theological difference separates us from table-fellowship each time we celebrate the eucharist, when gender difference takes priority over God's call to women to the ordained ministry of the word.

Rachel, a second-year student at a theological college in Australia, lives with the pain caused by polarizing difference and equality. Some time during her second year of training for ordination, the leaders of her church voted to amend the constitution of their denomination to enable them to rescind the ordination of women. Rachel was devastated. The options of seeking ordination in another denomination or of becoming a deaconess in her own denomination were suggested to her. But as Rachel said to me on more than one occasion, God had called her to be ordained within her denomination, not in another one. To opt for one of these paths would also absolve her church council from dealing with the injustice of their actions. Rachel is still an active member of her denomination; she continues to worship regularly in her parish as she attempts to find ways to address the antagonism of some of its leaders — especially that of some members of the clergy. She persists in her struggle for ordination. She is different because of her gender and she has been declared unequal to men when it comes to ordination by the policies of her church government. But her call from God to the ordained ministry does not differentiate between genders, neither does it treat her as a lesser being when compared to the men who train with her in college.

Difference cannot be ignored. Therefore we must learn to view difference not as a basis for division and conflict but for right relations. Such an approach will move difference and equality from opposing ends into relational positions within human society. It will challenge dominant power that exercises control. When we affirm difference as a relational force we recognize the depth and meaning of human relationships. Carter Heyward claims that "resurrection is a relational movement, the revolutionary carrying-on of a spirit of love and justice that does not and will not die".[7] When we accept being in relation with each other and with all of creation as the outcome of resurrection relationality, then the many forms of difference that exist will cease to separate us. Mutuality will become the foundation for our interconnectedness. The possibility for true inclusivity will become an experienced reality. Power-over is replaced by power-with, and power and difference become partners in creating healing and wholeness.

Power and identity

How does one experience mutuality and being in right relation as power-with, rather than as shared power?

Sri Lanka has been in the grip of a racial war for many years. The churches continue to grapple with issues of ethnic and racial identity within their congregations. Neelum is a member of a church that is in the forefront of the struggle to bring about peace in this island nation. She is a Tamil and therefore a member of the minority race who are fighting for justice and equality in the country. Neelum has grieved through the deaths of her father, two young brothers and a cousin. All of them met violent deaths in the north of the country where the war is being fought. She has been the sole supporter of her aging mother, whose health continues to deteriorate as she relives the horrors inflicted on her family and replays in her mind the acts of violence she has witnessed in the town she once called home. For Neelum and hundreds of others like her the possibility of being in a mutual relationship with members of the Sinhala majority community is not an intellectual exercise. It is a continuing reality that challenges the centre of her Christian teachings — that she loves and therefore forgives. Experiencing power with members of the Sinhala dominant race who are also members of her church community is a painful proposition for Neelum. In one of her conversations with me she asked: "How can I even begin to think in terms of Christian love and justice, when I see none in this war? I cannot see myself connecting with particular persons in this congregation, who I know are Sinhala racists. You are asking the impossible." Answers are hard to come by for questions such as hers, even within the community of faith.

Similar questions are heard from women who are victims of other forms of violence. How can they be in community with the person who has perpetrated a crime on them? I have heard women in church congregations pose the same question as they continue to live with violence in the home because church leaders quote biblical texts to sanctify that violence.

For women like Neelum whose identity is rooted in her racial and cultural heritage, the destruction of her identity by the arrogance of the dominant race is the central issue. For women caught in innumerable acts of violence across the world, the issue is the same. Their identity is being violated to the point where their loss of identity is cocooned within the security of powerlessness. Within this environment they continue to experience their sense of who they are as social beings. They learn to accept their identity all over again, but often as powerless victims feeling secure in their powerlessness. Hanna Papenek, an anthropologist exploring the question of identity and control, claims:

> A sense of identity can be shaped and reshaped — often very powerfully — by external forces, bent on their own agendas of building new solidarities, new group boundaries, and new political alliances. These transformations may be experienced as a "violation of identity" but may also be embraced with enthusiasm and experienced by the person as a process of growth. Paradoxically, therefore, one's sense of identity may be simultaneously stable in some aspects but also volatile in terms of changing loyalties evoked in response to changing circumstances.[8]

Changing loyalties and changing circumstances often reinforce images of powerlessness and strengthen the dominant power that controls relationship and robs identity. Such expressions of power are rooted in the expression of arrogance: arrogance of race, gender, religious beliefs, class, sexual orientation, and all the other labels that we use to categorize and control.

The reality of identity

Warren is a friend who is experiencing the effects of power as arrogance in relation to sexuality and identity. He is currently working towards ordination within my church in Australia. Because his journey is now an open story, I do not hesitate to share it as an example of the community of faith dealing with the reality of identity.

Warren is gay and is open about his sexual orientation. I was his elder and friend as he continued to deal with his absolute certainty that God had been calling him over a long period of time to the ordained ministry. He had responded to the call many years ago, but the church had gently but firmly advised him to rethink the matter. Warren continued to be an active member within the church as he rose successfully within the Australian public service. When I first met him, I was struck by the person he was, his talents, his gift for friendship, his academic abilities, but above all his capacity to care. It was obvious that his call from God was a continuing struggle for him. As his elder it also raised many issues for me. One of the main questions I kept coming back to was, if his sexual orientation was not a barrier to baptism into the community of faith and lay leadership in it, why was it now a barrier to his exercising an ordained ministry within the same community? His identity has not changed. His sexuality is as much a part of his identity as his concern for justice, his commitment to Christ, his faith in God and his acceptance as a baptized member of the body of Christ.

One of the issues for Warren was how he could be faithful to his call without inflicting pain and division within the congregation, should he decide to be a candidate once again. After many lengthy discussions I remember saying to Warren that perhaps he should allow the parish to make the decision as to whether they would support his application or not; perhaps he should stop trying to protect us from the pain and the struggle to come to a decision. I felt strongly that as a parish we had to make the decision as to whether Warren's identity was defined only by his sexual orientation or by his humanness. We had to examine our own arrogance as heterosexual persons who would prefer to extend our understandings of sexuality to our understanding of God. Once we made our decision, we would have to own it and live with it.

Warren's application for ordination is still being processed. The parish voted unanimously to support it. However, like many church structures and systems my church government, too, is not equipped to deal with difference and identity — only with conformity. Therefore, while committees of presbytery, synod and assembly continue to debate and seek consensus by calling "meetings about meetings about meetings", Warren continues to be an active elder, parish secretary, leader of worship, preacher, activist, and a high-ranking public servant in the Australian public service. His own sense of identity is secure. The parish continues to walk with Warren, to be connected to his struggle as an issue of faith and discipleship for the whole community of faith.

Warren's struggle has created the climate for a recognition and affirmation of identity as personal identity and collective identity. When all of us — including the Warrens and Neelums of our societies — are prepared to address issues of difference and identity from the position of relationality and mutuality, the equation of power changes and ceases to be power-over. This vision for a discipleship of equals begins to emerge within a community living in true partnership. Elisabeth Schüssler Fiorenza identifies a discipleship of equals as *ekklesia* ("believing community") that can make present the *basileia* ("God's world"), the alternative world of justice and well-being intended by the life-giving power of God. She goes on to amplify this reality by claiming that like Jesus we

> are called to proclaim the "good news" of God's alternative world of justice and love and to make it present by gathering people around the table and inviting everyone without exception to it, by feeding the hungry, healing the sick, and liberating the oppressed. The discipleship of equals must be a *basileia* discipleship.[9]

Within this understanding of a discipleship of equals, concepts of power have to be changed radically. Power as dominance, arrogance, separation, must not be permitted to polarize and subordinate. For women to "reclaim the ekklesia as community" we have to permit ourselves the right to own and claim power for ourselves and to use it for wholeness, for empowerment and for building community. Perhaps as women our socialization makes us react negatively to this proposition. Yet we continue to see evidence of change when the collective power of women is harnessed to challenge political, economic and military systems. The United Nations' women's conference in Beijing, where 30,000 women were able to demonstrate the positive aspects of collective power, emerges as a powerful icon for harnessing the power of those whom society traditionally labels as "weak". While issues relating to difference and identity were strong factors in the debates, discussions and negotiations that formed the tapestry of the conference, they also provided the platform for the naming of all forms of injustice and violence that continue to be a part of our human journey. The collective naming then became the voice of all women, speaking for each woman in her time and place.

The power of the weak

However, as women we unfortunately prefer to use the "power of the weak" in our personal lives, to hold us in a form of inertia. Rosine Perelberg, a social anthropologist and psychotherapist examining issues of gender and power in families, makes the observation that:

> The concept of the power of the weak is important to an understanding of the ways in which women in different societies may exercise powers... The fact that power can be exercised from a subordinate position is fundamental to both the way in which gender roles are constructed in different societies and the respective positions from which men and women perceive themselves.[10]

The negative concept of the power of the weak exercised from subordinate positions is visible within what I term "de facto" power. Rather than claim power as a human reality and not as a gendered reality, many of us learn to use our many roles and functions to own power through the social systems that define our behaviour as women. We continue to claim our identity through the various ways in which we exercise subtle control over those whose lives impinge on ours. Many of us have learned to create dependency cycles within our families, our places of work, and even within our church communities. We become indispensable to the work of our communities while we simultaneously claim to be powerless or victims of social networks. Yet by creating dependency we also create avenues for controlling and exercising power over our small communities. We will not own power, but we will use it in a de facto manner to influence and control. Such an exercise of power can polarize women against women and women against men. The negative use of power from a subordinate position can polarize the many layers of structure within the body of the church. It undermines any democratic process that is established for the good of the whole community. It cannot assist in re-imaging power as transforming power.

Transforming the community

Transforming power is the vision that can keep us on the journey towards creating a partnership of equals within the community of faith. It is embedded in experiencing power-with as the basis for our being connected to each other. This is not power-sharing, as that may contain elements of arrogance and dominance. Who decides how the cake of power is to be cut and shared, or when it is to be cut or not cut? Inequalities can be incorporated into power-sharing. However, when we are able to experience power with each other, the transformation of one leads to the transformation of all. Similarly, the oppression of one leads to the oppression of all. In experiencing power with each other we are interconnected. We are drawn to work together while respecting each one's identity and affirming our mutual need for each other. At such moments we become aware of power-within each individual and the community as a whole. Letty Russell, theologian and writer, creates the image of staying well connected as we "discover the church in the round in and through the many table connections that disturb and nourish us day by day".[11] Rita Nakashima Brock, the Japanese American theologian, names power-within as "the power that heals and allows the touching of heart to heart, the most sacred power I know".[12]

Power-within has the potential for transforming both the individual and the community. It guarantees inclusivity as "the radical openness to otherness and difference whose incorporation constantly creates identity anew". In an inclusive community, perceptions are constantly transformed to correspond to the reality that makes up the concrete life of persons. It creates a healing community where victims of dominant power have a voice and are believed and loved into healing and wholeness.

Power-within guarantees justice for all within the community. This includes accountability from those who would use power to control and dominate. It becomes the catalyst for creating processes that will challenge and change all forms of power that legitimize unjust structures and systems, including all forms of leadership within the community.

Power-within has the potential to transform our understanding and experiencing of God as we work in mutuality and inclusivity. It can replace our kyriarchal theologies, which create God in our male images, with God as "God who lives within the relational web as a fully active and interdependent partner with creation". It connects us to God as the source of life-giving power that created us different and equal.

Power-within continues to challenge us into the creation of community where peace with justice, freedom with equality, and love with vulnerability become foundational to all living. It is reflected in the "resilient hope of the human spirit, which can resist abuse and create new communities for the restoration of communion and freedom of self, others and God".[13]

NOTES

1 For further discussion on the topic see "The Ubiquity of Power" and "The Contemporary Question of Power", in *A Theology of Power: Being Beyond Domination*, Minneapolis, Fortress, 1993.

2 *The Abuse of Power: A Theological Problem*, Nashville, Abingdon, 1991, p.12.

3 *Ibid.*, p.24.

4 *Gender, Power and Promise: The Subject of the Bible's First Story*, Nashville, Abingdon, 1993, p.23.

5 For further discussion on difference see her chapter on "A Christian Perspective on Difference", in *After Eden: Facing the Challenge of Gender Reconciliation*, Mary Stewart Van Leeuwen ed., Grand Rapids, MI, Eerdmans, 1993.

6 *Towards a Feminist Christology*, Grand Rapids, MI, Eerdmans, 1994, p.112.

7 "Mutuality: The Power of God-with-us", in *Staying Power: Reflections on Gender, Justice and Compassion*, Cleveland, Pilgrim, 1995, p.20.

8 "The Ideal Woman and the Ideal Society: Control and Autonomy in the Construction of Identity", in *Identity, Politics and Women: Cultural Reassertions and Feminism in International Perspective*, Valentine M. Moghadam ed., Boulder, CO, Westview, 1994, p.44.

9 *Discipleship of Equals: A Critical Feminist Ekklesia-logy of Liberation*, London, SCM, 1993, p.12.

10 "Equality, Asymmetry, and Diversity: On Conceptualization of Gender", in *Gender and Power in Families*, J. Perelberg and A.C. Miller eds, New York, Routledge, 1990, p.45.

11 In *Church in the Round: Feminist Interpretation of the Church*, Louisville, Westminster/John Knox, 1993, p.208.

12 *Journeys by Heart: A Christology of Erotic Power*, New York, Crossroads, 1992, p.xvi.

13 Poling, *op. cit.*, p.23.

9. Power and Minorities:
Indigenous Women in South America

MANUEL LARREAL

In order to understand the situation of indigenous women in South America, it is important to remember the original causes of the impoverishment of indigenous peoples in general. The process of conquest and colonization that began more than five hundred years ago is still a reality in their lives. Two historical cases can help us understand how colonization is still going on.

In the beginning...
  This is what happened to Anacaona, the wife of Canoabo... She was courageous, magnanimous and resourceful and remarkable tales were told of her throughout the island... When Nicolás de Ovando received the cargo from the governor of La Española, she decided to go to Xaraguá... Anacaona prepared a royal reception with singing and dancing... But the conqueror already had his own plan: to perform a great massacre as a warning... He made them all go into a large log cabin..., gave the signal and the massacre began. Anacaona was handcuffed; they set the building on fire and burned it; the lords and kings were burned alive on their lands, poor wretches, until all were reduced to embers with the straw and wood. As for Queen Anacaona, "in order to honour her, she was hanged". Everything corresponded to the sadistic sentence: to suspend the beautiful body of the chief's wife as an honour three months after forcing her, as a prisoner and in handcuffs, to watch as they burned all the men of her court alive.[1]

Thus we can say that the violence of the conquest found all kinds of justifications for imposing itself.

Not long ago...
  Seven colonists who hunted Indians acquitted in Colombia: Villavicencio, Colombia, 23 June (AP). Seven colonists accused of having assassinated 16 Indians in cold blood on 23 December 1967 were acquitted because they had acted "in absolute good faith resulting from incorrigible ignorance", a conscientious jury decided here today... The accused did not deny their participation in the collective assassination of Indians which caused an outcry and indignation in Colombia; they simply said that they did not know that "killing Indians was a crime"... The Indians of the Kuiba tribe had been lured to the farm La Rubiera in the eastern plains along the Colombian/Venezuelan frontier with offers of food. The Native Americans accepted the provisions and, while they were eating, the colonists riddled them with bullets and finished them off with machete blows. Then they dug a trench, poured petrol over the corpses and set fire to them. At the trial, which lasted twenty days, the partly blackened bones of the 16 Indians were exhibited; they included women and children.[2]

It could hardly be clearer: killing Indians is not thought to be a crime, and legal acquittals are justified through laws made by the heirs of the conqueror.

Some figures

The indigenous population of South America has been estimated at more than 36 million (5 percent of the total South American population). Today's indigenous panorama has its own peculiarities and differs from that of previous decades. The marked increase in the population of the world and of this continent is reflected in the indigenous population, but this is also closely linked with a strengthening of its identity.

Pluralism as a force, a contribution and a creative value is gaining the upper hand over homogeneity. The presence of indigenous peoples is a recognized fact, more significant and determinative in some societies than in others, but with a clear and precise form: their goal is to be in control of their own destiny. They are endeavouring to discover who they are, how many they are, what they are doing, and how they can live in the context of complex societies, in order to make themselves better known and to end the discrimination and indifference reflected in official population analyses.

Despite the persistent aggression of incorporationist policies and erosive processes from which they have suffered for the past 500 years, indigenous peoples have preserved their life-style, their cultures, languages and traditions — the elements which now support their ethnic identity. There is more interest in and attention to the emergence and presence of indigenous peoples within the United Nations, among financial bodies at the world level, and in national governments.

The modernizing process after the second world war had a substantial effect on all the countries of South America, including its indigenous peoples. Modernization, population growth and other factors precipitated the disintegration and collapse of the agrarian regimes to which they had been subject for centuries and gave rise to three closely related processes: substantial agrarian reforms, a massive and continuing flow of migration from the country to the cities, and the appearance and rapid growth of an active and widespread Native American movement supported by a clearly ethnic ideology.

In their search for modernity, well-being and justice, the indigenous peoples of South America have become engaged in innumerable activities and processes, three of which have stood out in the past few years because of their size and growing importance.

Throughout the continent there are dozens of indigenous communities which have succeeded in dynamizing and recreating their local economies, using their own technologies and management capacity. They have not abandoned their ethnic identity but, on the contrary, have seen their traditional culture as an additional value for their products.

Over the past forty years, the cities of Latin America have more than doubled in population and the urbanized proportion has shifted from a minority to the majority. In cities like Lima, La Paz, Guatemala City and Quito indigenous migration has comprised the major part of this growth.

The most obvious and promising process is the mobilization of indigenous peoples throughout the continent which started with the emergence in the past decade of dynamic organizations and indigenous leaders occupying important places in the political and social scene of their respective countries and at international level. Thus, indigenous people are becoming protagonists. Their absence in the past gave rise to the development and success of "indigenism", meaning management by well-intentioned third parties on behalf of the Indians. Now Native Americans themselves are taking the defence of their interests into their own hands. Their most active organizations and leaders are supported by ancient forms of community and local government that are still alive and well today. Their common ideology is ethnicity, understood essentially as a doctrine which states their right to endure as ethnic groups with different cultures and languages, and to achieve well-being, development and modernity without losing their identity.

As far as Latin American countries are concerned, the serious crises which have affected and still affect the whole region have demonstrated the exhaustion of the Western type of national social model with its cultural homogeneity. Today, there is a growing appreciation of cultural diversity in those countries. In leading circles attention is now being paid to the American Indian nations, their past history, their present demands, and their importance in the process of building up modern, ethnically pluralist societies. Over the past decade, far-reaching constitutional and legal instruments have been promulgated which recognize, protect and encourage the presence, permanence and development of indigenous groups as specific sectors.

Indigenous women in South America

The majority of indigenous oral traditions affirm that women arose from the entrails of Mother Earth so that they can continue the process of creation, reproducing and generating life in their communities. Myths about origins tell us about a matriarchal rather than a patriarchal creation. On the basis of this cultural principle, the role of the indigenous woman is determinative in community life: she is the preserver and transmitter of cultural values; she is the most familiar with the medicinal plants, she has the best knowledge of the shamanist world, and she does the most to care for the health of the community.

The imposition of individualistic values from the West had a negative effect on community relations in the indigenous world. Indigenous men learned the characteristics of male dominance (*machismo*) and asserted them perhaps more strongly and savagely than the conquerors themselves.

The marginalization of indigenous women can be seen in two ways: one is internal to the communities themselves; the other is external and depends not on the community but on the dominant society.

Internal aggression

From girlhood, women undertake responsibilities within the home, helping with domestic chores, caring for children, working in the kitchen garden, and so on. This deprives them of the time for recreation and restricts their opportunities to study. Because of the lack of social, economic, educational and political openings, many women are leaving their communities and going to work in urban centres. This problem of migration is linked to processes of acculturation and loss of identity.

There is a clear subordination to males in the family and the community. In such a context women have less access to education. They are the first to leave school, and it is they who have to take responsibility for supporting their children. A large percentage of women are engaged in activities which generate no income or are not included in official statistics. They contribute not only by their domestic work but also by working in the garden, caring for animals, making handicrafts, selling on the markets, etc.

Responsibilities as mothers and wives prevent women from performing organizational work. Women are also frequently restricted by their husbands, who do not want their wives to be active in such fields; if they continue, they may become victims of violence.

Very often the work done by women in their communities is not valued by their male companions. They shoulder all the responsibilities in the home, a form of work which does not yield monetary gain but is indispensable for life in community. If they are abandoned by their male companions or remain alone for some other reason, they have to bear the full burden of supporting the family.

External aggression

Exploitation, rejection and marginalization also affect indigenous men, but they are experienced more severely by indigenous women.

The health problems of communities are aggravated by the lack of state support and are felt more by the female population, because it is the women who bear the responsibility of caring for the sick. One serious problem is the lack of health care when they are pregnant, have difficult deliveries, and need care for their children. The authorities are indifferent when demands are submitted by women. Very often women are confronted with the response, "We do not serve women, only men." Women suffer the negative treatment of some health programmes which render them sterile without informing them or consulting with them beforehand.

With regard to land tenure and agricultural credit, most indigenous women have little access to such benefits, in spite of the fact that they are the ones who spend most working days on the land.

Indigenous women are the most vulnerable to the attacks of religious movements of the sectarian, fundamentalist kind. These groups are divisive factors in the communities because of their alienating, individualistic preaching.

In the majority of cities, young indigenous women spend their best years working in factories, suffering all kinds of abuse for being both indigenous and female. Dismissals, threats and unfair wages over-ride their right to work at a salary which would allow them to live like human beings. Domestic workers suffer violation of their dignity, molestation and humiliation, including salary exploitation, denial of labour rights, sexual abuse, etc.

In the words of a group of indigenous women who participated in the International Conference on the Health of Women, Reproductive Health and Justice, held in Rio de Janeiro in January 1994:

> As indigenous women with a collective consciousness we are working for the recognition of our territorial rights; for our religion not to be clandestine; for our language to survive in our children; for our traditional healers to obtain

legal recognition; to be able to decide freely where we live; for access to education to become a reality; for food for our children who have nothing to eat, who cannot find work, who want to change their faces in order to be accepted and who are frequently used as "cannon fodder" in armed conflicts. We want our husbands to have decent jobs and not to beat us. We want our grandfathers and grandmothers to enjoy a dignified old age and not to become beggars. For these reasons we ask for solidarity and for help in trying to make these dreams come true, because we also need the support of you who live in the same countries as we do.

NOTES

1 Olivia de Coll, *La Resistencia Indígena ante la Conquista*, Mexico, Siglo Veintiuno, 1974, pp.28-30.
2 *Excelsior*, 29 June 1972.

10. Communion and Economic Power

RUTH BESHA

In the past two decades, and particularly since the mid-1980s, there has been a proliferation of literature which dealt first with women and then gender. Today, no development agency worth the name can talk of development projects without stressing the "gender aspect". It has become a magic phrase, especially when used in relation to the poor in the "third world". It would be simplistic, however, to argue that this apparent interest in women is recent, or that it is the result of a new "donor mentality". In Africa, at least, politicians have emphasized since the immediate post-independence days that "women are the backbone of the countries' economies", that "women work hardest of all groups", that "they keep families going", etc. Similarly, in the developed world women have been glorified and praised at one time or another. There is no reason to doubt the sincerity of all this, but it is still pertinent to ask where all the rhetoric has led.

In this essay I shall refer to the majority of women in the third world: the poor women in rural areas and urban slums who are the subjects of developmental theories and the target groups of development agencies. I shall focus mainly on Africa, and in particular on the country which I know best, Tanzania. All those who come from countries which have had to bow to the dictates of major international money-lenders and who find themselves in the web of the debt burden will see many similarities with their own situations.

But first a word about the words "communion" and "economic power", because words mean different things to different people in different contexts. I take "communion" to mean simply "mutual participation", as this is the agreed definition in many dictionaries. The other two terms have various meanings, but in combination they can be defined as "the ability to control and manage the complex of human activities undertaken for profit and concerned with the production, distribution and consumption of goods and services at community, society, household or other levels". So two issues will be discussed: how much economic power women have, and whether that economic power has any effect on their participation in the affairs of the community. I shall try to determine whether in fact women in the target groups identified above have economic power and then go on to discuss the issue of "communion" or "participation".

Women's economies

There are certain facts which are taken for granted but which need to be stressed in order to contextualize this whole discussion. The first is that there is no time in history when women have not been involved in production and reproduction in society. In traditional rural Africa, women have always been in control (i.e. had power) of the production, distribution and consumption of what went into the cooking pot, over and above their roles in childbearing and nurturing; in short, they have always been "managers of the household economy".

But the second fact is that the criterion of "profit" (read "monetary profit") in the above definition has been missing in these women's economies. This, however, was not problematical as the whole household was involved in ensuring its own welfare. The introduction of money-power made all the difference, as women found that the absence of that "commodity" deeply affected the welfare of the household. I shall not describe the separation between what a woman controlled and what a man controlled, except to mention that it came to be taken for granted that a woman had no control of money, whether from the sale of the cash crops which she helped to produce or from the salary of her husband if they lived in an urban area. But so long as she could produce surplus from her home-consumption plot, she could manage to ensure the survival of the household.

The economic crisis of the late 1970s deepened these divisions. Increasingly, the survival of households was threatened, in rural as well as in urban areas. Of course, it fell on the women as managers of household resources to find ways of making ends meet. In Tanzania, it is estimated that while in 1977 wages constituted about 77 percent of total household income in urban areas, by 1988 wage earnings made up only about 10 percent.[1] Further income had to be acquired through informal means, and it was up to women to look for them. The era of "income-generating projects" had begun, and research has shown that about 80 percent of all these projects were started between 1982 and 1987.

The significance of these projects was that they were very small and revolved around the household. In other words, women started projects which could be managed together with their other "mainstream" roles. Examples of such projects include the doorstep sale of cooked items for women in urban areas, soap-making, tie-and-dye businesses in times of product scarcity and, later, the setting up of food stalls on construction sites. In both rural and urban areas, women used whatever little surplus they had to brew local beer to earn much needed cash.

A new dimension to all this was the sudden proliferation of development agencies. Their sole aim was to cushion the "most vulnerable groups" (that is, poor women and children) from the harsher effects of the deepening crisis. Thus, women were targeted as recipients of aid, but essentially even the projects launched with this aid remained small. Most analysts are agreed that, apart from creating a donor-dependent mentality, these projects did not address the bigger issue of the causes of the abject poverty into which the majority of people in affected countries sank.[2]

One effect of these projects was to increase disproportionately the workload of women, because as the cost of living continued to rise sharply women had to work harder and in different activities to compensate. Even the token loans given out by some aid agencies had little impact, except to create expectations among the majority who never benefited from them. All the same, whatever the pros and cons of small projects, they had the effect of putting some cash into the hands of women, which they could use to meet the daily demands of the household without having to beg from their equally over-burdened male partners.

However, it must be stressed that not all women had the opportunity to start small income-generating projects, for they required a small amount of initial cash which some women did not have. Some projects needed space, and sometimes women depended on the good will of their husbands. Many such women are unable to make ends meet in these circumstances, with inevitable consequences. The young ones find refuge in prostitution in the mushrooming guest houses in urban and semi-urban areas and in roadside bars, while many small children end up on the streets of urban centres. The rising number of street children is one indication of the disintegration of households and families. Much has been written about women in income-generating projects, but the plight of this other group of women has not attracted as much attention, except in general terms.

Economic power and participation

At the household level. It is clear from the above that the majority of women are involved in survival strategies. However, it is arguable whether these strategies bring them any sort of economic power. Mainstream economists would say No categorically, while developmentalists would want to believe that they do provide women with power, in other words the ability to act. These are essentially different arguments, because "economic power" and "power" are two different concepts. While these small projects do not give women "economic power", they do help them to create some space for themselves where they can act. There has been noticeable change at household level, inasmuch as women are able to take decisions about such issues as the education and health of their children without having to argue with their husbands. The fact that men are often heard to complain that women ignore them because of "their money" is an indication of this power.

But the most significant effect of these income-generating projects has been the creation of women's groups around them. These groups have done much to train women in leadership and give them the confidence to assert themselves. It is a fact that as long as women operated individually, they had no chances to network, exchange information and deal with common strategies for common problems. Quite a number of marriages have broken up because women have insisted on joining these groups.[3] Increasing numbers of women are attending seminars and workshops to learn more about how to manage their projects, and such skills as record-keeping, choosing the right raw materials and marketing are opening up avenues which were previously closed to them.

It is apparent in a country like Tanzania that today women are increasingly becoming the money-earners in their households and are having a say in matters about which they had not previously been consulted — for example, the acquisition of property and the building of houses. Sometimes, when women feel that they can no longer survive in an oppressive relationship, they opt to live on their own. Contrary to what is sometimes claimed — that women-headed households are poorer than two-parent households — the experience in many cases is that women who can have their own house, as in some rural areas where they can be given village land, are better off than others. But there are very few women who have the courage to take this step. In urban areas women sometimes do not choose to be on their own, but where men have extra-marital affairs women feel that they would be better off just taking care of their children without having to obey an often-absent husband, especially if they can afford to rent their own room, or even build their own house.

At community level. While at the household level women's economic power can be said to give them more room to participate in decision-making, the picture is not so good in the wider community. One reason is simply lack of time: where women are busy just trying to make ends meet, participation is considered a luxury reserved for men. But there are more fundamental reasons why women are still operating at the periphery in community and national affairs.

Women's organizations have helped to give women self-confidence, but as one researcher has remarked: "It is paradoxical that they [women's associations] continue to maintain an ideology of male dominance, and support traditional perceptions of gender norms and expectations."[4] For example, recently in one village in Tanzania women complained that men had taken the decision to grow tobacco as a cash crop, with the consequence that women's labour had to be divided between the production of food and working in the tobacco fields. The most strenuous part of this activity is gathering firewood to cure the tobacco. Carrying heavy logs has resulted in some women having miscarriages and many suffer from pelvic problems. In discussions, the women stated categorically that they had no power to argue with the men, and could not even talk about the dangers of frequent pregnancy and heavy workload. "Some matters are not in our hands," the women said, "they are sanctioned by tradition." In fact, in this particular village, women do control the cash from the sale of their own surplus produce and many of them engage in brewing local beer, so they are not obviously dependent on men for their daily needs.

Furthermore, it is also true to say that in spite of all the talk about the need to "empower women", a phrase which has become another cliché, efforts to do so have been very ineffectual. The main reason for this is that women have never actually been involved in needs assessment and subsequent planning, even in those projects which are supposed to be for them.

Many researchers have noted the tendency of government officials and development agencies to make decisions about what "people need" and then go on supposedly to meet those needs. One writer has called this the "count-cost-carry" approach and continues:

> Faced with programmes with fancy titles such as "integrated rural development", the ordinary small farmer had little or no opportunity to exert control over the aims and directions of development efforts. Nor did millions of women, farmers, pastoralists or fishermen. Indeed, the issue of popular control was rarely even raised by the development planners of the 1970s.[5]

This issue is not raised even today, especially when development agencies are so anxious for quick results. In many cases, recipients have just been too grateful for their handouts, and have not questioned their underlying assumptions. As Beckley notes:

> In spite of the underlying message of goodwill which the basic needs strategy conveys, it remains undoubtedly conservative in its maintenance of the status quo and its mystification of those larger social and political issues which must be addressed for authentic development to come about.[6]

Conclusions

Two conclusions can be drawn. One is that apart from the few women who belong to the small middle class in most third-world countries, the majority of women do not posses economic power in the orthodox economic sense, because their undertakings are mainly survival tactics which do not realize any profit and which are concentrated around their traditional reproductive roles.

The second conclusion is that real participation is not automatic; it has to be consciously cultivated by involving women right from the grassroots in discussing their own needs and offering their own locally appropriate solutions. This is because women traditionally have not been exposed to decision-making situations, and even their major acknowledged production roles have not changed this. They still feel uneasy in mixed groups, and there is a tendency for them to be neglected or marginalized in male-dominated situations. Major events such as the UN Conference on Women in Beijing in 1995 are trivialized as "those women's affairs" (witness the media coverage of such events), and the feeling still persists that women cannot cope with issues other than those concerning themselves and their children. Somehow, most men do not take women seriously even when women are far superior in terms of education and earning power.

What all this means is that the concentration on earning cash and on survival has had the effect of neglecting wider issues surrounding a real "communion of equals". While it is important that women continue to struggle to keep body and soul together, there should be no slackening in efforts to make sure women assume more important roles in the management of community affairs. Since they are so close to human needs, they might be able to reverse some of the more disastrous decisions which have landed their countries in tragic situations, not only of perpetual poverty but also of civil strife.

NOTES

1 M.L. Swantz, "Women Entrepreneurs in Tanzania: A Path to Sustainable Livelihood", 1994, draft paper, Helsinki.
2 B. Wisner, *Power and Need in Africa: Basic Human Needs and Development Policies*, 1988, Earthscan.
3 R.M. Besha, ed., *African Women: Our Burdens and Struggles*, Institute for African Alternatives, 1994.
4 S.M. Beckley, "Women as Agents/Recipients of Development Assistance: The Sierra Leone Case", in *Women as Agents and Beneficiaries of Development Assistance, AAWORD Occasional Papers*, no. 4, 1989.
5 Wisner, *op. cit.*, p.17.
6 Beckley, *op. cit.*, p.52.

11. Rethinking Economic Power

MARIAMA MARJORIE WILLIAMS

What do women want from the economy? The question is a lot less banal than it might seem, for the way we answer it will affect the practical, conceptual and methodological issues that feminist scholars, researchers, social and economic justice activists and policy-makers must tackle in analyzing the relation between women's social and economic status and macro-economic policies. At the simplest level, one answer to the question might be: adequate fulfillment of basic human needs and parity in care-giving responsibilities. Thus, from the vantage point of women, the objectives of economic policies should be to sustain life, to promote general human development, and to eradicate poverty. Thus, ultimately the quest of a good economy should be to work towards meeting the fundamental needs of all people.

To what extent can any economy fulfill these obligations? What are the roles and obligations of the economy and government regarding its citizens? Needless to say, most governments would pay lip-service to a commitment to social welfare. Yet today the empirical evidence shows that for many people worldwide this is not the reality. In fact, for countless numbers of women the day-to-day reality is a frustrating search for food, fuel and water.

Economic insecurity due to rapid changes in the world economy has made women's lives increasingly vulnerable to exploitation and violence. In most countries — in both North and South — women are fighting against poverty, crimes of hate and violence in the home. Worldwide, women comprise the majority of the dispossessed, the refugees and the unemployed.

The North

Ethnic violence in Eastern and Central Europe is creating enormous hardship for women. In addition, the end of the state as a central player in economic, political and social life has created a great backlash against women in many countries. This is evidenced in the reduction of social and economic rights. Many women have difficulty obtaining paid work; as a result, they turn to informal activity and increased household production. Underpinning much of the violence is the end of the central state and the subsequent struggle for control and ownership of key sectors of the economy.

In this struggle, as with the Structural Adjustment Programmes (SAPs) utilized in the transition to a market economy, power and control of the economy are in the hands of those who are able to wrest control of the former state apparatus. Women and ethnic minorities are the disenfranchised and the poor. They also shoulder much of the cost of economic adjustment and political and social realignment.

In countries of the Organization for Economic Cooperation and Development (OECD), such as Canada and most of Western Europe, the engineered breakdown of the social contract is tearing away the safety net that once prevented many women from falling into dire poverty. Hard-won benefits and social guarantees have been drastically altered or eliminated. This phenomenon is forcing women to operate in a labour market in which the terms of participation have hardened significantly against workers.

In addition, the increasing importance of regional and international trade agreements such as the North American Free Trade Agreement (NAFTA) between Canada, the USA and Mexico, the single market in Europe, and the European Economic Agreement that extends European Community laws to the European Free Trade Area are reshaping and redefining power relations within and between governments. They are also "harmonizing" wages, benefits and standards of living downwards.

These "new" forms of agreements and institutions are the result of intensive international competition among multinational corporations. They are pressuring countries to restructure their economies to increase profit and maximize accumulation for the rich and the powerful owners of capital. This has created dramatic changes in both the nature and organization of work and production, which have led to severe hardship among women, especially those at the margins of the world economies. Poor working women, immigrant men and women, ethnic minorities, and people of colour are the bulwarks of economic growth worldwide: years of economic and social warfare have systematically deprived them of the means of ownership of economic resources.

Women as a group are most severely affected by changes in the world's industrial base. Increasingly, women are joining the ranks of the unemployed, and those able to find work are forced to work part-time or temporarily.

The impact of restructuring on women

It is well known that capitalist economies undergo periodic bursts of stops and starts. We are all familiar with the upswing and downswing of business activity and the attendant problems of inflation and recession. Ideally, over the course of this cycle, those who have lost jobs regain them and life resumes. However, the kind of changes we are experiencing are not temporary interruptions in profitability, solvable by bursts of business and consumer confidence. We are witnessing a fundamental reorganization of the industrial bases of the world economy.

Driven by advances in micro-technology and telecommunications, which have heightened competition within and among firms and nations, the world economy is being feverishly reorganized. Crucial to this reorganization is the realignment of other political and social forces. This includes structural liberalization (adjustment) policies to deregulate national labour and financial markets; restructuring of the public sector; redefinition of the social contract; and (as mentioned above) the widespread proliferation of regional accords such as NAFTA.

While the phenomena of economic, political and social dislocation and disintegration are common to all countries, their speed, intensity and direct manifestations may differ greatly within and across countries.

Globalization and Northern (OECD) economies

In the USA, this process (ongoing since the late 1980s) has become more pronounced. Economic restructuring has created tremendous insecurity and fear across a broad spectrum of workers: plant closures, "downsizing" or re-engineering which results in massive layoffs have created havoc, from the upper levels of management right down to the plant floor. However, given the vast disparities in access to resources and family incomes, the people likely to experience the most severe effects are those of colour and women.

In other OECD countries — such as the United Kingdom and Ireland — there has been great pressure to promote a fall in real wages (euphemistically called "wage flexibility") and erosion of the collective bargaining process. The Canadian government has yielded to the pressure of the giant industrial and financial corporations to realign social and labour market guarantees so that workers have no choice but to rely on the dictates of the market. For example, since 1990 the Canadian government — under the pressure of its free trade deal with the USA and the need for local capitalists to compete with US corporations — has modified its unemployment insurance by reducing the maximum duration of benefits and increasing the minimum period of work required to qualify for benefit. It has also lowered benefit rates and tightened eligibility requirements for unemployment compensation. Similar trends are developing in Belgium, Denmark, the Netherlands and Sweden. This creates significant hardship for women and immigrants who are forced to accept part-time or temporary work.

In Spain and France (as in the USA) there is a resurgence in and predominance of part-time work, temporary work, subcontracting, casual employment and home-working. In all countries most of these so-called contingency workers are women. Since these jobs have no security, little room for advancement and pay low wages, they have increased women's vulnerability to poverty.

In Eastern and Central Europe — presently undergoing structural adjustment similar to many developing countries and the complete realignment of political, cultural and social systems and values — there is widespread economic insecurity. This has made daily living increasingly hard for women in ethnic minorities. In many countries, labour-market participation as an option for women is under attack. In general, the availability of meaningful income-generating work is minimal. Thus women, like their counterparts in the developing countries, find themselves shouldering much of the burden of International Monetary Fund and World Bank SAPs. They must increase their household production and complement it with informal activity for the survival of their families.

As we can see from all this, governments everywhere are bowing to the corporate imperative to increase profitability, spur economic growth and improve productivity. In rich and poor countries alike, government policies and budgeting priorities are being redirected and redefined to meet this corporate agenda: an agenda that will benefit the few, while working to the disadvantage of women, ethnic minorities and people of colour.

While government monetary and fiscal policies are directed towards bolstering the investments of corporations and the rich, social and welfare policies are severely constrained. At the same time that a government strives to expand the value of investments by corporations and the wealthy, it trades off meaningful job creation and programmes which support the poor. High interest rates to prevent inflation and therefore protect bondholders come at the cost of higher unemployment. Low corporate and capital gain taxes and increased subsidies to corporations for research and development of high technology simultaneously reduce inflows of revenue and increase outflows of cash, thus creating high budget deficits which are then used to justify eliminating programmes for the poor.

Additionally, the push for privatization of public services entails the complete marketization of the state welfare function and a dismantling of the social contract in favour of a new social dispensation. This process of privatization and deregulation, which is common among all countries, is more intense among developing economies, especially those undergoing SAPs. In these countries, as well as in the North, people are being stripped of their rights as citizens in a democracy to have the state provide and ensure the basics for human survival: cheap and affordable housing; reasonable quality health care; meaningful education that enlivens the mind and expands human potential. While in the North privatization can be a simple process that leads to marginal reductions in services and marginal increases in the price of such services, in the South it can be a matter of life or death. The sell-off of public utilities and government firms can result in significant increases in the cost of electricity, food and medicine.

So even as states everywhere accept, promote and protect the rights of (foreign) investors in the bond market and stock markets, they reject and renege on any commitment to ensure the rights of every citizen to food, clothing and shelter simply on the basis of their humanity. This commitment was implicit in the full employment agenda that was a cornerstone of macro-economic policy up to the 1970s. Everywhere, the state accepts the right of corporations to make enormous profits and to be taxed minimally, but it does not accept the right of women (as mothers and wives) to receive a social wage for their immense contribution (investment) to the economy.

Today, every aspect of social life is being brought under the direct control of the market. Thus, freedom of the market has now become synonymous with universal freedom, and hence the "hallmark of democracy". What is often ignored in the conversion to free-market religion is that the logic of the market is simply the logic which firms use to expand options for profit-making. This logic is inimical to the liberation of people from hunger, poverty and widespread inequities and injustice. Thus, the more the market encroaches on our lives, the more intense and dramatic profit-making becomes, the more we observe widespread social and economic inequality, dehumanization of people and their creativity, and increasing spiritual and emotional deprivation.

In the final analysis, structural change and restructuring of OECD and East and Central European economies and SAPs in Africa, Asia and Latin America are the result of a more systematic process to subordinate the world economy to the imperative of transnational corporations. This process — part and parcel of the phenomenon we refer to as "globalization" — has been greatly advanced by the demise of the Soviet Union. The fall of communism as a counterbalance or alternative to capitalism has engendered "the celebration of the market both as a concept and as a process".

Women and global economic structures

The impact of global economic structures on women can be examined in three areas: labour market, deregulation/privatization, and macro-economic policies.

A dominant feature of global restructuring is the feminization of the labour force worldwide. However, this is occurring in patterns prescribed by the sexual division of labour. Women are still segregated into occupations and tasks based on their gender ascription. For example, in the free-trade zones and export-processing zones of the developing countries, women are recruited for their "nimble" fingers and their "docility". Predominantly, women are the production workers while managers and supervisors are mostly male. A similar pattern of occupational segregation exists in the labour market of OECD countries. The vast majority of female workers are over-represented in a few occupations which have very low wages, little room for advancement and few benefits. As a result, a disproportionately large number of working women are poor or live on the brink of poverty. When they retire, older women find themselves with inadequate pensions and in dire economic straits after a lifetime of hard work. The plight of working-class women is intensifying as labour-market restructuring creates more temporary and part-time work relative to well-paid full-time positions. In general, in OECD countries there is a subtle shift in the sexual division of labour: more women are working for wages in the business and government sectors. However, this shift is a double-edged sword: even as it engenders the crossover of larger numbers of women into paid work, it reinforces their marginalization by deepening occupational segregation in the labour market. Many women were incorporated into the labour force in industries that were experiencing lower profitability and so turn to women as a way of further lowering the cost of production. Once women entered into certain fields they then received less pay than departing male workers. In all cases the sexual division of labour in the household sector remains intact, so that women who hold paid jobs end up working a double or triple day.

There is still no formal recognition that women's work in households undergirds all social, economic and political processes and is the basis of economic growth. Without women's paid and unpaid labour there would be no "magic" to the market. The market's presumed efficiency depends fundamentally on extracting women's social labour without adequate compensation.

The increasing productivity of women in the household and in the labour market has been the silent factor behind structural change and adjustment in both the North and the South. The main effect of SAPs and global restructuring has been to ensure that women work more hours and with greater amounts of capital than before. Further economic liberalization will not inherently improve women's economic and social status; rather, there is a strong possibility it will increase their exploitation and marginalization. Yet women's work is under-counted and under-valued. This is fundamental to the economic subordination of women. In the arsenal of economic measures which assess the performance of an economy, there is no economic measure which takes account of the increasing numbers of unpaid hours women are forced to contribute in support of the economy and overall economic growth. Hence, there is no recognition of the distinct contribution of women to economic activity.

Restructuring is also occurring in all aspects of civil society, creating fewer viable alternatives within the existing framework. As a result, poor women's lives are becoming more tenuous. This situation calls for dramatically new approaches to the labour market and restructuring and increased vigilance on the part of working-class women and their supporters.

Macro-economic policies are the set of strategies, principles and rules pursued by a government to achieve low inflation, high output growth, high employment and an acceptable balance of payments. The achievement of these goals depends on the behaviour of business in producing and supplying goods and services and on the behaviour of consumers in purchasing those goods and services. It also depends fundamentally on women's work activities in the home and the community.

A government uses fiscal policy and monetary policy, its main macro policies, to affect economic growth by altering household behaviour as well as general business conditions. *Fiscal policy* is the government's use of its budget and taxation (for example, government investment, minimum wage policy, unemployment compensation policy and tax changes) to redirect investment and spending.

Fiscal policy has asymmetric effects on women. It typically focuses on ensuring the proper rate of growth of the capital stock, so its general prescription is often to offer tax relief to capital (either in terms of tax credits on structure or equipment or tax cuts on corporate income). In either case this imposes an increase in the tax burden on the poor in terms of loss of benefits and loss of earnings, as the government reduces expenditures by laying off workers and cutting social services. Hence, women have to work harder by increasing part-time work activities and increasing household maintenance.

Monetary policy relies on movements in the interest rate. It is used primarily to manipulate the money supply and stabilize inflation rates. Nowhere is gender neutrality assumed to be stronger than with money. But this is not so. Raising real interest rates to prevent inflation can create unemployment which may affect women quicker and longer than men. Tightened credit conditions are also inimical to fostering the economic independence of women entrepreneurs and in securing mortgages for homes.

Structural reform (embedded in SAPs) is facilitated by neo-liberal applications of restrictive monetary and fiscal policies. The base of these policies has been a single-minded focus on restraining inflation at any cost. Coupled with a pronounced anti-egalitarian bias, this has led to the proliferation of pro-business policies and the retrenchment of the state. In its wake there is widespread poverty, unequal distribution of income, and a pervasive rise in structural unemployment in both developing and developed countries. In general, there has been a noticeable increase in homelessness and hunger among women and children in many OECD countries. Though these phenomena have been a pervasive and enduring feature in Africa, Asia and Latin America, the plight of poor women in these countries has worsened drastically with the implementation of SAPs.

Women's activism

Women worldwide are intensifying their fight against the entrenched features of exploitation in the work-place and society at large. They are fighting back by seeking creative alternatives and pushing for more comprehensive solutions to economic turmoil and social disintegration. The success of poor women's struggles, however, depends on an accurate assessment of the nature and consequences of economic and social restructuring and a thorough understanding of its impact on women's lives.

This process involves coming to grips with the discipline of economics, economic policy, business and financial language and procedures which hide oppression and exploitation. Undergirding this there must be a clear and strong vision. The nature of the vision, its content and the process of its articulation, will differ across cultural and national boundaries. But its fundamental force — its essence — has a common foundation in the desire for peace with economic justice. Thus, we return to the question posed at the beginning. What do women seek from their economies? What do women want as the objective of economic policies? What are some of the basic material needs that must be satisfied? Can these be accomplished with or without the state? What instruments are to be used? How do women gain control and effectively participate in the decision-making process?

How can women help to redefine, restructure and recapture the commanding heights of the economies? How can women redirect economic operations so that they sustain life and do not destroy it? How can women rebuild and reshape societies to ensure economic justice characterized by equitable distribution of income and wealth, economic security and economic freedom? While they do all this, can women also broaden their understanding of economic security and economic freedom so that they encompass the following:

— the right of every woman to a safe, secure home, good health care and child care, and a wage that will sustain her family whether she desires to engage in the labour market or remain in the household;
— shared responsibility between men and women for social production;
— the right of working women in the labour market to advance unimpeded by wage discrimination, gender bias in promotion and sexual harassment;
— the right of women to choose self-employment without fear of falling into poverty;
— the right to own property and other economic resources.

Some of this work has already been undertaken in many regions and at many different levels by a diverse group of women activists, researchers and non-governmental organizations (NGOs). Independently and jointly many of these groups:

— support research into the impact of restructuring on women;
— campaign for economic literacy based on the popular education methodology used in Latin America;
— advocate a return to the broad macro-economic goals of full employment and income security;
— run programmes to institute rapid growth of meaningful jobs and wages;
— campaign for the enforcement of international fair labour standards to shape "upward harmonization" of wages rather than the current downward trend;
— urge the transformation of political parties to fight for economic justice as defined above;
— support new forms of advocacy groups which are multi-racial and culturally diverse and which seek to strengthen women's voices;
— campaign to enforce rules and regulations for the international financial oligarchy, and the taxation of bond and stock markets to finance job creation.

12. An Agenda for the Whole Communion

ISHMAEL NOKO

The Lutheran World Federation has shifted and widened its focus by understanding that issues about women are not just for women but are societal issues. They concern both men and women; in other words, they concern the whole church, the whole community and the whole nation.

Since both men and women are called through faith in Christ to the priesthood, it is a priesthood of the bearers of witness to the mysteries of God's salvation. Faith in Christ is the foundation for joint participation in God's mission. Traditions and theological perspectives that impede the living out of this priesthood and this call to witness should be challenged and changed. In this connection, let us recall the profound words of Ruth, the Moabite woman, speaking to her mother-in-law, Naomi:

> Entreat me not to leave you or return from following you; for where you go I will go, and where you lodge I will lodge; your people shall be my people, and your God my God (Ruth 1:16).

This statement contains many layers of theological, ecumenical and spiritual significance — so many that space and time would not allow their full exposition. Suffice it to say that Ruth's words are a foundation for our search for *communio*, for the unity of the human race, for peace and reconciliation among communities and nations, and for reconciliation between women and men. Are we really and honestly ready to appropriate and own the words of Ruth — "your people shall be my people" — and practically to demonstrate a life that transcends racism, tribalism, sexism and negative images and attitudes about "them" out there? We know too well the pain and brokenness that are in the world today. Ruth's words are an invitation to be a community of women and men bearing witness to God's love, grace and forgiveness.

It is clear that we must not lose the opportunity to reflect critically on how the churches, made up of men and women, have lived out the Reformation principle of justification by grace alone, and how they have translated into action the understanding of the priesthood as a gift to all believers.

Solidarity

How do we as member churches of the Lutheran World Federation live out solidarity with women? Can we say with confidence that the decade which started in 1988 is indeed a Decade of the Churches in Solidarity with Women, or is it "the women's decade"? Has the Decade found its way into the structures of the churches and influenced the way they are organized, and the way decisions are made in dioceses, synods, congregations and parishes? What about the constitutions and other instruments that govern the formal life and work of our churches and institutions, which make it possible for both men and women to participate in decision-making in God's mission? Have they been amended to accommodate a ministry of partnership between women and men? I am not talking about cosmetic changes, but changes that involve awareness-building and genuine participation.

What about the whole area of theological education and ordained ministry? Has progress been made in doing theological reflection from an inclusive human point of view, rather than from the perspective of patriarchy?

We are at a very important point in the history of the ecumenical movement. The ecumenical scene is marked by interconfessional dialogue at various levels — national, regional, international. Some of these dialogues have concluded their work, others are still in progress. They must involve and include men and women on an equal basis. The participation of women in these dialogues remains a concern for the LWF at every level. We must move forward with teams in which men and women are equally represented, otherwise the next vital stage — namely the reception of conclusions — will never go beyond the paper on which they are written. Not least, since women constitute the majority of church membership, one would hope that common sense will guide us to draw the only conclusion there is, namely that meaningful reception will be impossible unless this part of the body of Christ is involved.

In Mexico in 1989, Lutheran women met around the theme "Open Our Eyes". They made recommendations to the LWF on issues such as poverty, the debt crisis, militarism, violence against women, children, integrity of creation, and women and church structures. The content of the consultation was not only *eye*- but also *ear*-opening: it enabled us to hear the cries of so many "silenced" women. There is no doubt that it had an impact on the conclusion of the LWF eighth assembly in 1990, and on the life of our church community. The commitments adopted by the assembly require the member churches to:

— "...intensify our efforts to be a sign of an inclusive communion in the world", and to that end to

— "work out a clear plan of action in every member church which fully expresses the equality of men and women within the life of the church and enables the churches to benefit from the potential which women are able to give to all areas of the church life", and

— "undertake practical efforts to open the way for women to enter the ordained ministry of all our member churches".

We need to reflect on how this commitment has been implemented, and go forward into the future being accountable for our commitments. An important step in implementing the commitment undertaken at the eighth assembly was the elaboration of "A Clear Plan of Action", to facilitate the focus on women's issues and to accelerate action in our member churches. It provided guidelines on how to implement the assembly's call to achieve equality between men and women, and identified the areas of highest priority.

The LWF council recommended that each church should:

— develop its own clear plan of action which expresses the equality of men and women;

— initiate studies and actions which motivate people to change;

— adopt monitoring and evaluation methods including appropriate performance indicators in order to document progress towards full equality for women;

— designate a person in every church and every country to serve as liaison to the LWF Desk for Women in Church and Society in fulfilling the church's plan of action.

"A Clear Plan of Action" has been shared with all member churches. Some translated it into their national languages as a first step towards making it accessible to the whole church and particularly to women, and it is being used in church seminars and similar gatherings. A pledge of commitment has come from several member churches.

What do these commitments mean in the daily life of the community of Lutheran churches? What have the member churches done to achieve the goals set out, where do we stand, and what needs to be done? We are on a journey together, a journey of faith in the confidence that God goes before us. It is a journey which calls for unity of purpose and mutual concern, acceptance and respect for one another; a journey which invites the participation of all without exception or discrimination; a journey undertaken in the context of a community of sojourners in communion with one another.

The skills and expertise of women and men together are needed to make the LWF fuller and richer in carrying out its mandate and in clarifying its self-understanding. We have policies in place which show that the Federation is committed to the inclusion of women, for example, in its study programmes, projects, educational resources and so on. Yet we live with tension in implementing this policy, for example, when member churches are unable to provide names of women who could serve on the staff of the Federation, act as resource persons in meetings, or receive educational support. How can we possibly claim that there are no qualified women to serve on various committees, to attend meetings, to write theological papers, or to apply for staff positions?

Theology and gender bias

We all know that gender issues in the church are not only culture-determined. They are also heavily theological, and we need to address this. In the tenth chapter of the gospel of John, Jesus tells the Pharisees that he has come not only to bring life to all people, but *fullness* of life. There is much in the world which prevents women from enjoying this fullness of life that God intended; for example, traditions and laws which not only assign women to second-class status, but which make them believe that they deserve such a status.

Unfortunately, gender bias exists everywhere. Church structures, which are hierarchical and masculine, are but one example. This state of affairs has been legitimized by tradition, theology and church practice throughout the ages. We must commit ourselves to challenge and to review these practices. We know very well that changes will necessarily bring discomfort, but they are necessary if progress is to be made.

There is insufficient participation of women in theological events, ecumenical dialogues and leadership of meetings. On the other hand, participation of women in training events, youth and women's gatherings on special topics and in areas of diakonia and Christian education presents a more favourable picture. At present, there are some positive signs that we are on the right track. Many women are being educated on a variety of issues and especially in leadership skills. The challenge is now to give these trained women the space to use their skills.

Setting numerical goals is not without problems. But it is a *corrective* measure, necessary in order to achieve our main goal, which is the change of attitude towards women.

Local gender inclusivity

The LWF has a mandate to carry out mission, development, advocacy and communication work. It provides financial support and offers training and consultative services to projects initiated and implemented by member churches, church organizations, and other organizations whose projects have been endorsed by a member church. It is up to the women and men in the churches to make sure that these projects are gender-inclusive and that they empower women. International efforts alone will not move us into the next century — work for change happens at the local level as well.

The LWF is *not* involved in recruiting and seconding personnel to projects and programmes of the churches, and we therefore cannot influence the choice of personnel. However, it is imperative that the commitments member churches make together at formal gatherings such as assemblies and council meetings are also carried out in the everyday life of the home church and congregations.

The Federation supports projects of member churches in almost all sectors, and they all need a strong dose of women's empowerment in order to succeed. Unfortunately, development projects in general tend to address the symptoms of what one could call "lack of development" and are often reactive. They respond to human needs but do not necessarily address the root causes of the problem. Empowerment of women involves the painful process of challenging these kinds of projects to bring about change. There are choices to be made and these need to be discussed.

Women, emergencies and long-term development

The LWF is also called to assist those most vulnerable in a given emergency. The most vulnerable groups in a crisis are often women and children, and as a result the major components of field programmes are specifically designed around their needs. A good example of this can be seen as the LWF plans to make the transition from emergency relief to long-term development work in programmes such as that for Rwanda. LWF staff have gone into the field to assess situations and identify needs which a development programme might meet. Their observations and investigations have shown that those who lack land and are generally disadvantaged are households headed by women.

The critical need at this point is for these women to begin to produce their own food. While projects will focus on goals such as increased agricultural and livestock production, access to credit, environmental protection and clean water, it is recognized that women are already overworked because of distance to water and wood, hand grinding of grain, etc. Cultural restraints also hinder their involvement in decision-making, both in the family and society. We all need to address these basic and interlinked problems.

Gender inequality contributes to women's poverty. Therefore, LWF projects aim to help women to economize their time through improved access to water, wood and milling facilities, and to have better access to credit. The ratios between women's free time and work time, as well as the way they schedule their time, will be taken into account when training and other activities are carried out. It is vital to have a holistic approach to gender issues. Only when a society achieves improvement in conditions for both women and men can it embark on a just, sound and sustainable development path.

Development can only take place in a peaceful and just environment. Women's role in bringing about peace and reconciliation is often forgotten and neglected, yet their contribution is vital and needs to be recognized. Only recently I was at the fourth ecumenical consultation on Guatemala, with the participation of the parties to the Guatemalan peace process. I was deeply impressed by the courage, strength and constructive attitude of the numerous female participants, most of them of Mayan origin. In the present stage of the Guatemalan peace process, women are taking the lead and the results are very positive. They have, as models and sources of inspiration, women like Rigoberta Menchu, Nobel Peace Prize winner, and Rosalina Tuyuc, a powerful leader of the widows' association. The Guatemala consultation once more confirmed that we can achieve peace with justice and reconciliation only if we work together, women and men. In this context, our commitment is to uphold the voice of the silenced: women, children, the marginalized, indigenous peoples, and so many more.

Women are very seriously affected by armed conflicts, militarization, the dissemination of weapons, and the landmine threat. In this respect, the situation of women and children has deteriorated considerably since 1989, and we need to reflect seriously on how to address these problems.

International efforts

Efforts to promote partnership between women and men cannot be seen in isolation from other endeavours at the international level. For example, the step forward taken at the Beijing conference in 1995 is a decisive one. For the first time, world governments acknowledged the vast potential present in women and committed themselves to work towards unleashing and utilizing that potential. The Beijing commitment, expressed in a document called "Platform for Action", is a powerful agenda for the empowerment of societies through empowering women. It is the agenda of a true partnership between women and men.

The Beijing document contains a number of goals which are in accordance with LWF's goals and mandates, and member churches have been urged to commit themselves to the implementation of the outcome of Beijing. The spirit of Beijing is a pointer, entirely compatible with the theological and spiritual self-understanding of the LWF regarding inclusivity and the ministry of the church. Despite giving directions on the way to go, it respects diversity and the possibility of exercising choice.

According to the secretary-general of the United Nations, "the empowerment of women is the empowerment of humanity". This means that the empowerment of this part of society is a must. Here again, the international agenda, with its focus on empowerment, partnership and justice, must be our own.

Among Basotho and Batswana there is a saying: *Goruta mosadi ke goruta, kegorutu sechaba* — a free English translation of which would be "to empower a woman with education is to empower the entire nation". This wisdom is in most instances sung as part of the traditional songs in gatherings of different kinds.

What is significant is that it is a distillation of experiences accumulated over many generations. Basotho and Batswana have come to realize — although not fully to put into practice — that women play a very important role as bearers of the basics and essentials of their cultures. As one of those nurtured in that culture, I am not only convinced that *Goruta mosadi ke goruta, kegoruta sechaba*, but also that *Goruta mosadi ke goruta kereke le secheba* ("to empower a woman is to empower the *church* and society").

13. Theology in the Communion of Churches: What Are the Implications?

ELISABETH PARMENTIER

Communion

The Lutheran World Federation, initially a "free association of churches", is now defined as a "communion of churches". In 1990, the constitution of the LWF was reframed thus: "The Lutheran World Federation is a communion of churches which confess the triune God, agree in the proclamation of the word of God and are united in pulpit and altar fellowship." The Budapest assembly in 1984 had already stated that "the aim of unity" is for a "conscious and responsible community capable of taking decisions and acting together", which goes well beyond a simple federation of churches in which each remains autonomous. Furthermore, the bilateral dialogues and commitments of the Lutheran churches and the LWF likewise place emphasis on a quest for unity as communion. All the Christian confessions have made this concept their governing idea — their leitmotiv — and all the recent programmes of the World Council of Churches and bilateral conversations have seen the key to future unity in this idea.

This concept of *koinonia* concerns not only the structures of these churches but their whole life, common witness and quest for unity: "The central issue is the 'quality' and depth of our common life as Christians and as churches."

Factors constituting koinonia

Koinonia is not a new word but a biblical and patristic concept which has existed since the beginnings of the Christian tradition. The concept has various meanings, which are summarized in what follows.

1. Koinonia is sharing in Christ. The Greek verb *koinoneo* means "to share in, contribute a share, participate, give a share to someone". Koinonia is not a translation of the word "church", which is *ekklesia* in Greek. The latter term defines the characteristics of the church. It reminds us that the church is a "communion" of individuals who "share in Christ". Therefore, the church is not to be understood simply as a human association founded on common interests or aims. Applied to the church, the concept of koinonia reminds us that the centre is not to be found in the individuals themselves, nor in the ideas they hold in common, but in the gifts of God in which these individuals can have a share. Many New Testament images develop this idea: the vine and the branches, the wild olive grafted onto the cultivar (Rom. 11:17), the people of God (1 Pet. 2:9-10), the temple (1 Cor. 3:16-17). The Johannine texts take this idea of "being in Christ" further. Paul also says much to this effect, above all in the theme of the "body of Christ" (Rom. 12:4-5). Diversity is constructive and plays a part in

building up the body of Christ. Paul develops this theme in relation to the Lord's supper: the community shares in Christ when it celebrates this meal (1 Cor. 10:16-17). The movement is between participation in the life of Christ and sharing in the gifts of his body and blood.

2. Koinonia is expressed and becomes a reality first and foremost in baptism and the Lord's supper, which bind believers to God and to each other and make it possible to celebrate this salvation together. This communion or fellowship in the sacraments is linked to communion in the gospel, which affirms that Christ has brought about salvation for human beings. These gifts of God which visibly express the salvation that is offered to everyone make it possible for the community to overcome its divisions in becoming "one body". This becomes particularly meaningful against the background of the challenge for the first Christian community represented by Gentile and Jewish Christians living to-gether. Communion called for two things: receiving the faith and sharing with others, considered as partners who give each other the "right hand of fellowship" (Gal. 2:9) as a sign of communion.

3. Koinonia, sharing in the joy of salvation, is also compassion and sharing in the sufferings of Christ and of human beings. For the authors of the New Testament, the Christ who gives himself is always the one who has suffered his passion, the crucified whose death cannot be dissociated from the resurrection. The apostle Paul greatly stressed the suffering which he experienced, not only in his flesh but also in his ministry as a preacher, and which he lived through in communion with the sufferings of Christ (Phil. 3:10; Rom. 8:17; Gal. 2:19). He reminds us that by participating in the sufferings of Christ we also bear the sufferings of others (Heb. 10:33). Between Paul and his congregations there are also mutual sufferings and joys (2 Cor. 1:6; 7:7,13) and an exchange between the spiritual benefits lavished on them by the apostle and the material benefits coming from the congregations (Phil. 4:14-16). This is where koinonia is given very concrete expression. "The concept of 'communion' is thus trying to tell us that the communion [or fellowship] of believers is essentially, and not only by reason of good will, communion *in solidarity*. It calls for joint participation in material and spiritual suffering, in material and spiritual riches."[1]

4. Koinonia finds expression in sharing what we possess. There is no devaluation of material benefits in relation to spiritual, but a reciprocal relation. Moreover, in the context of the collection which Paul organized for the Jerusalem congregation (Rom. 15:26 and 2 Cor. 9:13) — which is a practical expression of the solidarity between Jewish and Gentile Christians — the collection of funds is itself called koinonia. "The gift which originates in koinonia is an act of faith in God and not an act of mere generosity... It is the direct consequence of being one in the Lord." Thus, there are not two stages — a spiritual koinonia with Christ among believers and then a material implementation — but two simultaneous aspects of the same communion which "commits" the two partners and calls for implementation in the life of the churches, particularly in four areas: the communion of confessing the faith, of pulpit and altar, of the church's ministry, and in joint decisions and actions.

5. Koinonia in Christ is communion with God through the Holy Spirit. We are called to share in God's life through Christ, who is one with God (John 10:3; 14:10). Koinonia is possible through Christ. Through him we can be sharers in

the divine nature (1 John 1:3,6-7; 2 Pet. 1:4). He initiates the possibility of a more intimate relation, a life based on unity and diversity in the image of the unity and diversity of the Trinity.

6. Koinonia has an eschatological dimension. It is to be regarded not solely as a present reality, but refers also to its final consummation (1 Cor. 9:23), which still lies ahead. This is why "our hope for you is unshaken; for we know that as you share in our sufferings, so also you share in our consolation" (2 Cor. 1:7).

7. A final element which is less in evidence in the biblical text than in ecclesiological reflection is the link established by koinonia between the local and the universal church. "The fellowship of believers is *at once individual and universal.*"[2] The sense of universality challenges us to go beyond particularisms just as, conversely, sensitivity to each individual situation calls for the universal community to take action. Different confessions place different emphases on these two aspects, but it seems that the concept of koinonia accords greater importance to local needs. The fellowship of believers does not imply any pressure or demand for conformity. This communion is intrinsically *plural.* The ecclesiology of koinonia requires diversity as a foundation simply because it is not an association of individuals coming together on the basis of their common tastes or identical opinions. It is a communion gathered together by God in and beyond divergences. Consequently, it includes all believers and makes itself available to human beings as a whole. "The fellowship of believers could not be simply inward-looking. It lives on the foundation of communion with the Lord... whom it serves as an *instrument and sign for the world's salvation.*"[3]

We find precisely all these elements in the Budapest assembly's declaration on the LWF's identity and mission: community among the Lutheran churches is founded on:
— unity in the faith, given in scripture and attested in the ecumenical confessions of faith and the Lutheran confessional books;
— unanimous agreement in proclamation of the gospel and celebration of the sacraments.

It is expressed by:
— pulpit and altar fellowship;
— unanimous witness to the gospel of Jesus Christ in the sight of the world;
— fulfillment of the missionary task and joint ecumenical work.

Ecumenical progress is linked to the fact that all churches regard these elements of koinonia as fundamental. But the difficulty in dialogue is that churches do not give them the same priority. Thus, for the Reformation churches full communion requires only two elements: unity in the proclamation of the word and in the celebration of the sacraments. For these churches the ministry, though it is important, is not constitutive for communion, whereas it is for the Roman Catholic, Orthodox and Anglican churches.

Communion and inclusiveness

For women, the question is how to grasp what the concept of communion can contribute and whether it meets women's aspirations. I should like first of all to show the opportunities that this concept opens up, and also its difficulties.

The LWF's theological reflection has always been Christocentric. However, at Curitiba the new constitution referred to the *triune* God. I think this point is important both for the LWF and for women. It reminds us that we are not the church because of our good will or our plans, but because we are sharing together in the life of God. The link that unites us comes first and foremost from God, who calls us together. Because we are in communion with God we are able to be in communion with each other — not the other way round. Metropolitan John Zizioulas said at the World Council of Churches' Faith and Order world conference in Santiago de Compostela in 1993:

> We are not called to koinonia because it is "good" for us and for the church, but because we believe in a God who is in his very being koinonia. If we believe in a God who is primarily an individual, who first *is*, and then *relates*, we are not far from a sociological understanding of koinonia; the church in this case is not in its *being* communion, but only secondarily, i.e. for the sake of its *bene esse*... God *is* trinitarian; he is a relational being by definition.[4]

In other words, God *is* koinonia.

Hence, the church also exhibits its relational *esse* in its structure, both locally and universally. The idea of communion makes it possible to transcend the classic dichotomies of the institutional and the charismatic aspects of the church, of the local and the universal church, etc. On the basis of this statement, Zizioulas stresses the aspects which women stress: "interdependence" and the rich diversity of all the members that make up the church. He is careful to specify that this diversity embraces at one and the same time differences of race, sex, class, culture and spirituality without this causing exclusion or marginalization. He is against spiritual elitism in speaking of the variety of "spiritual gifts". He stresses a relation of communion and "perichoresis" even between the bishop and the other ministries:

> This one minister should be part of the community, and not stand above it as an authority in itself. All pyramidal notions of church structure vanish in the ecclesiology of communion. There is perichoresis of ministries, and this applies also to the ministry of unity.[5]

Such a wording would certainly also be acceptable for the Reformation churches. In this view of koinonia, authority in the church is also relational, as it lies not in an ecclesiastical office but in the event of communion among believers, brought about by the Spirit. While the supreme authority in this Orthodox presentation remains the council, that does not mean that its standpoints would be imposed on believers from above. Rather, these must be "received" by believers and integrated in the spiritual and worshipping life of congregations prior to claiming "full authority". Here the *sensus fidelium* takes on its full value.

To the extent that the church's mission is also relational there is likewise interdependence between the world and the church. The question of inclusiveness arises not only within the LWF but also in relationships with other churches and with the world. Likewise, it concerns not only women but also other groups which till now have been marginalized, such as, for instance, the churches of the South. These have come into the ecumenical movement since the 1960s and are also of great importance in the LWF. But these churches have brought with them different priorities from the traditional preoccupations.

Women's concerns and the priorities defined by the churches of the South run along the same lines: they state that racism, sexism, poverty, exploitation and violence must also be taken into account in dialogue between churches and in their reconciliation. The churches cannot be reconciled if, in a disunited world, no heed is paid to human poverty. For the churches, as for women, ethical questions appear to be priorities and cannot be separated from doctrinal reflection. As an example, let us take American Reformed feminist Letty Russell.

Russell devotes the whole of her book *Church in the Round* to setting out a different view of the church based on a new hermeneutical centre: the church is a "round table" like the open tables of the New Testament and the table-fellowships presided over by Jesus Christ. The figure of the table expresses the community sharing in the meal (the "round table", the "kitchen table", the "table of hospitality"). The authenticity of the church is measured by its ability to be a welcoming table and a table for the exchange of ideas for those who are marginalized:

> The critical principle of feminist ecclesiology is a table principle. It looks for ways that God reaches out to include all those whom society and religion have declared outsiders and invites them to gather round God's table of hospitality. The measure of the adequacy of the life of a church is how it is connected to those on the margin.[6]

Thus, the issue is no longer that of being faith communities, but of faith and *action*, linking together the church and the world in a dynamic spiral. In Russell's view, which is shared by feminists and liberation theologians, this involves a shift from an "ecclesiocentric" (church-centred) outlook to an "oecocentric" (literally, "house-centred/home-centred") outlook, giving the church a more modest role in relation to the world, where it is only a sign and instrument of this action which God is taking everywhere.

This position matches that of the churches in an important point: for the concept of koinonia, witness and service in the world are central and not secondary. The church's calling itself is both to bear witness to the gospel and to serve others, and to participate in the coming of peace and justice. This is true for all the churches, which are trying to answer the call to diakonia for the world.

A problem arises for the churches and also for the LWF when moral commitment becomes a prime element in koinonia, where works on behalf of others *constitute* the church. Lutheranism is particularly sensitive to the temptation to put the believer's works before faith. Love cannot replace faith but it is the result of faith. Hence, Lutheranism stresses that the *common faith* is what creates koinonia. There may be many other forms of koinonia with human beings, and with non-believers, but this common faith in God is what brings Christian unity. This also has great potential for women.

Conclusion

Koinonia is defined from a centre; our life, our commitment and our unity are given us in God. This has two consequences for women.

Women share fully in the life of the church. The inclusiveness of koinonia is at present a concern shared by all the churches and by the ecumenical movement. The Reformation churches have been pioneers in this emphasis on full participation by women at all levels, even if there is some distance still to go. But this inclusiveness concerns not only women but also other churches, cultures and contexts, the differences among which are regarded as enriching dialogue. Koinonia is deeper than unity because it extends to integrating believers in life in God. An important advance is made here, opening up an ecclesial life without any hierarchy of values or functions and giving access to the greatest possible diversity.

Hence, the need to define what is central to koinonia if it is to be inclusive. When we define our centre as life granted in abundance by God through Jesus Christ in the Spirit, we are calling to mind the idea that nothing other than this gift of God unites us. The LWF is not an association of ideas held in common or of individuals who get on well with each other. Koinonia is created on the basis of God's calling and God's gifts. Hence, the limits of koinonia: it does not depend on our efforts!

Salvation does not depend on women! Women — or feminist theologians — are in general against calling to mind limits. They are more ready to claim that love can embrace everything, that it must be open to all humanity and to the cosmos, and that it is typical of a masculine church to set limits. The church has set *faith* in the triune God as the primary and specific aspect of koinonia, thus recalling that koinonia cannot be created solely by joint action but rests in God. In reminding us of this, the concept of koinonia is also helpful to women: they must not depend on their own strength or on their commitment in order to make a success of koinonia. Women — who often cannot rely on anyone in life — can rely on God and share in commitment for the world on the basis of God's gifts. That is why we believe that salvation has already been bestowed on us and that we are together as koinonia; and this frees us for service to the world.

NOTES

1 *Communio / Koinonia: A New Testament-Early Christian Concept and its Contemporary Appropriation and Significance*, Strasbourg, Institute for Ecumenical Research, 1990, p.9.
2 *Ibid.*, p.10.
3 *Ibid.*
4 "The Church as Communion: A Presentation on the World Conference Theme", in *On the Way to Fuller Koinonia*, official report of the fifth world conference on Faith and Order, Santiago de Compostela, 1993, T.F. Best and G. Gassmann, eds, Geneva, WCC Publications, 1994, p. 104.
5 *Ibid.*, p. 107.
6 *Church in the Round: Feminist Interpretation of the Church*, Louisville, Westminster, 1993, p.89.

14. Women in the Lutheran Communion

MUSIMBI R.A. KANYORO

We at the Lutheran World Federation Women's Desk understand our work as ministry. We do this work in the conviction of our calling — which comes from God — and which has been affirmed by women. Just as an ordained minister receives a call from God for ministry and the practice of that ministry is implemented through a call from a congregation, so we feel that women are our "calling congregation", because it is through the efforts of women that a women's desk exists at all.

The year 2000 is almost with us. What do we want to see happen in our churches and in our societies? We hope to make a link between the issues we raise in the church and the issues we raise in society.

The LWF and the agenda on women in church and society

The LWF Desk for Women in Church and Society (WICAS) exists to encourage the participation of women in the total life of the LWF and its member churches. Advocacy and the empowerment of women are the over-riding tasks of this office. Advocacy is the attempt to influence a certain target group, so that they accept and implement a specific idea, approach, policy or programme for the benefit of another target group. In order to advocate effectively one needs to know the people and the issues that call for that advocacy, for an advocate always speaks on behalf of someone or something. They often take on the multiple roles of advisor, educator, activist, ombudsperson, motivator, planner and lawyer. They use techniques and resources such as persuasion, empirical data, diplomacy and — not least — the law, policy, or other binding agreements. Effective advocacy must start with objective facts. Therefore, an advocate needs to be extremely well informed and know how to use facts effectively.

The LWF's agenda on women is organized under six programme priorities:
— to promote leadership development and to equip women for full partnership in the life and mission of the family, church and society;
— to focus on justice for women, with particular attention to poverty, violence, illiteracy, health, militarism, displaced women, refugees, migrants, foreign workers, prostitutes, HIV/AIDS-sufferers and widows;
— to promote the education of women in the social, cultural, economic, environmental and political realities of the world, and to help women to organize and promote networking;
— to expose the violation of women's rights by men (also by women) within social, political, economic and ecclesiastical structures;
— to involve women in theological studies for a deeper contextual understanding of the biblical message and its implications for the growth of the church;
— to encourage LWF member churches to incorporate into their thinking and teaching women's perspectives in theology.

WICAS operates under the general mandate of the Department for Mission and Development, and relates specifically to the commitment to an inclusive communion. In order to carry out its task, over the years WICAS has enabled women to meet together to share stories of their own experiences and to examine obstacles and strategies for action. These gatherings have empowered women to speak for themselves and have enabled Lutheran women to build international and ecumenical solidarity with other women. Lutheran women today do not work in isolation, either as church women or as individuals. In addition to gatherings of women, other programmes in the LWF, such as exchange programmes, visitation programmes, development support and scholarships for the furthering of education have all helped towards forming a new image of women in Lutheran churches. Twenty years ago the emphasis of the work was on conscientization of women to stand up for their rights. Today, in every region and country where there is an LWF member church, there are conscientized and empowered women doing their own advocacy and empowering others in their communities.

Well-organized activities by women in member churches challenge the style and nature of operation of the LWF WICAS office. I contend that there is a need for the LWF to shift emphasis and energy to follow up activities in member churches on agreements that Lutheran churches make together. Assemblies, council meetings, regional meetings and national church governing bodies are the places where joint commitments are made. The promotion of women's participation in the life of the churches is one over-riding commitment that Lutheran churches have often agreed to make. There are two parts to making women's participation meaningful. The first is through an increase in numbers, and the second and more difficult is to let women's thinking and presence affect the nature of the church and life in the churches, and to make both church and society safe places for women. While we acknowledge progress in increasing the numbers of women, other aspects of participation are still far from being realized and require urgent attention. Changes at local level are much harder to realize.

Such a shift of emphasis constitutes a celebration. It acknowledges that we have made some progress. It stretches and challenges our imaginations into developing new methods of work, and it maintains the creative tension in our memories between past, present and future. We look back to learn from history and to affirm those who have paved the way for the progress we have made. We look to the present because the issues we are addressing are not solved once and for all. Traditions take a long time to change and there are repeated backlashes even as we continue to make progress. We know that human beings often do not learn from history. We look to the future because we are a people of faith and hope.

One of the major strategies for WICAS is to keep the records of "herstory" in order. In this respect, WICAS produces and archives all reports of women's workshops, seminars, consultations and other gatherings. WICAS also selects and archives letters and other documents important in telling women's story in the Federation. For several years now, WICAS has been compiling a data bank of Lutheran women and facilitating its use in the Federation and in the ecumenical family. WICAS has also been responsible for a number of publications. The magazine *Women* is a regular bi-annual publication with a distribution of about

2500 copies. Currently, there are two "siblings" of *Women*, one in Spanish under the title *Mujeres Luteranas en Acción*, which is produced by the regional coordinators of Latin America, and the German-language *Frauen in Aktion* produced in Poland and Hungary through the regional coordinator's programme for the Lutheran churches in Eastern Europe.

To celebrate the twenty years since the LWF established the Women's Desk (1972), WICAS initiated a study which led to two publications. *The Continuing Journey* records the history of women's participation in the LWF, using assemblies as landmarks (1947-90). *A Clear Plan of Action* is the programme priority of the LWF WICAS agenda. It was developed in response to those issues which women in LWF member churches identified as needing programmatic action in the whole of the LWF family.

The first task of WICAS was to communicate to the Federation and member churches the results of the research coming from the women's constituency. After council approval, *A Clear Plan of Action* thus became a programme document for all member churches. Each member church made a commitment to:
— develop its own clear plan of action which expresses the equality of men and women;
— initiate studies and actions which motivate people to change;
— adopt monitoring and evaluation methods including appropriate performance indicators in order to document progress towards full equality of women;
— designate a person in every church and in every country to serve as a liaison to WICAS in fulfilling the church's plan of action.

Every member church of the LWF was requested to designate a contact person. Out of the 122 member churches, 68 responded positively. Our joint task is to monitor how our churches implement joint commitments and to bring those issues that we see as needing joint advocacy to the attention of the whole communion. To begin this work, we sent a questionnaire asking for a report on the general status of women in the society in which each member church is situated, and on the status of women within the member church itself. The questions covered such things as general conditions, how women are organized and where they feature in the structure of the church, pressing issues for women, the ordination and theological education of women, women in decision-making, how decisions are made in that church, and whether the church has a plan of action for women. We also asked for some reflections on the assembly theme and for issues which could be discussed in a consultation. Some of these reflections were published in the study book, *The Witness of Women*.

Status reports are still coming in, but sample summaries of those received at the time were published in *Women* (44). The summary results outlined below represent respondents from 50 churches: 16 from Africa, 6 from Asia, 19 from Europe, 7 from Latin America, and 2 from North America. The analysis was made by two independent non-LWF, non-Lutheran researchers, one man and one woman, one from the North and the other from the South. These results need to be discussed so that recommendations can be made to which we all can commit ourselves, and so that we can request our member churches to implement them programmatically.

Pressing issues for women in Lutheran churches

In this report the multiplicity of issues raised has been rationalized where necessary under more general subject headings, which are then listed in priority order of frequency as mentioned by respondents.

Access to leadership and decision-making (1). This was an explicit concern of many respondents and an implicit concern of most others. It is a common refrain that women are responsible for much (indeed, most) of the work at the "grass-roots"/congregational level, but are unable to penetrate the decision-making apparatus of the church. Even when the church has ordained women pastors, women's participation in committees, councils and assemblies is often notable by its absence or else limited to token representation. This under-representation is a source of much frustration. It is sometimes the case that even when women are participating in greater numbers in decision-making (around 30 percent is the usual maximum representation), the "chain of command" is such that their views may be ignored and their advice unsought. Women also recognize the shortage within their own ranks of people qualified for leadership (for further information, see also the WICAS Report, *Women's Participation in the LWF, 1984-1994*).

Education and training (2). This is something of a catch-all heading, taking in a wide range of issues relating to schooling, vocational training, theological study and training for leadership. The nature of many women's lives, the society in which they live, and the limited expectations of them mean that many women have been denied access to educational opportunities. The extent of these educational opportunities varies from country to country; many women from Africa and Asia lack even elementary primary education, while those in the West have greater access to education but are still not sufficiently visible in decision-making positions of leadership.

Everywhere there is a great hunger for education and training. Women's increasing confidence and self-awareness — results of their enhanced perceptions of feminist politics and gender issues — have led to expectations about themselves and their daughters which they feel can only be fully realized with education and training. So, for example, the education of their children is a great concern — they want their daughters in particular to be educated beyond primary level, so they need school buildings and other resources. Other practical measures include literacy training and vocational training, so women can earn their own living.

Specifically within the church, women recognize the need for training so that they can gain responsibilities and competences. Training in administrative, management, finance and communication skills is viewed as particularly important. Theological training is being taken up by greater numbers of women almost everywhere, irrespective of whether their churches ordain women. Such training may be undertaken in the hope of becoming a pastor in the future, for other church work, and for personal development and effectiveness.

Clearly related to education and training, personal development encompasses a range of aspirations relating to literacy, human rights, economics, law and politics. In short, many women wish to know more about themselves and the world in which they live, so that they can improve their lot as individuals and as a whole, inside and outside the church.

Theology, doctrine and ordination (3). These three areas are mutually reinforcing and potentially revolutionary. The campaign for women's ordination (whether successful or yet to be so) is couched in terms of a theology from a woman's perspective, which in turn leads to an examination of doctrinal matters, which again has implications for ordained women.

Ordination is an emblematic issue for women in most churches. If their church does ordain women it is usually in very small numbers, so the focus is on increasing the percentage of women pastors to at least the 40 percent level, and on women becoming bishops. Other churches allow the ordination of women in theory but have yet to do so, while others do not ordain women at all. There is also a new and increasing trend for some churches (specifically in Europe) which have ordained women to reverse the practice. Whatever the church, overcoming prejudice and oppressive attitudes involves the development and discussion of feminist theologies, an inclusive theological language, feminizing liturgies and alternative forms of worship. Women everywhere, it seems, are vitally interested in these approaches; they want to know more and to do more theology for themselves.

Judging by individual responses, this process leads to an interest in and a desire for a fresh interpretation of Lutheran doctrine — the doctrine of sin, and justification by faith are specifically mentioned. The theologizing and politicization of so many members of the church will continue to reach levels of complexity and sophistication that go beyond the repudiation of sexist theology to an even more basic reappraisal of traditions and interpretations, especially those manifested in an apparent backlash and return to conservatism.

Health issues (4). Women's traditional roles as carers and nurturers of the family mean they are acquainted with a host of health-related issues affecting their families, themselves and their aspirations for the future. Reductions in spending on social welfare are universal, but their effects are felt most of all in poor nations of the South, particularly in rural areas. The relative strength of Lutheran churches in many such areas means a great many church women are deeply concerned about such things as access to and information about family planning, abortion, nutrition, prenatal and maternal health care, AIDS and first aid. There is often a desperate need for health facilities. Women want access to information so that they can help themselves, but they also recognize the need for health care to be provided as a human right.

Traditionalism, conservatism and oppression (5). Mentioned specifically by many, these related issues permeate everyone's responses to a varying extent. They occur everywhere but their specific manifestations differ from place to place. Culture and theological biases seem to play a great part. The church, of course, comprises ordinary men and women who are themselves culture-bound. Churches are therefore themselves "enculturated": they exist within a specific culture and take on many of the attitudes, beliefs and values of that culture. The ways in which many churches act as receptacles of cultural values are somewhat ambiguous. When it comes to women's issues, Christ is more often than not seen as the preserver of the status quo rather than the God of surprises. Women in especially traditional, male-dominated societies often have to endure the self-same imposed silence within their church as they do in their society.

Women (particularly the older generation) have often internalized prevailing values and thus become accomplices in the oppression of their own sex. This becomes apparent in attitudes towards the ordination of women. In some churches, older women oppose it and younger women support it. Occasionally, ordained women come to be regarded with suspicion by lay women as representatives of the distant church structure which oppresses them. These kinds of fissures between women are a source of concern to many who believe that strength lies in solidarity. Some church women's organizations, for example, are said to be alienating to those women who do not agree with the way these organizations are run. A number of respondents claim that some of these organizations promote exclusion by reserving leadership among themselves, or promote certain programmes which younger women and professional women are unable to fulfill. Respondents express concern that churches often focus their acknowledgment of women's presence and participation in church only through women's organizations, and thus exclude women who for one reason or another are not members of organized women's work in church.

Violence, poverty, unemployment and migration (6). Increased awareness of all sorts of violence directed at women has led to concern over such things as rape, sexual abuse (including within the church), domestic violence and racism. The use of such violence towards women by police and armed forces as a means of intimidation, torture and control is perceived both in the North and the South.

Many of the respondents live in areas of extreme poverty. Such poverty not only is severely debilitating and life-threatening, but it also eliminates most if not all possibilities for women to engage in church work and self-improvement. As one respondent said, if a woman walks many hours each day simply to fetch water, she will not have the time to attend literacy classes. Cutbacks resulting from Structural Adjustment Programmes (SAPs) have affected women most. Economic liberalization and the dominance of the market have meant that those with the least earning power have to seek work which more often than not is unavailable.

Prostitution, drug abuse, trafficking in and migration of women, national instability, lack of employment, environmental issues and increasing crime were also often listed as concerns.

Expectations of the LWF

The process of ranking and categorization applied to the issues raised by respondents was also applied to their expectations of the LWF. The expectations listed below are not mutually exclusive.

Education, information, research and training (1). This, the most frequent expectation, is commensurate with the importance given to education and training in the issues listed above. It includes a variety of specific requests: besides "education and information" there were also requests for theological seminars, awareness programmes for church leaders, study programmes on unspecified themes, and a French edition of *Women*.

Some requests were made for research, but the nature of the research was not specified. It is worth mentioning here because research is implied by virtually all the other expectations of LWF WICAS listed above.

Pressure, encouragement and consultancy (2). A theme reiterated in many responses is that women see themselves as exerting pressure from below on a more or less conservative church hierarchy, while the LWF exerts (or should exert) pressure from above (the terms "below" and "above" are simply spatial metaphors and are not meant to imply relative importance or effectiveness). As already indicated, women find it difficult to get into the "middle manage-ment" of leadership and decision-making within churches. They see themselves as allied with an LWF WICAS which is on their side, advocating with the leaders of their churches from a different context.

Just how the LWF should act as a "pressurizer" varies between respondents. Continued campaigning and awareness-raising is largely assumed. Some want the LWF to "remind" churches and to ask them for progress reports on the implementation of the 40 percent resolution. One or two want stronger action, with churches "promoted" and "demoted" (in an unspecified way) according to their progress or lack of progress on this resolution.

Specifically stated and implicit in everything else is the expectation of encouragement. Women value and expect the (unspecified) "active support" and encouragement of the LWF. This support and encouragement stems both from the active work of the LWF WICAS and from its providing the opportunity for meeting other women from different backgrounds. Indeed, providing a forum for meeting others is almost always seen as a very positive part of the LWF WICAS's mission and as a great source of encouragement.

The LWF WICAS is also regarded as a sort of outside consultancy, which should provide advice and help to women on specific matters as requested. Where the LWF does not have the necessary expertise it could call in experts to help, either on the spot or in meetings elsewhere. It should be emphasized that this is not a request to be told what to do, or for women to have something done for them. Rather, it is a recognition that it is sometimes necessary to seek advice and help in order to attain one's goals.

Financial support (3). It seems that although financial help is undoubtedly welcomed, women's primary emphasis is on changing attitudes, self-help, soli-darity, communication and other resources. A number of respondents mentioned support for women's activities geared towards economic independence, although they were mostly small in scale and entrepreneurial. It is interesting to note that financial support was not among the most frequent expectations of the LWF. While the importance attached to money should not be forgotten (financial help is, after all, tremendously significant), the combination of related requests listed above by far outnumber this one expectation. Women do not look to the LWF principally for money but for advocacy.

Issues for discussion by the global Lutheran gathering

Strategy (1). Strategic thinking on how to maintain and enhance women's solidarity, overcome obstacles and attain goals takes a variety of specific forms, from "the power of united women/mobilizing", "women's problems and oppor-tunities", "ending male domination" and the "advocacy of the advancement and participation of lay and ordained women", to "overcoming men's fear" and "overcoming opposition to the ordination of women".

Theology / philosophy / doctrine (2). This encompasses a number of related issues, the most frequently requested of which is a discussion on the biblical and theological foundations of women's ministry. Another important theological interest centres on feminist spirituality and liturgy, while doctrinal concerns focus on sin and justification by faith (perhaps, as one respondent put it, on their relation to justice in today's world). Philosophically, questions as to the meaning of the "inclusive community", the problem of forming a specifically Christian Indian culture, and the concepts of peace and democracy are also raised.

Education and communication (3). Education and training for women inside and outside the church are frequently requested over a range of practical issues, no one of which ranks higher than any other. The diffuse nature of these issues may make them difficult to tackle under a single rubric, but they testify to the need and desire for training and education as a means of empowerment and self-improvement.

As has already become apparent, women want to train for leadership. This is reflected in suggested topics like "communication for leadership", "gaining confidence to overcome cultural barriers", the setting up of seminars and workshops for leadership training, challenging existing structures of leadership which exclude women. The Budapest LWF assembly 40 percent resolution was often cited and claimed.

Violence, discrimination, and "silence" (4). The number of requests related to this complex and interdependent network of issues reflects women's position in the frontline and highlights the interdependence of society and church. "The silence of the church on women's subordination" is an especially resonant theme.

Social / ethical analysis (4). This includes such topics as "the younger and older generations of women", the rights of single women and mothers, and the ordination of homosexuals. Reproductive health, sexuality and abortion were also suggested as topics for discussions.

Networking (5). Largely extrapolated from other topics, the theme of meeting and working with other women is a strong one. Suggestions include "establishing a network of women working on liturgies", "establishing regional activities" (seminars and workshops) and "pairing local groups affiliated to the LWF", visitation and exchange programmes.

Environmental issues and sustainable development (6). How to preserve and enhance the environment and to plan sustainable development, the problem of fuel, waste disposal, drought and desertification are listed as general topics for discussion.

Women and the church and the ordination of women (7). This seems a burning issue for many women and there was a definite request for its discussion.

Synthesis and response

The status of women within their church is a microcosm of their status within the society of which the church is a part. Even when the law enshrines the rights of women, custom, tradition, popular attitudes and values lag far behind and continue to oppress women. Regrettably, the church is more often than not a part of this oppressive culture. Even when the church has the institutions and mechanisms for the participation of women, it has few of the practices. Democracy is more apparent than real. Tokenism often limits women's participation in leadership and decision-making. Even when women are ordained they very rarely move above the role of pastor.

Individual churches' responses to the needs and aspirations of women are usually inadequate. It is often claimed that no clause prevents women from becoming members of the church board, for example, but there is no clause that actively helps them to overcome prejudice and opposition in order to do so. Traditional church opinion can regard "the preaching of the gospel" and "women's liberation" (as it persists in calling the women's movement) as mutually exclusive and antagonistic aims, rather than as a step towards establishing Christ's kingdom.

An important development for which women campaign is the establishment of a separate women's desk or office within church structures. Although its work can be stifled by a lack of resources and the unchanged attitudes of the church bureaucracy, such an office can begin to ensure that women's needs are recognized; that a budget is allocated; that women can begin to participate in decision-making; that women have a say in their own affairs.

Of course, the picture is not all gloomy and many churches have done comparatively well. However, the stress should be on the word "comparatively". Much still needs to be done. The good news is that women are doing it. Women in the church are organizing and empowering themselves to an astonishing degree, for which they have just cause to celebrate and rejoice. They address their own problems and operate their own solutions. The numbers of women theology students appear to be increasing in all parts of the world. These are all tremendously hopeful signs, but there are enormous difficulties still to overcome.

The ordination of women is a crucial issue in itself and as a symbol of progress, perhaps because it necessitates the dismantling of such archetypal barriers as patriarchal theologies, the conservatism of male elites, and the attitudes and values of traditional cultures.

An overarching theme which runs through most of the responses (and one which can hardly be over-emphasized) is the importance women place on networking — meeting one another, learning from one another's experiences, and the sense of solidarity, support and encouragement it provides. To me, this above all other things is the key to the continuing effectiveness of LWF WICAS.

The participation of women in the LWF has been an issue since 1947, when the Federation first convened. At the first assembly in Lund there were one or two women present. Even though numerically women's representation was woefully inadequate, concern at that time was about the representation of clergy and laity. Five years later, however, in the assembly in Hanover, women prepared and presented a study document *The Living Word Gives Woman Her Place in the Church and Society*. In Hanover, women and youth were present in small numbers but were described by the general secretary as "sociological divisions", while everything else was seen as having theological ramifications. Women rejected this categorization and stated: "Something much more vital is at stake, the proper place — the God-intended place — of women in the fellowship of the Christian church. Women should find their place not in a separate section, but according to their interests, experience and gifts."

We still live with these two tensions today. In all our member churches, we still have less than a handful of women as general secretaries, presidents, bishops, heads of seminaries or teachers in seminaries. Few women have served as area secretaries or as members of the cabinet in the LWF. In June 1994, the LWF organized a meeting of church leaders; from the then total of 122 member churches of the Federation only two women could be said legitimately to come under the category of "leader". The LWF is committed to the policy established in 1984 at the assembly in Budapest which requires at least 40 percent women's participation in events organized by the Federation and the member churches. The Federation issued a special invitation to women bishops. At that time, there were three: Maria Jepsen from Germany, April Larson from the USA, and Rosemarie Köhn from Norway. It helped us to see these women in positions of high ecclesiastical leadership, but it did not do very much when we saw all the male leaders of our churches.

How can we advocate effectively to get more women in decision-making positions in our member churches? Where are the women in the local leaderships of member churches? Why do our churches continue to say that there are no women capable of leadership, either locally or in international forums? How can we women change the image of leadership in our churches?

Women in ordained ministry

Lutheran churches have ordained women for nearly seventy years. The Evangelical Lutheran Church in Thuringia, Germany, ordained the first woman in 1927. The Evangelical Lutheran Church in the Netherlands approved the ordination of women in 1922, and ordained the first woman in 1929. Many other Western, Central and Eastern European churches followed suit within the next three decades. For example, the Evangelical Lutheran Church of the Augsburg Confession in the Slovak Republic ordained its first woman in 1951, and in Sweden the first woman was ordained in 1958. Lutheran churches in North America, Latin America and Asia all held their first women's ordination in the 1970s. Lutheran churches in Africa only began to ordain women in the 1980s but the numbers have been increasing in the 1990s. So far, 68 percent of Lutheran churches which are members of the Lutheran World Federation ordain women, and the numbers continue to rise, especially as churches in Asia and Africa join the others.

The churches which do not ordain women are often those which have relationships with both the LWF and other Lutheran groups or churches that do not ordain women. Discussions continue to take place at some level. The situation in Eastern Europe is somewhat different. During the communist era, women served the church in a number of ways; a few churches ordained women. After the demise of communism, there is more freedom of worship, and some men in the churches have began to question the ordination of women. The archbishop of the Evangelical Lutheran Church in Latvia has publicly rejected the ordination of women, which has caused great concern in Latvia and all over the world. Such a reversal of a practice already in existence for nearly twenty-five years has also raised concern in non-Lutheran churches. Many groups have condemned the action, and the Lutheran World Federation has attempted to persuade the church not to institutionalize such a decision. While at this writing the decision has not yet become an official position of the whole church, it certainly has much support among younger clergy who claim that it is theologically incorrect to ordain women.

Despite this setback, Lutheran churches continue to affirm the ordination of women, and the LWF council has passed many resolutions in support of it. Women are being considered for the post of bishop in their churches and presently there are five women Lutheran bishops.

Advocacy and women's perspectives in theology

Promotion of women's participation also requires re-reading and rewriting the theology of the churches. Culture, tradition and biased interpretation of the Bible and theology have conditioned many women and men to be insensitive to discriminatory practices against women. In the last twenty-five years a rich library of theological research has been compiled — mostly by women — which provides us with new theological challenges. Advocacy work in women's participation must include promotion of theological thinking in women which comes from women's own experience, the theological education of women and the ordination of women, the incorporation into the curricula of theological schools of some core subjects on the concerns raised by women theologians, and equipping libraries with books by women theologians.

In the office for WICAS we have tried to do some of this advocacy, sometimes via existing structures and sometimes by other means. After the Curitiba assembly in 1990, we organized four regional consultations under the theme of "Women in the Lutheran Tradition". As a result, we have published four reports from Asia, Africa, Europe and Latin America. These regional consultations were followed by an international consultation for Lutheran women, which took place in Finland in July 1992. This meeting suggested setting up networks of women theologians in the regions to continue to reflect and implement ways of getting more women's theology into our churches.

Of these regional networks, the Latin Americans have been most active; they have held two regional meetings and a number of national ones. The Europeans have been the next most active, with a smaller group gathering followed by a meeting of European women theologians in May 1996. African Lutheran women opted to work within the ecumenical group of African women theologians, still in its infancy, called the Circle of Concerned African Women in Theology and Culture. Through this group, Lutheran women have met and contributed to publications currently emanating from the African continent. The Asians chose to work through the Asian Programme for the Advancement of Training and Studies, but there is a need for someone to take responsibility for women's theology in that setting. The North American region is still difficult for us in that there are only two churches and each seems self-sufficient. While we have a good relationship with the women's organizations in both the Evangelical Lutheran Church in America and the Evangelical Lutheran Church in Canada, in both cases we have no joint programmes with the whole church in relation to women. This is something which questions our understanding as a communion. There is certainly a need to strengthen the theology of women in the LWF and member churches.

Empowerment of women for participation

Equipping women for participation is the basis for women's own empowerment. We have asked for larger budgets to assist those member churches that are initiating educational programmes for the empowerment of women. We have also defined the criteria of the Special Fund for the Promotion of Women, which is our Ecumenical Decade fund to cover leadership development. Since 1990, this fund has sponsored about seventy projects totalling US$235,000.

We have also carried out leadership training in all regions except North America. Within Europe we have concentrated on Eastern Europe, where we have worked closely with the women's organization in Austria and carried out five workshops. All LWF member churches in Eastern Europe have sent representatives to these workshops and now Eastern Europe has for the first time its own regional coordinator in the person of Martha Pinter Brebovszky.

Advocacy and human rights

The last ten years have witnessed a breaking of the silence about violence against women. The issue was common to all the reports to the fourth world conference on women held in Beijing. It took a lot longer for us in the church to speak out, but now there is no going back. Whether this violence is perpetuated by organizational structures, persons or systems of thought, it degrades women. Advocacy to end it must be based on promoting equality and ending discrimination against women everywhere.

Since the Budapest assembly in 1984, the LWF has passed a number of resolutions about violence against women, asking member churches to take action. In 1984, studies on violence against women were requested. At the council meeting in Kristiansand, Norway, churches were asked to develop policies and procedures to be used in cases of sexual abuse or harassment in the church. Also in 1994, at the council meeting in Geneva, churches were asked to take deliberate action to stop all forms of violence, including female genital mutilation and all other culturally based violence.

In so far as specific actions on the human rights of women are concerned, we have continued to include the topic in every consultation. Three major workshops have taken place with the focus on women's human rights: two for Asian churches and one in Jerusalem. Women's human rights comprise a large part of the agenda of such workshops, which are carried out by area desks and the Office for Human Rights and International Affairs.

It seems that the six programme priorities and consequent strategies established by LWF WICAS are of continuing relevance and importance. If they can begin to be properly addressed (or, rather, if the LWF member churches can help to equip people to address them), then much can be achieved. If the responses upon which this report is based are at all typical and genuinely representative, these are the things that LWF WICAS should seek to be and do. Many of the issues point to obstacles still to be overcome. Despite all these, a revolution is in progress, one of small changes in the midst of ambiguity and struggle. Every time a member church announces another decision to ordain women, the revolution goes forward.

We must welcome these encouraging signs and stay well connected to our churches and communities, and to all those who have been sidelined and marginalized. We need to stay inside the church to stimulate and nurture one another and the whole church day by day. Many are leaving the church these days because they are not able to put up with it any more. Listening to stories of women globally makes us aware of this growing worldwide phenomenon. We have to respect the decision of women who opt out of the church and we need to accompany them in their journey by not isolating them from church women's organizations. However, I think that by opting out of the church we women are denying ourselves our God-given place in church. The clergy alone are not the church. The leaders alone are not the church. The men alone are not the church. All the baptized people of God — children, women and men, ordained and lay, people with various physical or economic disabilities — *we* are the church. Why should this important institution be left to only some selected groups? We need to keep our pain and our struggles inside the church.

We make the church credible when we make it aware of its own shortcomings and need for repentance. Ensuring that the church makes commitments and then implements them is our urgent task. The call for doing so is here and now.

15. African Women and Lutheran Tradition

ANNA E. MGHWIRA

Women everywhere want to get together, tell their stories, exchange experiences. These meetings are forming the basis for a deeper understanding, and are resulting in new forms of solidarity, support and advocacy among women for the common good of all. Because of the isolation many women have experienced, this precious phenomenon of caring and sharing builds up our strength, not only as Lutherans but also as global and ecumenical women.

It is significant that we should take time to know each other better in our own Lutheran family. Together, we can discover who we are, where we come from, and where we are headed. This self-knowledge will enable us to face realities courageously as well as critically, as we examine and develop our perspectives in theology with the commitment that we are all God's children and co-heirs in the heavenly kingdom.

We should also remember our diversity — for our differences should help us discover each other more — and should act as intermediaries to reconcile different parts of our body, which is the temple of the Holy Spirit. In certain respects, our diversity is not a result of personal differences but rather a reflection of the way in which we have each been incorporated into the one body. Thus, transcending our differences in order to claim oneness is the real challenge before us. We need patience as we listen to each other. At this juncture in the history of the church it is especially essential for those of us in the so-called "first world" to listen to the cries of those in the so-called "third world".

We must struggle to move beyond ourselves into a deeper examination and critique of our theology and of Luther's theology. Our contexts and our perspectives as women doing theology need to have a place in the mainstream of Lutheran theology. The perspectives we share should help reshape Lutheran theology globally. As women theologians we want our theology and our tradition to centre on the gospel of Jesus Christ, the good news of salvation to all who believe. Therefore, what unites us is the affirmation of our faith and commitment to God in Christ Jesus and its relevance to the ministry to which we have been called.

Luther and us

Luther comes into our context as one who dared to speak of the priesthood of all believers. Luther models those who overcome servitude based on conviction. Ebeling states that Luther

> shattered faith in authority by restoring the authority of faith. He transformed priests into laymen by changing laymen into priests. He liberated man from external religiosity by making religiosity that which is innermost to man. He freed the body of chains by putting the heart in chains.

Luther himself spoke of those who did not understand the mass because of their belief that only the priest could conduct the sacrifice before God, whereas in fact anyone who receives the sacrament is or should be exercising such an understanding. According to Luther, true priestly ministry inheres in everyone who has the faith:

> Faith must do it all. This is the real priestly ministry and there can be none other. Hence, Christian men and women are priests and priestesses, young or old, master or servant, learned or lay. Here there is no difference, unless there be a difference in faith.

Today, societies are greatly challenged by the fact that women are taking on many new roles, especially those which used to be men's sole prerogative. For some people these changes are very difficult to accept. Yet some women's qualifications and capabilities are so self-evidently God-given that there is no way to hide them. This development of women's roles and abilities is what we all hope for; a change from one stage to another, simultaneously painful and joyful, like the first pangs of birth.

It is a pity that many churches today still refuse to see and accept these facts. This should not discourage us, since we women have opened the Pandora's box and have understood the extent of the freedom we have in Christ: our consciences are captive to it, not as a mere awareness, but as a "lived power" just as our brother Luther said: "My conscience is captive to the word of God... It is neither safe nor right to go against conscience."

What is often lacking with us is a source of sound authority over our various dilemmas. We have to realize, however, that it is not possible for one woman to come up with authoritative ideas and actions for all other women. Again, we need to know each other and to know the men and women who support us. We must then work together for change, for we ourselves have received freedom in order to help free others.

Luther's teachings

Luther's work comprises a wide variety of material which covers many aspects of the life of the church during his own time and which is still relevant to us today. His interpretation of the scriptures made them the supreme authority over matters of faith, but at the same time he examined them critically in their context. It is very important that our interpretation of scripture also "promotes Christ", who is the basis of our faith and commitment to ourselves and to others. It is also important to be able to distinguish between different revelations of God to different people at different places and times.

African Lutherans or Lutheran Africans?

In the African context, interpretation and revelation have to come to terms with the fact that Africans normally danced out their religion and lived their faith practically. There is nothing mutually exclusive about the spiritual or the material: in other words, there is no disintegration of the different parts of the body. They are all one and all are important for the well-being of the body.

To take an example, in my community whenever there was any disaster or damage to property or person, people gathered together and slaughtered a sheep as a sacrifice. The sheep is considered a calm animal; its blood was thrown on the place of worship. This act was performed with a very deep concern for the well-being of any guilty person who had gone against God's will. Any persons involved in the wrong-doing walked away quietly and remorsefully (confessing their sins?), while at the same time wishing (praying) that God would not punish them severely for the grievous harm they had caused to the community and to themselves. In this context, the question of how God responds was not a big issue. However, it was important that the "guilty" did not re-offend. These kinds of ethical standards in African society are never referred to in the context of the church.

The point I want to make is that the interpretation of scripture in Africa is quite often removed from the very context that could enhance its understanding. Scripture becomes distant and not genuine, nor is it truly presented as worthy of our faith. This failure to build on African experience puts many of us in a kind of limbo. Who are we? Lutherans who happen to be Africans or Africans who happen to be Lutherans?

Luther's emphasis on faith that has come through experience is a relevant point here. Luther was a man of principle who dealt genuinely and committedly with the goal of his calling. His problem was that he was not accepted by the very system within which he believed he was called to minister. I am sure this is familiar to many women today in their involvement in religious circles.

Often, I have found myself denied the freedom to confess what I know, what I have seen and heard. This has helped me to be more courageous, to stand for that which I believe. The confession of a blind person whom Jesus healed — whether the one who healed me is the Messiah is not my question, but that he healed me I cannot deny (John 9:1-34) — is a testimony that speaks to me, too.

It is my firm belief, therefore, that our interpretation of scripture in the light of our different contexts will lead us to a clearer understanding of who we are and who we could become even as we strive to make our faith more meaningful to our lives in and out of the church. Our experiences should therefore impel us towards a better understanding and application of scripture. They should not for any reason distance us from the realization that God called us to service in specific ministries.

The priesthood of all believers

Luther's doctrine of the priesthood of all believers is seen by most women as an invitation to ministerial functions solely on the basis of their faith. This was not an invention of Luther's but an affirmation of what Paul said and wrote. Luther gave it a practical meaning in the course of his ministry. His expansion of the text was made possible by his experiences in the hierarchical structure of his church. Luther and other reformers felt very strongly that the pyramid of authority had to be turned upside down, so that it could allow more space for the majority of believers (the people) to participate in the priestly function, rather than bestowing all authority on a few people on behalf of the majority. Thus Luther said, "All Christians are really of the spiritual estate, and there is no difference among them, unless it be in the degree of service."

Luther claimed that if we are all priests, "no one may arrogate to himself what is common to all without the will and order of the community". Here again, the question of representative democracy in matters of faith must face critical examination. We must ask whether the special priesthood of some believers can meet all the needs of individual members. Luther and other reformers objected to the institutional church's jurisdictional power to interpret and mediate between the people and God, even though Luther did in fact argue that the institutionalized church could possess such authority provided that it did not abuse its power.

The basis of the reformers' objection to too much power in jurisdictional authority was the reduction of ecclesial authority by emphasizing the authority of the Bible, which had been overshadowed by strict tradition and the cumbersome bureaucracy exercised by the church of the time. This bureaucracy had become a tool of the human lust for power, one which served traditions more than people. This type of "spiritual oppression" was made possible by the mystification of priests, monks and bishops (all those within the spiritual estate), whose firm beliefs were grounded in their different statuses.

If we compare Luther's idea of service and what we see as the needs for our parishes in Africa today, it is obvious that we need believers to *become* pastors more than we need the guarding of special positions and functions *for* pastors. The problem is that too many of those who become ordained pastors fail to free themselves from the reasoning which confers on them an eccentric priestly aura, which puts them in a very special class. This makes it difficult to restore the "priesthood of all believers" to every individual and also makes it impossible to press successfully against the claims of pastors about their professional class. Luther himself said:

> I do not understand why anyone ordained a priest cannot again become a lay person, since the only difference from the lay person lies in the office of the ministry... but now they have invented the priestly office and state that a priest can never return to the lay state. All of that is just talk.

Thus, "special priesthood" has been made a dogmatic and infallible proposition which cannot be changed by any other authority. It has itself become like scripture to some people, both lay and clergy. It would be different if those accorded the office of priest did not abuse it, but since this is not the case then they should be more accountable, and power and resources should be shared among all church members.

Luther was used by God to remind us of many things which Jesus and those after him taught about leadership in the church. Thus, Luther and other reformers did not in fact reject dogmas, but acknowledged them as historical entities which could be changed and understood in different contexts. On the one hand, dogmas can be fallible; on the other, they could be a meaningful basis on which to build faith.

Luther's way of doing theology and his interpretation were definitely influenced by his own experiences in the church. This is a very touching and convincing encouragement for feminist methodology. Sometimes I see myself in Luther's mirror! African women with theological training who are denied opportunities to answer their call to ministry lament the blindness of our churches. Many women are also denied opportunities to study theology. Others have no chance of offering their skills to the church in leadership capacities. Despite all of this, we are sustained by the scriptures as we are reminded that what is happening in our lives has happened to others. Humanly speaking, we are sometimes discouraged, but we should remember that no person in the world has lived without temptation.

Are our contemporary Lutheran churches living up to the expectations of the Reformation? Is the process of reform still continuing? What do we see in most of our "church houses"; peace, love and hope, or confusion, misunderstanding, pain, hatred and hopelessness? Are our churches worthy of the label "Reformation"? These questions challenge my faith every time I think of myself as a member of the Lutheran church. In a way, it is even difficult to claim Lutheranism as one church. There is too much uncertainty even on very basic matters, such as worship and ministry (the issue of women's ordination is but a small part of this). In some of our churches there is no sense of humour at all!

African women's experience in the Lutheran tradition

During the African Lutheran women's consultation in Addis Ababa in December 1990, participants pointed out that the Lutheran tradition in the African context comprises Lutheran teachings from the time of the Reformation, as well as the teachings and interpretations of the missionaries who brought Christianity to Africa. Another aspect of Lutheran tradition is evolving out of the African context and only began to grow after the independence of most African countries. It is still in its infancy, simply because church culture finds it difficult to cut the umbilical cord even for its own good.

Through discussion and listening to stories about each others' churches, women concluded that the Lutheran heritage in Africa is alien to African Lutheran Christian members. Luther and all his contemporaries are only the subjects of seminaries. For most people, it does not really matter that they should adhere to the Lutheran tradition. In any case, the only available Lutheran tradition has been sifted by a particular mission group. The Lutheran tradition in Africa has passed through many hands, thereby intermingling cultures and nationalities. We speak of being either Swedish Lutherans or German Lutherans or Missouri Synod, and so on. Even the practices in our churches are not based on what Africans are or what they want or experience, but what the missionaries or the "mother church" indirectly dictate. This is a painful thing to say, especially for our male leadership, who might not have the freedom to say it so bluntly.

Taking into account the history and current affairs of our political and religious colonialism in Africa, how do we dare embark on a new journey of global sisterhood, be it in theology or something else? Is it really possible? Humanly speaking, will it be possible for African sisters (and brothers, too) to be fully open in bringing our gifts to the table for sharing? And if it is, shall we be scorned, humiliated, dominated or ignored? Will other sisters around the world continue to ignore our voices just because we come from a continent that has so many problems? Where, indeed, is our Lutheran identity with our global sisters? Can we transcend our biases of race, nation and ethnic group? Is it possible that in Christ we all are one, and no longer simply European, American, Asian or African? Can Christians in the world claim any unique genuineness of commonality based strictly on their faith and commitment? Can women in the Lutheran world communion really make a difference in the way they relate to each other?

As an African theologian, I wish to help find a way to welcome Jesus to an African home, with all of its characteristics. In Africa, women are mainly found at home. Jesus should be seen visiting these homes and not just church headquarters and seminaries. African women's theology will not be imprisoned in books: we shall attempt to record it in the hearts of those who spend their time at home making a world of difference to a world that does not acknowledge them.

The experience of Lutheran women in Africa today has little to do with what Luther himself said or did not say about women, but much to do with what is happening to women in Lutheran churches now. This should be our concern and our obligation, which we have to fulfill as we work and live.

African women's international participation

The Lutheran World Federation — especially the Desk for Women in Church and Society — is a very important tool for us women. However, we must be aware that the LWF itself is far ahead of its member churches in the way it works with women. This is part of our dilemma as women in these churches. I often do not see any clear relation between our participation in the events and work of the national churches and those of the LWF or international ecumenical gatherings. We feel more accepted outside than we do at home, where we could render our services and use our talents in a more intense and consistent way.

In some cases our international participation is looked upon by our churches as rebellious, or with aggressiveness and often indifference. We are not given an opportunity to maintain the continuity of what we are doing. We do not have a platform from which to report what we have gained from international events. There is nobody who takes responsibility for the outcome or for follow-up. We have neither the resources nor the permission even to do the least that we can do. We have no chance, therefore, to implement most of what we gather from these meetings.

However, I am encouraged by what some of our sisters are saying. Often, it is men who are weak and who need to be empowered to face contemporary issues and developments. In my experience, those men who wield power are often the weakest. I do not judge them as oppressors, but I recognize them as persons whose view of the partnership of men and women in community is underdeveloped or deficient.

We need to create more awareness in men and women in our churches. There is a need to focus the education of the clergy; although they have learned many things and have seminary education, they are often unschooled in matters of women's participation and women's dignity as persons created in the image of God.

16. Cultural Elements
and Women's Ordination

DATUK THU EN-YU

In the beginning, God created humankind, men and women. They were made separate and independent; each inherited God's image and dignity. God entrusted them with a common task to manage his creation. This was the beginning of the power institution of mutual responsibility and sharing. In order to be sustained, this institution stipulated that men and women respect each other and practise interdependence. This is the biblical teaching on partnership and stewardship; sexual equality is established right from the beginning.

With some exceptions, most Asian cultures uphold the concept of sexual equality. In the process of evolution, cultures eventually become more integrated, with the assimilation of foreign elements and the influence of mores, superstitions, creeds, economics and politics. Therefore, when Asian cultures are discussed, it is preferable that their original cultural elements are separated from their sub-cultures.

Asian cultures, especially Chinese, emphasize the harmony of *yin* and *yang* and observe moderation. These values uphold both biblical teaching and sexual equality.

Women's ordination and Asian culture

Women's ordination is not only a recognition of the contribution women can make; more important, it is a restoring of their original and legitimate image and dignity. It invariably causes men and women to reflect on their respective cultures. As an Asian, and especially as a Chinese, I do not treat women's ordination as an alien cultural peculiarity. On the contrary, it is embedded in the source of Asian culture, awaiting discovery by Christianity.

The Chinese people, like the majority of Asian peoples, were originally an agricultural community. Each has a similar worldview, with an emphasis on the harmony of nature; humans must seek the favour of earth and heaven in order to survive. They pray for the cooperation of natural forces in return for a plentiful harvest. To lead a blessed existence, they fear and worship nature, something beyond their control and manipulation. They perceive an active cosmos and hence personify it. Thus they identify heaven as male, or *yang*, and the earth as female, or *yin*. *Yin* and *yang* become one in harmony and interact with each other. Such a state of nature is the basis for natural harmony that permits peaceful human existence. Moreover, Chinese acclaim women as "the other half of heaven". This is indeed a profound philosophy of equality and partnership.

From a religious point of view, with the exception of Islam and Hinduism, most mainstream Asian religions assign both men and women important and distinct roles in religious affairs. In Buddhism, Taoism and Confucianism, women occupy an all-important position. In folk religion, female ritual specialists enjoy a higher status than their male counterparts.

What in fact makes Christianity treat the issue of women's ordination with reservation? The problem lies with Western Christianity and not with Eastern cultures. When Christianity was first preached in Asia, many Western missionaries treated Eastern cultures as thoroughly anti-Christian; along with this, they rejected the bases of local cultures. Sexual equality was and still is a very recent phenomenon in the West. Hence, it can be argued that the negative attitude of Eastern Christianity towards women's ordination derives from the teaching of the West. The West is the source; the West needs to correct a wrong concept.

The BCCM and women's ordination

The Basel Christian Church of Malaysia (BCCM) shed this particular facet of Western missionary culture when a resolution to ordain women as pastors was passed in 1983. The process was not an easy one. Initially, there was a substantial number of open-minded church leaders who favoured and accepted the employment of women pastors. The proposal was tabled for comprehensive deliberation covering all aspects of the issue. Previously, in 1979, I had presented a paper on women's ordination for the first time in our synod. It was hotly debated and the proposal was rejected. It was noted that the opposition was never cultural in nature, but primarily based on misguided theological concepts about women. To reiterate, objection to women's ordination is the outcome of the theology of the West. The theological objections were:
— God and Jesus are referred to in the masculine gender;
— the twelve apostles were all men;
— Paul forbade women to preach.

The opposition had neither a firm biblical/theological basis nor a strong Asian cultural background. Their claims revolved around a certain interpretation of the Jewish patriarchal tradition, and an unholistic theological view which ignored the priesthood of all believers.

The BCCM spent the next couple of years re-educating its members. Finally, the proposal was reintroduced at the 1983 synod, and women's ordination was formally accepted. Pang Ken Phin and Chong Fui Yung were subsequently ordained as the first women pastors of the BCCM.

The BCCM practises two-tiered ordination. The first ordination is essentially sufficient to enable the candidate to be eligible to perform all holy sacraments, while the second serves to denote senior status. To date, the BCCM has twenty-five women pastors, of which five are senior pastors.

Now women's ordination is a closed issue in the BCCM. Women pastors enjoy completely equal status with men pastors: the same benefits, the same job structure and the same remuneration. They have not only fulfilled the task entrusted to them by the church, but in some cases their performance surpasses that of their male counterparts. This positive development has led a modest section of the initial opposition community to become supporters.

From the point of view of a social institution, women's ordination is a recognition of the rightful status of women. Its inherent meaning lies in the concepts of partnership and stewardship, because recognition and acceptance result in motivation, encouragement and hence full participation.

Nowadays, women's participation in the BCCM is holistic. Women can seek election freely in any hierarchy; at each and every level, they are the *bona fide* colleagues of men. The way is therefore open for women's specialized gifts and ministry to be utilized to the utmost.

There is no doubt that concepts decide the outlook of a person; the nature of a concept dictates the consequence. The BCCM has the right concept of women's ordination and therefore elicits a positive response. At present, we have more than a hundred pastors and evangelists, 35 percent of whom are women. Female seminarians comprise a bigger proportion: among forty seminarians, twenty are female. Women's representation looks set to grow.

BCCM tradition emphasizes collective leadership. Such an excellent tradition is further enhanced by women's participation, and we are thus in the process of achieving a very holistic leadership structure. This helps the leadership to comprehend better the needs of all the people, and hence the church is in a better position to provide a holistic service. Holistic leadership paves the way for a new model of the priesthood of all believers; it facilitates consolidated lay participation. Irrespective of sex and age, all participate in the service of the fellowship. Increased participation enables all to identify with the church. Hence, all have a common identity while each retains his or her own identity.

The church should be the forerunner of a good society, and its testimony can lead the way to change. For example, recently more and more indigenous communities in Sabah have readily identified themselves with the BCCM. The response of indigenous communities to the holistic leadership pattern promoted by the church is more than welcome. Traditionally, indigenous women worked in the fields and seldom took part in social organizations. Moreover, they lacked opportunities for education. Now, women are accorded status within the church; they are trained and then return to serve their respective communities; they provide effective service as well as leadership in the church and in their societies.

This new development has motivated women villagers to take pride in themselves and has resulted in changes in tribal social concepts. There is a growing emphasis on the education of daughters as well as sons. Mothers have also gradually increased their own involvement in church as well as in society. One indigenous woman leader has commented on how the position of women has changed as a result of women's ordination:

> These days, we see changes among the women in the Bahasa Malaysia Congregation. There are ten lady pastors; we also have lawyers, teachers, bankers, a chairlady of the congregational council, seminarians, university graduates and others. They are the present and future leaders of the indigenous group in the church and also in the society. Women's roles in the interior are changing as well. Most of the girls go to school; they don't get married as early as before or become mothers at the usual young age. They are looking for a bright future in their Christian life with dreams and hope.

It cannot be denied that women pastors face some technical and practical problems in their ministry (men pastors also have their problems, but they are different). Owing to differences in physical abilities, talents and backgrounds, some women pastors are not able to work in isolated rural areas, while others cannot be transferred because of their husbands' work or the education of their children. Even if a husband and wife are both pastors, they must make adjustments in order to strike a balance between their ministry and their family commitments.

These sorts of problems are not linked uniquely to gender. Men pastors and women pastors have their respective problems, but many difficulties cannot be characterized as specifically female.

We face problems in transferring women pastors from church to church and in assigning them positions and tasks. Each church needs to be flexible in evaluating a woman pastor's capacity, especially when children are involved. Policies are undoubtedly important, but compassion and the reality of family situations are equally important and have to be taken into consideration.

Each church's institutional and personnel management has a definite structure. It is hard in practice to balance policy, compassion and reality. In spite of this, the churches are required to be open-minded and understanding about impending changes to accommodate the rightful claims of women's ordination; otherwise, they can be accused of prejudice and mismanagement.

Conclusion

In the Bible, the concepts of partnership and personhood are interconnected. Personhood is an inclusive term that includes the whole of humanity, men and women. Hence, any alienation between men and women must be done away with; reconciliation and harmonious relationships render partnership possible and meaningful.

The perfection of God is to be found in the cultures of the world, waiting for us to discover it. When it is realized that concepts in original cultures are in accordance with biblical teaching and therefore beneficial to the communication of the gospel, the church should employ them to its advantage. Thus, a thorough study of biblical hermeneutics and culture is necessary to distinguish what is the gospel and what is culture, in order to facilitate the orderly planting of the gospel in the soil of culture.

Therefore I propose that the churches look at women's ordination positively and:

— identify whether the attitude of the church towards women's ordination is a result of their own culture or the influence of Western Christian culture;

— explore the position of theology and ecclesiology on women's ordination and the priesthood of all believers, and determine their relationship;

— explore whether the Asian theology of reconciliation and harmony can shed any light on the theology of communion and women's ordination.

17. Women Pastors in Indonesia

BASA HUTABARAT

In the Protestant Christian Batak Church (HKBP) the procedure for the preparation of ordinands is theological study, followed by two years of practical ministry. My practical ministry was in a rural area, among people whose way of thinking is very different from that of city-dwellers. It began in 1988, two years after my church first ordained women pastors. As a vicar I was responsible for Sunday school, teenagers, youth, and women's groups. At the time I thought such an assignment was not very rational because much of it could be done by Sunday school teachers and chairpersons of the youth and women's groups.

Physically I am a small woman, so when I met people I always introduced myself as a vicar, so that they would know I was a pastor-to-be. I felt I needed to do this because the attitude of people towards women was not encouraging. With the supervision of my pastor, I learned to chair congregational meetings and perform other duties related to the ministry of a pastor. Very often during church meetings participants would ask me to provide and serve tea or food. I felt sorry for myself and I could not accept that it was quite natural or a matter of divine will that it is the responsibility of women to serve at table. But I had to cope with it because I thought of myself as "just a vicar".

Opposition

Although a number of women have been ordained as pastors, Batak society cannot yet accept their presence in the HKBP. The reason given is that "women are not suitable to teach in the church, advise men and speak in public to a crowd. They are a lower class than men". This view has carried some weight. For instance, church members male and female have great difficulty in accepting a woman pastor at a wedding ceremony or a baptism; particularly when the woman pastor is not married. In Batak society, women do not have the right to speak in a formal cultural meeting, especially when the audience is male. Men ignore the sermons given by women pastors and the views they express. Biblical verses such as 1 Timothy 2:11-12 and 1 Corinthians 14:34-35 are very often quoted to defend such attitudes and to weaken the integrity of women as the image of God.

The welfare and salaries of women are neglected. Most HKBP women pastors are unmarried, and their salaries are lower than those of men. The reason given is that the needs of women pastors are fewer. We have to accept this discrimination because we are ashamed to speak out to the church board and to church members. Very few women are on the decision-making body of the church, and this is an obstacle to the development of women's potential.

The offices entrusted to women are normally in a specific category (i.e. children, youth or women), or have to do with social matters, finance and things related to technical administration. Almost no women are in positions dealing with formation, education, law or politics.

To be acknowledged as women

There is no success without struggle. After learning about the Ecumenical Decade of Churches in Solidarity with Women, the HKBP launched programmes aimed at demonstrating the concern of the church for women. I have used the opportunity to acquire as much information as possible. As a young woman pastor I have felt very inadequate among male colleagues. As a result, whenever I am with them I frequently attempt to get their attention by my appearance, by putting forward ideas about the issues we discuss, and by expressing opinions and working hard. I have also tried to approach decision-making officials. I have learned from experience that one has to have courage to perform serious tasks and take responsibility for them in order to achieve anything.

Moreover, a woman pastor in such circumstances must face challenges. For instance, in the matter of assignment she must be prepared to be sent anywhere; men have no choice in their assignments so a woman should not seek a choice simply because she is a woman. She must show that as a woman she can accomplish the task assigned to her.

For a woman, knowledge and skills are essential: not simply the ability to operate a sewing machine or manage a beauty salon, but more importantly general skills, because she serves congregations with complex problems and characters. Without learning continuously and keeping herself informed a woman pastor cannot serve well.

My own experience of administering holy communion is very encouraging in terms of the value a congregation places on the ministry of a woman. After a while, I noticed that people did not refuse holy communion and, surprisingly, church members now *prefer* to be served by a woman pastor. This really is a new phenomenon, and I am quite convinced it has something to do with the work of the Holy Spirit. For church members, understanding of the ordination of a pastor is more than simply a "church" thing: it has God's blessing.

Living with Christ

In life one experiences sufferings. For a woman pastor, cultural and family obstacles limit movement. Some who are married have to quit, mainly because they are unable to divide their time between their family and their ministry; they have to follow their husbands. For our people, the Bataks, it is unworthy if a woman is responsible for the family income and the husband follows the wife in her ministry. The ministry of a pastor is no longer seen as a prophetic calling but simply a profession. It is this prophetic calling that has to be fought for by women pastors. It is in suffering that the essence of the calling lies. If a person is called, she becomes the possession of God, and her status changes; she is no longer the possession of a particular clan or class. If we are Christ's possession, it is God who really cares for us.

In my calling as a woman pastor I have a heavy task and responsibility. But this is the consequence of my calling and at the same time a joy. I have to learn to obey God. Obedience is not just about obeying an order, but about the willingness to give up one's thought, will, belongings and everything else. For me, obedience to God is demonstrated in my attitude to heeding God's calling and plan irrespective of place and situation. Frequently, I have heard criticisms and accusations by church members or pastor colleagues about things they do not like in me. But I must have the courage to say that somebody is wrong when he or she is wrong, even though people will not like me for it. In facing this situation, I have only Christ to defend me. I have to be very close to Christ in my ministry, even though I may not be respected.

In his suffering, Jesus Christ acted as an example to his disciples. That God never left him was the certainty of his hope. Jesus is always with a woman pastor in all her struggles; he suffers with her and cries over the condition of women in Indonesia. Therefore, women pastors generally should not be too overcome by their suffering, for they should know that God never leaves them; God is there for suffering women.

In the long-standing crisis of the HKBP which began in 1992, congregations badly need church workers and pastors who are not afraid for their lives. In facing the crisis, I myself have experienced the hand of God guiding me in solving various problems. The crisis of the HKBP has had negative effects on the lives of members. The violence committed by the military and people backed up by the government — expulsion, arrest, torture and intimidation — are the results of a crisis caused by the election of HKBP leadership by the military. In witnessing this violence a woman pastor cannot remain silent. As a pastor she must uphold the truth and encourage church members not to take violent action themselves, even when they are tortured, because violence never solves problems. Jesus Christ never taught violence. The struggle for freedom of worship and religion is costly. Church members have suffered for the freedom of the HKBP to govern itself. But I have told them not to seek revenge. It is the cost of following Christ.

During the crisis in the HKBP, I have witnessed the courage of women pastors. Along with church members, they have demanded freedom of religion from the military and the police, and have put themselves in a dangerous position. One day, I had to preach in the open on a street, because the church had been occupied by the military and thugs. Church members were not allowed to use the church building for worship. After the service the police summoned me to the police station to be interrogated; I answered all their questions as best I could and afterwards I was sent home. This has happened a number of times. Together with other women pastors I have been involved in risky work. But we have done it without fear and have witnessed God's protection. I know that Jesus himself had to choose between temporary happiness and lasting glory. He chose the glory even though it meant great suffering.

During this time we have seen the role of women in seeking to discover solutions and to put them into practice. When sacrifice is needed, the women of the church have stepped forward to offer their lives for its freedom.

Women pastors in society

Even after all these years, many people in our society are still surprised when I am introduced as a pastor. They frequently ask: "Is a female pastor allowed to marry?" I have discovered that this question is based on the belief that to be a pastor is very difficult and involves heavy responsibility. This view renders the activities of women invisible, inasmuch as it asserts that in order to be a pastor a woman must be able to do things which a man cannot do. For instance, a woman pastor should not marry, or if she is married it should be to a pastor. She must behave well. If she makes one mistake, then her whole character is questioned.

At first, the general public could not accept the presence of women pastors. They also thought that the work of a pastor had to do with spiritual things, detached from social and political/legal matters. This understanding also used to be indoctrinated into the minds of women pastors, but after a while it was criticized. A pastor is a teacher in society; therefore he or she must communicate with society and the community. A pastor is responsible for encouraging congregations and society generally to care for the needy as a means of sharing God's blessing in society. Congregations must be encouraged to "do ministry" and to witness.

A pastor does various things in society, including encouraging people to repent. Women pastors are expected nowadays to work with women's groups which are in contact with a prostitution network, with the purpose of encouraging prostitutes to leave the profession and empowering them to find a new job. In doing this women pastors need to be able to engage in dialogue. Through dialogue they can motivate prostitutes and give them a purpose in life.

Pastors must also be concerned about the life of labour. For a long time, no one cared for workers or fought in their struggle for their rights. A woman pastor can approach workers, especially women, and help them to empower themselves and know their rights and responsibilities.

The vision of HKBP women pastors is to create a partnership between men and women in Christ. Such a partnership will materialize if men and women accept that they are partners, created according to the plan of God for the development of the world.

18. The Ordination of Women in Africa

MUSIMBI R.A. KANYORO

In Africa the first women were ordained only in the 1970s. It is a subject about which very little has been said and written in comparison with the other parts of the world. Most of the debate in Africa has not received extensive coverage because it has been conducted at the level of church committees and elsewhere rather than in books. The subject is therefore wide open for discussion. One might, for example, wish to consider whether or not the ordination of women is an issue that keeps the church in Africa awake, or simply to document Africa's contribution to this controversial debate, be it minor or otherwise. Whenever issues of justice for women are raised in international circles, an excuse is given for African women. It is often said that they are content with the church as it is and the agenda of women's participation in leadership is foreign to them. This essay listens to the voices of women in an attempt to answer the question, "What do African women say on this issue?"

It goes without saying that to deal adequately with this subject requires a great deal of research and long experience with church life in Africa. Although I have had some ecumenical experience in a number of African countries, I have not followed local debates. I shall therefore try to avoid inaccuracies by drawing my illustrations from situations of which I have first-hand personal experience. My comments will be limited to the Lutheran experience.

I also propose to be somewhat unsystematic in an effort to say a little about many things, so that I can provide an overview of the African situation. I will concentrate on issues that I feel have not been recorded and which will therefore contribute something new.

The African situation

Is the ordination of women an issue for African churches? There is no one answer to this question. A number of churches in Africa ordain women, and to reach this point one may assume that it was an issue of importance for them. There has been a marked discrepancy over time in regard to the practice of ordaining women. For example, the Anglican Church in Uganda ordained women long before the world Anglican communion voted to do so, whereas the Anglican Church in neighbouring Kenya ordained women in only one diocese and those women were not recognized by the other dioceses until the vote took place in the whole communion globally. Similarly, in Namibia the Evangelical Lutheran Church in the Republic of Namibia (ELCRN) ordained women long before the Evangelical Lutheran Church in Namibia (ELCIN) — another church of the Lutheran confession in the same country.

These examples show that in Africa the discussion and practice of women's ordination have been centred on each particular church and not necessarily according to confession or country. At most it may be said that, in some instances, the decision as to whether or not to ordain women has until today depended largely on the practices, the vision and the wish of the "mother" church. In Namibia, the Lutheran church that ordained women has its roots in Germany where ordination had taken place for a long time. The ELCIN on the other hand has its roots in Finland and only entered into the debate after Finland had made its decision in 1988. When discussions on controversial subjects take place in the "mother" church, the "daughter churches" are often not invited to take part. They are also prevented from initiating similar discussions in their own local churches by resident missionaries, who in some cases left their homeland before such issues had become important. In Africa this "protection" has been carried out by both expatriate missionaries and the African clergy, who in many cases have received their theology and training from the "mother" church in former times and are reluctant to accept change.

In spite of the variations in the practice of ordaining women in the churches of Africa, ordained women are still a curious minority. The sight of a woman in a collar raises the eyebrows of practically everyone. The phenomenon is such a recent one that even ordained women themselves are still excited — as well as insecure — about their role as pioneers. They are still finding their place within the male-structured church and male clergy system. Unlike in some other parts of the world, where ordained women have begun to question or examine their contribution, African women ministers are at the point where they are being "put to the test". They are doing their best to justify their existence and calling and to convince the church and society that they are in the right vocation. Some of the new women pastors are engaged in an extremely difficult journey, and in some cases it is a journey in the dark. One woman pastor recently ordained was sent by her church to a parish where no male pastor wanted to go. The parish had been without a pastor for several years. While the male clergy had the courage to refuse the assignment, she could not. Being the first woman, she feels that whatever she does will be used as a judgment on other women who feel called to the ordained ministry. Therefore, she is under pressure to comply, to obey and to please. She has no role model of what a woman pastor can or cannot do. Hence, she is conscious of the fact that she will be a role model to other women and she wants to be an assuring one.

Only time will tell the worth of the self-sacrifices these pioneer women pastors are making. I suspect that on the whole African continent there are no more than 100 ordained women. I shall use the Lutheran case to illustrate the situation further.

Resistance

In Africa there are 25 Lutheran churches which are members of the Lutheran World Federation. In some countries, several churches with different mission origins have amalgamated to form a national unit. For example, the Evangelical Lutheran Church in Tanzania (ELCT) is made up of 19 dioceses, some of which have different mission origins. Each of the dioceses has its own autonomy and more often than not a bilateral relationship with its particular "mother" mission. Even though the ELCT is a member of the Lutheran World Federation, each of the dioceses reserves the right to implement or not to implement decisions made by the national ELCT, let alone the LWF.

It is often said that male clergy rather than parishioners are the most strongly opposed to women's ordination. This may be because male clergy are familiar with the various arguments and have opted for those against ordination. The other reason could be professional jealousy: the fear that monopoly power might be challenged by women can cause resistance. Some constitutions of the African Lutheran churches bar women from ordination; in fact a number of them spell out clearly that the clergy must be male. The Evangelical Lutheran Church in Namibia (ELCIN) was one of the churches that had to revise its own constitution in order to ordain women. The Evangelical Lutheran Church in Sierra Leone has the most inclusive constitution within the LWF membership in Africa on matters concerning the ordination of women. It stipulates that the bishop of the church:
— shall be its executive officer, the president of the corporation and chief minister and counsellor in matters spiritual and temporal;
— is the spiritual head of the ELCSL;
— a man or a woman may fill this office.
Similarly, all other church offices are open to men and women alike. Whether it is the office of treasurer or secretary general, the constitution in each case spells out that the incumbent may be either male or female. But in addition to training enough women for ordination, the church in Sierra Leone will need to educate church men and women to elect women. The constitution is explicit in affirming the role of women: I confess joy at such openness, but scepticism when it comes to its realization. It is not enough to have a beautifully written document, even if it is translated into local languages. The issue here is not whether it is understood, but whether it complies with what can be done according to Sierra Leone's society. The church in Sierra Leone has a difficult educational task ahead of it: its success will not depend on what it says in its constitution but how it lives out that constitution. It made a good beginning when it ordained the first woman in 1996. She was also designated as a delegate to the LWF assembly in 1997.

There are some churches, for example the Lutheran Church of Liberia, which have already changed their constitution in order to admit women to the ordained ministry, but other barriers such as theological qualifications still prevent the actual ordination of women. The Lutheran Church of Christ in Nigeria (LCCN), for example, removed the barriers to ordaining women at its top administrative level, but it took a while to ordain for another interesting reason. A woman was trained for ordination and after her graduation she married an Anglican pastor. The church was very disappointed and hesitated to recommend any other women for ordination for a very long time. In 1989, a Lutheran pastor married a Methodist woman theologian. A debate ensued in the church as to whether she was eligible for the Lutheran priesthood and whether she could be called from a Lutheran congregation. It was only in 1996 that she was finally admitted to ordination.

The Lutheran churches exemplify an assortment of issues relating to the ordination of women in Africa. There are issues connected with the standpoint of the "mother" church, the local church's perception of leadership in society, preparation for leadership (such as theological training) and, not least, interpretation of the scriptures. With regard to this last, African churches with mission origins do not present different arguments about scripture or tradition from those made elsewhere. Many churches use the argument of "received" tradition. Why does a continent like Africa — fighting so many other issues of tradition — choose to align itself with this? Take the issue of slavery: Africa more than any other continent suffered from slavery, and the scriptures were used to defend it. No African can ever contribute to a debate supporting slavery with Paul's argument that slaves must remain slaves. The scriptures are also used to justify apartheid and other forms of racism. If African male clergy were to follow these lines of argument to their logical conclusion, they would also have to come to terms with the fact that there were no Africans or gentiles within the tradition of male Jewish priests or among the twelve apostles.

The argument about headship is often linked with traditional cultures. In some cultures in Africa men are the heads and leaders of the family. But this should not be given too much importance. In matriarchal societies found in many parts of Africa — such as the Chewa in Malawi and the Akan in Ghana — women's leadership is well recognized. In Akan society, for example, it is the queen mother who makes kings. Hence, the links between headship and culture should not be generalized as applying to all African cultures. In so far as priesthood is concerned, John Mbiti, one of the authorities on African traditional religions, says

> priesthood as a class is distinct and developed... Training may comprise seclusion from the world, instruction in laws and sometimes possession by divinity. The vocation of priesthood and devotee is highly honoured. It is generally open to both men and women.

In many traditional religions as well as African instituted churches (AICs) women play prominent roles as spirit-mediums — a role belonging to the priestly circles. Thus, the powers of healing, preaching and spiritual direction, typically understood by the Christian church to be priestly duties, are powers traditionally exercised by women and men in African societies. If there is to be any general picture of African women in ordained ministries, an inclusive study of the religious roles played by women in different types of societies in Africa is imperative. Whether or not African churches are conducting these in-depth studies is a crucial matter which requires more serious attention.

Pauline teaching on how women should behave in church is invoked both by men and women; in other words, this debate on the ordination of women is not determined along gender lines, with women holding one view and men another. More often than not, it has been claimed that African women are not interested in the priesthood; they are content in their present roles. For a long time, a majority of African church women believed and accepted this claim without question. Even the powerful Akan matriarchs were silenced by the scriptures quoted to them. Without themselves being authorities on scripture, church history and law, how could they state their case? But today African women theologians are beginning to address issues of church, the scriptures and theology with new eyes, new questions, new curiosities and new confidence. It is on this that I now wish to focus.

The women of Africa on ordination

A few years ago, one could have argued — maybe rightly so — that *ordination* did not rank very highly as an issue for African women. This is probably because the training of women in theology was something new; indeed, it is still rare even today. Theology as a discipline is not given a high profile, either by the churches or by women themselves. Perhaps women do not see a future for themselves in this area, or they do not have role models who have made vocations for themselves after training in theology.

Nevertheless, today the issue of women's ordination is being raised by women themselves, theologians and non-theologians alike. It is seen by African women within the whole context of women's participation in the life of the church and society. The lack of participation and recognition in decision-making structures is expressed by women of all ages and educational levels, from more Catholic churches such as Anglicans, Roman Catholics and Lutherans, to Evangelicals, independent churches and so on. The recently formed Pan African Christian Women's Association, an arm of the Association of the Evangelicals of Africa and Madagascar, states in its brochure: "PACWA is calling both women and men in the church to recognize that the call and mission of Christ are extended to the total family of God (men and women)." Even though PACWA itself has not yet raised the issue of ordination, many of its members come from churches which give women a high leadership role, for example, the Pentecostals. In some of these churches, women preach, lead services and sit on governing boards.

African women are no longer silent on theological issues, ordination being one issue among many. In villages they continue daily to sing and pray and live their theology in languages which are appropriate to them. Those who have done theology from the point of view of Western scholarship have reflected deeply and extensively on religio-cultural issues in the context of African society. Women have spoken on subjects ranging from rites of passage, motherhood, marriage, with its intricacies of polygamy and the church, and death, both in the contexts of mourning and widowhood rites.

The theological reflections of African women on these issues are the window through which we see their visions and hear their voices. One should not only research books published in Western countries, but also listen to the discussions of women as they go to fetch water from the river, braid their hair, meet in thousands of women's groups. The reports and the work of women in national councils of churches and the All Africa Conference of Churches also form some of the richest libraries for African women's voices. These voices have not made their way into church minutes because women are not yet on church boards.

The Ecumenical Association of Third World Theologians has provided a forum where women have talked and will continue to talk. Forums of international church organizations such as the WCC or the LWF also provide opportunities. In October 1989, the Circle of Concerned African Women Theologians inaugurated the Biennial Institute of African Women in Religion and Culture. The institute was created in response to the dearth of literature on African women by African women. Its primary concern is to stimulate theological reflection and literature by African women. The Circle women have held many meeting in their regions and also published reports and books on issue of concern for them. Ordination has ranked high on the list. During the meeting in Nairobi in August 1996, a number of ordained women were present and the ordination of women in Africa was one, although not the only issue needing attention. African women are speaking, and very soon the world will hear their voice. African women see ordination as one of the issues in the leadership of the church. Presently, there is a cry for a theological seminary to incorporate in the curriculum methods of ministering to the crucial concerns affecting women. Further reading of the voices of the Circle women can be found in the references at the end of this paper.

A godly vision

Anyone who is deeply involved, who knows about and values the ministry of women church workers, would never give up on God opening more avenues of service for them. A Tanzanian lay woman who was among the women who sang and danced in the streets after the decision had been passed to ordain women (1990) confided her feelings of joy to me:

> We have been blessed. At last God has blessed us with women pastors! We women can see ourselves in the ministry.

I believe God calls both men and women to complement one another, side by side, in ordained ministry as in other aspects of life together. The appearance of women in other professions formerly reserved for men even in Africa argues for similar actions by the church. Whatever the state of the debate on women's ordination, it seems reasonable to assert that the question is not so much whether the church is for or against it, but how the church handles such discussions.

It is not enough to argue that the will of Christ attested in the scriptures is the normative reason in the tradition of excluding women from the ordained ministries of the church. African male clergy will have to open themselves to other arguments, not least those by women themselves. The strong scriptural, theological and social reasons available today make a refusal to ordain women a kind of spiritual disobedience which ends in a loss of vision. The women of Africa do not want our churches to lose this vision. Will the churches listen?

READING

Ackermann, Denise et al., eds, *Women Hold Up Half the Sky: Women in the Church in Southern Africa*, Pietermaritzburg, Cluster Publications, 1991.

Kanyoro, Musimbi, ed., *Our Advent: African Women's Experiences in the Lutheran Tradition*, proceedings of the African Lutheran women theologians' meeting, Addis Ababa, 2-7 December 1990.

Kanyoro, Musimbi R.A. and Nyambura, J. Njoroge, eds, *Groaning in Faith: African Women in the Household of God*, Nairobi, Acton Publishers, 1996.

Oduyoye, Mercy Amba, *Hearing and Knowing*, Maryknoll, NY, Orbis, 1986.

Oduyoye, Mercy Amba, *Daughters of Anowa: African Women and Patriarchy*, Maryknoll, NY, Orbis, 1995.

Oduyoye, Mercy Amba and Kanyoro, Musimbi R.A., eds, *The Will to Arise: Women, Tradition and Church in Africa*, Maryknoll, NY, Orbis, 1992.

Pobee, John S., *Culture, Women and Theology*, Delhi, ISPCK, 1994.

Wamue, Grace and Getui, Mary, eds, *Violence against Women*, Nairobi, Acton Publishers, 1996.

19. Women's Ordination:
A Viewpoint from Tanzania

CUTHBERT K. OMARI

The ordination of women is simply a matter of decision, not for discussion or raising issues. Many of the questions women have been asked — theological or otherwise — have already been considered and answered, although the answers have not always satisfied everyone. So when we consider this issue from a sociological and cultural point of view, we do not expect to be able to answer every question about women in ministry. Rather, this paper takes account of the changes taking place in community and culture.

Women in leadership

General perspectives

When we consider the role of women in the ministry, we must do so from the point of view of leadership in the community as a whole. This point must be emphasized because the pastorate is a form of leadership which has been held exclusively by men for a very long time. When women are brought into this ministry by the community of believers, what are the sociological and cultural implications?

Sociologically, women have made progress in obtaining equality in various forms of leadership. Nevertheless, this progress has come through the struggles and efforts of women themselves, together with some men. There are still men who see no reason for women to be involved in leadership, since they consider that the place of women is in the home or that they should be given opportunities to serve but not to lead.

There are areas of leadership as a career which have in the past been an entirely male preserve. For example, women did not study medicine; those who wanted to do medical work became nurses and midwives. Similarly, women were not trained in engineering or mechanics; indeed, it was regarded as extraordinary for a woman to handle a trowel or a hammer on a building site or to direct construction workers.

Nowadays things have changed, though not as rapidly as we would like. We do have women doctors; we do have women engineers. Thus there are indications that the community is accepting a certain societal evolution. This situation will improve as more women obtain higher education and technological training. At present, according to the statistics available there are only a few women taking these studies, and therefore most high positions are not filled by women, especially those requiring experience in technology and engineering.

According to the information we have[1] women hold only 21 percent of the senior positions in parastatals and government ministries and departments in

Tanzania. Of these, only 3 percent have managerial responsibilities, that is, leadership roles and decision-making functions. Many of the high-level positions held by women are those relating to the division of career opportunities in accordance with sexual and cultural barriers and social trends. These careers include nursing, midwifery and teaching. In the whole field of human and veterinary medicine, only 8 percent of those with higher qualifications are women.

Since they are not present at decision-making levels in many sectors, we cannot expect women to have much influence in bringing about change in many social structures and attitudes. Men still lead and govern, and therefore most decisions continue to reflect masculine perceptions, especially in matters which concern the development of women and their role in the community. Culture and tradition, customs and habits are used to demonstrate and support this position.

Political responsibilities

Women's leadership in society is not measured only by looking at patterns of employment. We must also look at leadership in relation to political trends.

Among recent research in the field, an important study by Meena and Mtengeti-Migiro[2] examines the place of women in history and politics, especially in their struggles for various rights including that of standing for a seat in parliament. Nevertheless, this paper should be read in conjunction with Swantz[3] in order to obtain a complete picture of women in their struggles for development. The contribution of women in politics is only a part of the development of the community.

Meena and Mtengeti-Migiro provide statistics relating to women in the parliament of the United Republic of Tanzania. From 1965 to the 1985 election the number of women MPs increased in each election but not by very much. This is unsatisfactory, especially as there are in fact slightly more women than men in the total population. However, little by little women are beginning to hold positions of responsibility. Out of 25 current government ministers there are six women. And in the islands there are three women among the 143 government ministers.

It should be said that it has taken us twenty years since independence and ten years since the Arusha declaration just to take this small step in relation to the place of women in the community. It should also be made clear that not all women MPs have been elected by citizens in electoral districts. For example, in the 1985 election only one woman was elected in this way. The others were nominated by the president in accordance with the constitution, or they came through party channels. All other women candidates in the constituencies were defeated by men.

There are two conclusions which may be drawn from an election of this kind. First, it seems that the voters preferred to elect men rather than women to represent them. The reason could be that the women nominated to stand against the men lacked experience. Second, it seems as if women voters did not consider women capable of representing them. It could be that there were really no suitable women candidates, or it could be a lack of mutual trust among the women voters themselves.

Mutual trust and self-trust in the ministry of the pastorate is of the greatest importance. If women themselves do not have confidence in each other, we cannot expect much from men in bringing about change. There are plenty of men who are delighted when women fail in responsible tasks, so that they can say "we told you so". Therefore, whenever women hold leadership responsibilities we must recognize that opposition is unavoidable at this stage of societal evolution; those who oppose change will express their point of view.

The question is how we respond to these changes when they take place, especially in those areas which concern our culture and traditions, which are part of our very selves.

Women in the leadership of the church

The church came into being at a time when the community of believers were in an environment which was more favourable to men. To some extent the environment of the Old Testament and the New Testament at the time of the founding of the Christian church was not much different from the general situation and trend of our own society. On the whole, men are recognized as the leaders in society and women as the followers, although in some places women have proved to be very capable leaders.[4]

Our society is ruled by men and it is they who uphold weak arguments in favour of systems and structures which do not give women opportunities for leadership. Thus, even the systems and structures which we find in the church are the result of men's and not women's views. For this reason, we cannot expect to find good examples of societal systems and structures which throw any light on the topic under discussion.

In 1966 at the synod of the Evangelical Lutheran Church in Tanzania (ELCT) at Bukoba, I expressed the opinion that women should be given the same opportunity as men to study theology. My chief suggestion was to give all the young people of the church, who are tomorrow's leaders, the same opportunity to be fully involved in the church's life. I did not wish then to raise the issue of ordination because I knew it was only a matter of time. I saw no serious objection to women studying theology. Thus, the church's refusal to train women theologians at that time was in accord with the general view in society. In accordance with the division of service and ministry in the church, women are evangelists and assistants but cannot be pastors; so why should they study theology? It would be a waste of time and resources. They should stay where they are and where they are accepted by society.

But the Lutheran church is very progressive. Women have entered theological college, taken various courses and graduated along with the men. Any question of women not being able to cope with theological studies is purely theoretical. The question which arises is rather whether they should be ordained.

In 1986 when I was guest speaker at the graduation ceremony of Makumira Lutheran Theological College, I ventured to state openly that the refusal to ordain women as pastors was a matter of social education, not of theology. I also stated clearly that I not only expected to witness the ordination of women as pastors, but also looked forward to having a woman bishop in Tanzania.

What, then, is the cultural and sociological significance of the ordination of women as pastors? The views expressed below are extrapolated from the environment of Tanzania and ecclesiastical trends.

First, culturally the ordination of women is a progressive factor in the struggles of women to participate fully in the life and leadership of the church and its councils. For a long time, women and women's groups have upheld the church in a variety of ways. The task of stimulating congregation members and believers as a whole has belonged to women most of the time. In some congregations it is the women who are the reliable participants in worship services, while the men attend "men's" meetings and discuss "male" topics.

In the important lower levels of church leadership women have faithfully kept to their task. If we believe that leadership starts from such lower levels, then we realize that women have been leaders in the church ever since the time of the New Testament. When women want to take higher responsibilities in church leadership, they appear as a threat to men who have until now held onto them for themselves. This is not something new, except that now women are succeeding in obtaining these higher positions.

Aggressive reactions to this increasing success follow on from the notion that women are weak and therefore if they hold positions of leadership, especially pastoral leadership, they will only weaken the church still further. Such suppositions and perceptions are based on the present structures of society. In fact, men are just as weak as women, especially in spiritual ministries. It is true that women are inclined to be kind and compassionate, but this characteristic should be an asset and not a liability in the ministry of a pastor. Since the idea of ordaining women is seen as a threat by some people, it is our responsibility — all of us, men and women — to make every effort to erase such weak and impoverished notions by positive, progressive methods.

As already noted, the absence of women from the upper levels of responsibility is characteristic of the whole of Tanzanian society. We should not be surprised, therefore, to find the same attitudes in the church and particularly within its structures. The struggle to get rid of these attitudes is a difficult one and not something to be left to a few activists; it is up to the community as a whole.

It should be made clear that ordaining women must not be regarded simply as a demand for women to be involved in leadership or decision-making processes. Rather, it is a matter of principle in the fight for equal rights and equal involvement for all people, without discrimination based on biological or social differences. Therefore, it is the responsibility of the whole of society and of all who seek to defend the rights of every human being to speed up the overall development of society, and especially that within the decision-making bodies of the churches.

In society generally, the trend is for women and men to participate together in leadership and management according to ability. Therefore, the claim that women should be ordained is not due simply to the fact that they are women; it is made because they merit it and it is their right as faithful members of the community, in other words, the church. The basic principle behind this claim is that women should neither be denied the opportunity of holding responsible leadership positions, nor should they be granted those positions simply because they are women. We would defeat the purpose of achieving strong and firm leadership in our society if we ordained women without proper procedures. They must follow the same selection process as the men.

The second thing we have to recognize is that the ordination of women is a major step in raising their social status. The church's teaching has in all ages broken the bonds of cultures; and this church cannot be prevented by tradition and culture from fulfilling its calling to ministry. Cultural factors which are obstructive or which oppress believers or suppress their aims in one way or another must be scrutinized afresh and, if at all possible, changed. The ordination of women is one way of breaking down the cultural barriers which have prevented us from seeing that we are treating women unjustly if we do not give them opportunities of leadership within the church when they have the same abilities as men, and in some cases are actually better qualified.

The church, which has been supporting and defending human rights in accordance with its traditions and teaching, cannot avoid taking the next, revolutionary step of ordaining women and involving them fully in the leadership and structures of its congregations.

Third, since the ordination of women will be a revolutionary step, there will be opponents to it in the name of culture, tradition, customs and habits, or theology. When such opposition arises, we must be ready to listen even to those who disagree with us. We must be ready to examine their arguments, and if a certain church does not go along with the decision to ordain women this must not become a cause for division. We must recognize that there are different ministries and different ministers. We must simply agree that if such a situation does arise, we will continue our efforts and strategies for educating one another, until we reach the point where everyone recognizes that the question of ordaining women as pastors is one of sociology and not of theology.

Fourth, if this is the case we must not tire of explaining the importance of this matter just because people react to it in different ways. It is especially important to inform opponents, as to some extent it is they who have worked to perpetuate the system and support the structures which oppress women in one way or another.

Fifth, women who are ordained as pastors must have faith in themselves as leaders on equal terms with male pastors. They must build new attitudes by constructing different and meaningful patterns of ministry. Here a double strategy is needed: on the one hand, for those to whom the responsibility of ministry is given, and on the other hand for those to whom they minister. The strategies of both should be combined in such a way that the ministry provided by women pastors does not appear weak, or strengthen the negative image people have of women in comparison to men. Women who have the ability will come to be recognized on the same basis as men. It is up to the church to realize this and act accordingly.

Conclusion

Culturally speaking, the ordination of women is a result of the changes taking place in our society. It has taken a long time. Traditions, habits, customs and precedents have all lead us to consider women as "incapable" of taking responsible positions in society. As in the wider society, it will be accomplished one day, and with great rejoicing.

Those barriers which remain at the present time will undoubtedly be removed, because we are not the slaves of our culture but the creators of that culture. Culture at any given time results from the life of society, and when the church decides to ordain women it will be one major step forward in the creation of a new culture in both the church and the society of Tanzania. It will indeed be revolutionary, and a vital step towards the full involvement of women in the various leadership responsibilities of the church. There is no area of responsibility which a woman with ability cannot hold and fulfill. This step must be taken if the church is to stand firm on its principle of fighting for equality and human rights as a whole.

NOTES

1 C.K. Omari, "Women in Development in Tanzania", paper presented at Seurakuntaopisto, Jarvenpaa, Finland, 19 March-2 April 1989.
2 R. Meena and Mtengeti Migiro, *Women in Politics and Leadership in Tanzania*, Dar es Salaam, Educational Publishers and Distributors, 1988.
3 M.L. Swantz, *Women in Development: A Creative Role Denied. The Case of Tanzania*, London, Hurst, 1985.
4 C.K. Omari, "The Community of Believers and the Involvement of Men and Women on Equal Terms", paper presented to the seminar on the Decade of the churches, ELCT, 16-21 January 1989.

20. A Decade of Discovery

NICOLE FISCHER

Women's strengths and gifts

In spite of the fact that the church takes little account of their concerns, women have within them a tremendous latent power. They often love the church very deeply and are ready to commit themselves to work for it. However, they are also frustrated by the church's failure to receive and respond to their gifts and callings.

Women everywhere live under enormous stress: in charge of the day-to-day management of the home, they also work outside their homes and are often the sole breadwinners, although they usually earn less than men for the same work. Despite this double burden, they are still expected to have the energy and the will to volunteer their time to churches and communities. It is not money which makes the world go round, but women.

Women are active in many creative ways, even though they are rarely involved in the official structures and governing bodies of their church or society. They have instead established their own organizations within the churches. Frequently, church women link themselves with secular women's movements. For example, since 1986 in Japan the House of Emergency in Love and Peace (HELP) has supported migrant women workers and those engaged in the "entertainment" industry. In Cameroon, the women's department of a council of churches holds seminars and leadership training for and with women. It has also worked towards raising the consciousness of church leaders about the contributions of women. In the Philippines, several feminist church groups are members or associates of a secular, feminist women's advocacy umbrella organization, Gabriella.

Women all over the world are the pillars of the church. They are active, strong and ready to put effort into the church's mission: that the world may be characterized by justice and peace for all people today and in the future.

A question of uniform

Tensions sometimes exist between different women's groups in a church. It is manifested most clearly in parts of Lesotho, Togo and Cameroon, and also in Hong Kong. Women in these places speak of "uniformed and non-uniformed" groups.

Such tensions are known around the world. On one side, there are church-based women's groups or fellowships, whose members accept the role that society and church expect them to fulfill. They are faithful to the church, are usually very active, and serve it with all their hearts, well aware that they are the pillars of the church. Many women find their group to be like a home and family base. Some of them challenge the church for its patriarchal stance and support for oppressive cultural norms. They are often called "uniformed women" or "scarved women", because they cover their heads in obedience to Paul's injunction.

On the other side, in the same countries but also in many other places, new groups are emerging who through their education and training — often in the "uniformed groups" — are keen to challenge the preconceived roles given them by society and also by the church. They are assertive and question a tradition when it is oppressive. They also are dedicated to the church, but are ready to undertake new roles.

Both groups have much in common; they come from the same cultural background and above all they love the church. However, they seem severely to underestimate the negative effects of their public quarrels. In effect, they are unwittingly helping men and the church to maintain the status quo so as not to offend traditional women. It is painful to see how they thus militate against their own common interests.

Gospel and culture

It is vital to affirm the importance of respecting cultural contexts everywhere. We must remind ourselves that culture for women and men is an essential theological source, an inescapable medium for gospel expression. We should also understand that culture is capable of being both oppressive and liberating. If it is to be liberating, it must be rooted in the real lives of women, and both women's and men's experiences must be seen as an integral part of local culture. Church leaderships should note that the gospel is the basis for criticizing and transforming all human contexts and existences. This is very important, for culture is often cited as a pretext for the continued subservience of women, sometimes by violent means.

In Pakistan, for example, sexual assault, forced marriages and physical violence against women are seen by church leaders as culturally conditioned behaviour and thus not amenable to church influence. Some churches have even held on to very oppressive marriage liturgies, which establish and legitimate domestic abuse. In South Korea, Confucianism is blamed for negative attitudes towards women in the church, and it is cited as the principal reason why the heads of all major departments in the church are men. In the Cook Islands, explanations for the failure to speak out against hidden or secret violence in the home are couched in terms of cultural tradition. In one church in the USA, women have been ordained since 1970, but only four of the sixty ordained clergy are women. In another church, where women have been ordained for over 120 years, only thirty clergy women are serving as senior pastors of local congregations (this church has over 9000 ordained ministers). In Canada, native women speak of a triple oppression: gender, race and culture. While there is a struggle to preserve the integrity of native culture from white supremacy, women face within native culture itself a male dominance from which they seek liberation.

One of the goals of the Ecumenical Decade of Churches in Solidarity with Women is to help women realize the inadequacies of such cultural definitions for their lives, as measured by the gospel of love.

Theology of sacrifice and suffering

Theology can either help or hinder people's freedom and development. When it is applied only to women, imposed on them and taught in order to keep them subjugated, a theology of sacrifice and suffering is harmful to women and dangerous for the theology of the church. It hinders women's liberation and it distorts the purposeful will of God.

There are all sorts of theological "justifications" for violence against women and biblical misinterpretations of male-female relationships. In Indonesia, for example, church women victimized by their husbands are admonished to be patient and to pray. In Hong Kong, a theology of self-sacrifice operates when women are taught to sacrifice themselves for the sake of their family and church, when women pastors have to give way to male pastors, and when overseas contract workers have to accept low wages and endure abuse.

When women suffer due to poverty, racism or sexual violence, more often than not preachers or counsellors ask them to accept their fate and to sacrifice their health, life and dignity. Women are told that if they are really Christians they ought to bear their cross and suffer until they obtain their reward in heaven. One systemic way of imposing unnecessary suffering and silence on women is to use the Bible (especially Pauline texts) to keep women down, to justify male domination, and to load guilt on women if they do not comply.

Women must not be sacrificed in this way on the altar of power, domination and greed. Christ chose the way of the cross but triumphed beyond the grave. He came to give life for all. We need to develop and practise a theology of justice, empowerment of women and solidarity. Liturgical renewal, such as in marriage rituals, and biblical reinterpretations must serve the cause of the marginalized. Feminist theology and praxis need to be fully integrated into theological education and parish ministry.

Violence against women

In a recent report from one WCC member church, clergy (all male) stated that they would be opposed to violence "except in certain circumstances". It was made clear that this would not be spoken of from the pulpit, although individuals seeking support would be counselled. One church leader spoke of "disciplining" his wife and being "thanked" by her later. Several church leaders queried the definition of "violence" and wanted to distinguish between violence that resulted in death and "just hitting".

Unfortunately, violence against women is a global reality, and the churches' complicity in a conspiracy of silence about such violence is very evident. Often, indeed, the perpetrators of violence against women are in fact members of the clergy and the leadership of the churches.

There are at least three types of violence against women: physical, symbolic/psychological and economic/institutional. Concerns about physical violence are most frequently expressed. It apparently affects women equally across all boundaries of geography, economic status, race, culture, age, education and ecclesial tradition. Women note as one of their primary concerns the reality of violence in their societies, their homes and their churches. Many men admit the dramatic reality of violence against women. However, when men mention physical violence against women they often simply accept it, condone it as part of a husband's responsibility to "discipline" his wife, or even try to find theological justification for it as a way of helping women achieve "salvation". Other men do express disapproval of violence against women and are working to combat it. There is a group of Presbyterian men in North Carolina (USA) who volunteer maintenance work at a home for battered women. However, it is rare to find such men, who are as angry and shamed by violence as women are outraged and traumatized by it.

The good news is that women are beginning to speak out, to refuse to suffer in silence. The bad news is that they seldom feel able to turn to their churches for support and advocacy.

There is convincing evidence that violence against women is not only more openly reported, at least by women, but that it is also escalating. Women's courage in speaking out about violence in situations where the church leadership might condone it is impressive. The leader of a church in Hong Kong, for example, states that violence against women is not a major issue for the church; in the same meeting, a woman pastor reports the difficulty she has had in counselling victims of domestic violence because of the support of church members for the perpetrators. For reasons of shame, women too often refuse to admit that they are victims of violence. Such is the pressure to respect the conspiracy of silence that we seldom if ever truly hear the full story. In a church in Lesotho, for example, there are bitter complaints about the clergy's attitude towards violence in general and domestic violence in particular. When women dare to express to a pastor their fear of a violent husband, the only support they can expect are exhortations to patience and invitations for prayer. One woman said: "We are reminded by the priest that we accepted to marry for better or worse, so be faithful to your vow now that you get the 'worse'."

Women and some men speak of other types of violence: the violence expressed through biblical interpretations and liturgical practices which do not include women. They assert that when humanity is assaulted by biblical interpretations, it is a type of violence against the person. These are the cultural, social and institutional forces which undergird the subservience or unimportance of women, which are in themselves forms of violence.

Other women, mostly from poorer countries or communities, remind us of the violence of poverty. In some cases poverty leads people to commit violent acts. One of the effects of burdensome debt is that women are deemed dispensable in difficult economic times. Women and children are always the most vulnerable in situations of poverty.

What is the nature of the ecumenical fellowship between churches and their members when far too often churches participate in or condone in silence the violence perpetrated against women?

Racism

The churches of the ecumenical movement have long recognized the relationship between racism and sexism. This reality is particularly evident in countries like Australia, Aotearoa-New Zealand, the United States, Taiwan and India, where the plight of indigenous women and of women living as a racial minority within a different majority culture is especially acute. While many common issues seem to bring women into solidarity with one another, racism fragments that solidarity. Women of colour in many places report that the predominant women's movement does not address their concerns; in fact, women of the majority culture, along with men, are often the perpetrators of racial injustice or of the exclusion of other women because of race. The Decade is meant to address not only the solidarity of churches with women, but also the solidarity of women in churches with other women. It is important, therefore, to continue to address racism even as we challenge other forms of discrimination against women.

Theological education

It is cause for celebration that theological education is becoming much more accessible to women. In many regions women make up the largest percentage of student enrolment. On the other hand, the percentage of women in faculty and administrative positions is extremely low in almost every region and church. In addition, curriculum content and method generally reflect old patterns and assumptions and a lack of gender inclusiveness. There is a need not only for specific courses on feminist theology but also for the full integration of women's concerns and perspectives in the theological educational project as a whole.

In the United Theological College of the West Indies, for example, lecturers have often taken a feminist theological standpoint. However, the college was unable consciously to deal with the feminist perspective as a challenge to male-dominated theological research and teaching. Women have become visible in theological education; they need now to become audible.

At Vancouver School of Theology in Canada, a student remarked that her decision to study theology was motivated by the Decade, but she was disappointed that men did not show interest and solidarity. In Indonesia, at the Banjarmasin seminary, it is encouraging that 75 of the 130 students are women, that 50 percent of the faculty are women, and that women's issues and theology are part of the curriculum. Women continue, however, to face a double and triple burden. While they are encouraged to join men in the professional field, there is at the same time a widespread expectation that they will be the best in school and the best at home. Courses are required on the changing roles of women and men in society.

Theological education is emerging as an essential area of reform if there is to be an inclusive community for women and men in church and society.

Women in ministry

While some churches recognize the gifts and participation of women (both ordained and lay), many are quite slow, and even resistant, to recognize and support women in ministry. Theological formation and ordination are among the foremost concerns of women, but not, it seems, of the churches. In the Cook Islands, for instance, women are excluded from ministry and theological training unless they are accompanying their husbands.

Even if — through sheer struggle and initiative — women are trained and ordained, they are not guaranteed fair support and stable placements. In Indonesia, for example, while 55 percent of seminarians are women, they face problems after graduation. They are forced to choose between vocation and family. In many countries, the USA among them, male pastors obtain better and more secure placements than their female counterparts.

Women have very little, if any, access to decision-making bodies, no access to resources, and there is no women's leadership within the ecumenical movement. The Decade has highlighted tensions between lay and ordained women and between different groups, such as Pakeha and Maori women (Aotearoa New Zealand). These issues and concerns must be addressed comprehensively if we believe in the holistic ministry of the church.

Concluding reflections

The Decade is important in the lives of many women and for this we can be grateful. It has been the occasion for many women to articulate and address significant concerns. They have been prompted to look further at issues of ministry, theological education, gospel and culture, violence, racism and sexism, theological understandings of the relationships of women and men, and the leadership of women, including young women. The Decade has been a time to lift up and celebrate the strength of women and their gifts to the church.

The Decade has not yet had an impact on the total life and witness of the churches. Clearly, some member churches have been open to the possibilities for growth which the Decade presents. Unfortunately, many others have not taken the Decade seriously. In some cases, church leaders appear to have mastered a level of rhetoric which projects sensitivity to the gifts and concerns of women but which, in fact, masks a comfort with and commitment to the status quo: an ability to "talk the talk, but not walk the walk".

We must hope that during the remainder of the Decade and beyond, and through various processes within the World Council of Churches, the Council and its member churches will use the Decade as an opportunity for self-reflection and transformation.

21. What Does the Decade Offer Men?

ROBERT SHANTZ

The Ecumenical Decade of Churches in Solidarity with Women has not been "Churches in Solidarity with Women" but "Women in Solidarity with Women". For the Decade's goals to be met, it is critically important for the whole church, women and men, to be involved. Many men, I believe, are not actively supportive of the Decade because too many of their fundamental questions about the women's movement have not been addressed by men who see the good of the Decade. What follows are men's positive responses to questions about the Decade.

The men's forum at the University of Toronto has said that

> traditional notions of masculinity limit the potential of men. The lives of many men are focussed overwhelmingly on work, often to the exclusion of friendship, family and leisure. Expectations of mental and physical "toughness" diminish our potential for gentleness and limit our friendship with women and other men. The pressure to be in command frequently reduces our capacity to listen and to respond with emotion. Some things do have to be given up in order that relationships between women and men be on an equal footing, but the gains outweigh the losses.[1]

We are being asked to change personally and be politically active. Which comes first? Which is more important? The men's forum has said that

> both are important, and there's no one ideal way of making change. Personal growth entails opening up and legitimizing emotional responses to issues, and not restricting ourselves to dispassionate analysis. In order to fully understand and effect the kinds of social, economic and political changes that gender equality requires (in ourselves and the world around us), we have to open ourselves to change the way we think, feel and behave. If we are to think anew about "masculinity", we have to begin to discover all the ways in which entrenched notions of masculinity affect our personal lives.[2]

Am I responsible for patriarchy and for the actions of other men? After Marc Lepine killed 13 female engineering students in Montreal in 1989 because "they were feminists", I wrote:

> To say the killings were an act of a single madman, and end the analysis there, is taking our 20th century's emphasis on individualism to its most extreme conclusion. Surely, as a biblically inspired community, we have to identify Marc Lepine as an individual who was a member of society, of a people, and that we, the people of that society, are part of him. This is a basic Judaeo-Christian assumption that we are one in God. What you and I do as individuals is done in the context of the community in which we work and play and die. And thus we are accountable to each other. As a man, in this society, I am accountable to Marc Lepine for the suffering he endured from his abusive

father, just as I am accountable to the women in my society for their joy and sorrow, regardless of my personal contributions to either.[3]

Don't women have as many opportunities as I have? This is a question asked by men who see more and more women working with them as equal partners. It is true that some women have vocational opportunities their mothers did not dare dream of. But most women's vocational calling is compromised by religious and social expectations and economic realities.

Women and girls need to be encouraged to follow their vocational interests for their own personal fulfillment, so that they can participate as respected decision-makers in our societies.

How can women fit into the male-designed work-place? We need to consider how the work-place is structured and what our expectations are of women.

I heard a young, recently ordained woman who was working in a church peace office describe how she was expected to work such long hours that she did not have enough time for her children. Her male boss was working equally long hours, if not longer, driven by the importance of working for the noble cause of peace. But he too had children. Women can remind us that our work needs to be structured with a stronger commitment to family needs.

Bishop Desmond Tutu speaks of our expectations of women in a church designed by men:

> There is something uniquely valuable that women and men bring to the ordained ministry, and it has been distorted and defective as long as women have been debarred. Somehow men have been less human for this loss. But I would like to stress that women priests must not be tempted to emulate men priests. There will be many things where your sex will be an irrelevance in carrying out your ministry as an ordained person; but there are many other occasions when peculiarly feminine insights will be your unique and distinctive contribution. That is why I am myself unhappy that women dress like men priests with dog collars. I know they have to assert that their priesthood is equal to that of men in all respects. But I would hope that they very quickly assert their self-assurance and be women, not faint copies of men. They must not apologize for their existence, but celebrate their identity and personhood as women. That is what human liberation is all about.[4]

How can I work for Decade goals without being a "white knight" rescuing women? When do I speak out and when do I remain silent as women speak for themselves? This is a very difficult issue for those men who are attempting to be sensitive to their socialization to speak up and be problem-solvers. Often, unfortunately, it completely silences them. This is one of the most common questions men ask when they talk among themselves about the Decade. It is a concern of mine in every meeting I have with women. There is no easy answer. At times, we must risk speaking up; at times, we need to keep silent. Ray Whitehead's reflection is included here because of his emphasis on cooperative work as essential:

> If we have any hope for the future it is necessary to take a stand, to show courage and "en-courage" our male colleagues to do likewise. We men need to ask whether we are part of the problem of abuse or are working on its solution.

A woman colleague once said to me that women will never achieve full equality in an abuse-free society until men start to take greater responsibility for their power and use it to bring about change. I disagreed, using good revolutionary principles, that people must liberate themselves... Will it not take the power of women organized to overthrow patriarchy?

This woman colleague and I continued this conversation over a long period of time. Eventually I came to see that I was wrong. One cannot interpolate from wars of revolution to the creation of an abuse-free society. So far it is only in fantasies of science fiction that patriarchy is overthrown and women take power. A better analogy than wars of revolution for the issue of abuse and harassment would be environmental ethics. To overcome our polluting culture we need to create a new culture that lives with nature. That will be revolutionary, but not in the same way as class struggle, even though class issues are part of the problem.

In the revolution against abusive culture it is not that men will be liberators of women, but that women and men working together may liberate society from abusive patriarchy. This transformation will require courage of both men and women.[5]

Why are many women resistant to the goals of the Decade? To achieve the goals of the Decade, changes will have to be made in church and society. Change is always stressful and often frightening, whether you are in favour of it or opposed to it. There are no guarantees as to the outcome.

There are women, it seems, who are fulfilled in their traditionally prescribed vocations. There are many women who have not had direct experiences of extreme violence. There are women in satisfying positions of leadership within the patriarchal system (for example, leaders of traditional women's groups). I suspect that many women are afraid of men's violent response in their families and churches to their support of Decade goals. I assume also that many women have not been exposed to feminist theology and spirituality, much less had the opportunity to grant it authority in their lives.

It is understandable that many of these women will not appreciate the work of the Decade. The Decade has to earn trust, respect and authority from women as well as from men.

Isn't feminist theology severely limited because of its bias and focus just on women? In its anger with men has it anything to offer to the community of men and women? While its focus is on women, feminist theology's goal is the renewal of community for the sake of men and women. Thoughtful feminists know that their fulfillment cannot be solely dependent on men's sacrifices. They invite men to dream a dream with them of a new heaven and a new earth.

The media and many men in the church have focussed on feminists' anger and virtually ignored, for example, their emphasis on love of creation and on the gentleness of collective decision-making. The community of men and women would be living a lie if the reality of their anger was denied. We need to realize that the expression of anger and other emotions is critical if community is to be renewed, and that such expression need not hinder this renewal.

I have experienced violence by women. They may not trust me but I certainly do not trust them. Men and women do inflict pain on one another. We need to be sensitive to and patient with the mistrust we have of each other. (This is especially true for men working with women in the Decade, given women's mistreatment at the hands of a male-dominated church.) But we are called to respond, in faith, to the Spirit in the person standing before us and not to prejudge on the basis of our history. Obviously, this is a great emotional challenge which may entail some very real risk. It is a risk we as men and women must accept if we are going to be able to work together as equal partners.

We need to earn each other's trust, risking betrayal. Trust earned is healing balm for our wounds.

Is it not absolutely clear in the Bible and in church teaching and tradition that God is male and that religious leaders are male? How can women claim a feminine identity for God and justify their leadership in church and society? When my daughter Sarah was three years old I asked her who she thought God was. Without hesitating, she said that God was definitely like her grandmother, whom she experiences as warm, accepting, wise and delighting in life. It is probably true that not once in her participation in the liturgy since then has she had her early (and continuing) experience of God confirmed. Several questions come from this: Does she think the church is lying to her, trying to deceive her? Does she think the church is crazy for not seeing and celebrating self-evident truth, or is she wrong in her experience? How much of the reality of God are we missing by denying a wider range of metaphorical expression when referring to the divine?

When considering leadership in church and society, a fundamental theological truth for me is that God speaks through the voice and experience of women and men. Each of us is called by God to a vocation through which the Spirit can work. To limit or deny one's vocation calling is to compromise the work of the Spirit.

Cyril Powles, reflecting on male dominance in our culture, said that

> an increasing number of contemporary studies show that patriarchy (the social pre-eminence of men) as a social system is an historically limited phenomenon. That is, it has a beginning in history, and therefore could also have an end. In theological terms, God did not create males as the "head" of the females. Rather, patriarchy represents something that emerged out of a sinful human society. Thus even Paul is forced to admit that "in Christ", that is in a redeemed society, "there is neither male nor female" (Gal. 3:28).[6]

I am very supportive of the goals of the Decade but I know very few other men (if any) who are. What is the point of my becoming actively supportive? How can I be effective? Who will support me? We are called to be faithful, not successful. In the Canadian decade newsletter *Groundswell,* I wrote:

> I have been conditioned as a man to "go it alone"; to rely on another is a sign of weakness. Men who try to challenge fundamental assumptions of a culture will be overwhelmed. Well-intentioned men may find no plausible strategy for action and remain silent. The women's movement has reminded this culture (Canadian) that small-group support is crucial for people trying to change their lives and their society. Men can learn from this and be more intentionally supportive of each other. Men need each other's gentle, pastoral care. Great courage and support are required for a man to challenge, compassionately, this

male-dominated culture. Men must be in thoughtful, honest conversation with other men and with women to gain personal insight and prophetical clarity.[7]

We must remind each other that change usually happens slowly, but it does happen. There are other men who feel as we do. We must be very intentional in seeking them out.

I have heard women say that they find it increasingly difficult to honour Good Friday because they find it difficult to honour a parent who would sacrifice a child. Isn't that heretical? Redemption theology, with its emphasis on our fallen humanity in need of atonement (being brought back to being "at-one" with God) through the sacrifice of Jesus the Christ, has been a reassuring spiritual guide for many centuries. It has, indeed, become our dominant theological perspective. As helpful as it has been, it is only one of several theological themes which can be discerned from scripture and tradition.

Like all theological reflections, redemption theology has its weaknesses as well as its strengths. For example, the emphasis on our having sinned and our subsequent need for redemption leaves little room for affirmation of our having been made in the image of God and, thus, the great potential we have for doing the work of the Spirit.

Also, the Good Friday emphasis on the Father sacrificing his Son has, for many women and men who have become aware of the horrors of family violence, raised serious questions about why we have so emphasized this act of the "loving" Father. Good Friday could, from another theological perspective, focus on our experiences of not being in control (the parent watching helplessly) and of being deserted (the child calling out for the absent parent). On Good Friday at St Ansgar Lutheran Church, Toronto, which I attend, members of the congregation are asked to reflect on the meaning in their lives of the "seven last words of Christ". Together, we shift the focus from redeeming sacrifice to the pain of desertion and the mystery of suffering. We leave the church knowing we will return to reaffirm the baptismal presence of God in our lives.

As we rise to the task of caring for creation, surely we need a theology which inspires and motivates us for this challenge — a theology of baptism which celebrates the divine in us and all creation. And we need a theology of Pentecost which reminds us that we are indeed equipped with gifts of the Spirit to bring the promised "abundant life" to all.

How can I even understand what it is like to be a woman? How can a woman ever comprehend my experience? While women and men have many experiences in common, our biology and socialization give us radically different experiences of life. In some significant ways we do live in different worlds. Glen Nelson, in a sermon preached a few days after the murder of the 13 students referred to above, reflected on the difficulty of understanding what the world of women in a violent society must be like. He wrote,

> I can try to understand and empathize with that other world [the world of women's experience], but I cannot really know what it feels like to be female and walk home from a bus stop after dark and hear footsteps behind me. I cannot really know what it is like to be female and walk by the news-stand peddling pictures of my female body. I cannot really know how it feels to be assaulted by unwanted innuendo and leering looks where I work. I cannot really

know the helplessness of being dependent upon an abusive husband. I cannot really know how it feels to be patronized by men and then criticized for being over-sensitive or a poor sport when I object. I cannot really know how it feels when my female body is made into seductive decoration to sell beer and automobiles. I cannot really know how it feels to bury all that hurt and resentment for the sake of keeping peace in the family and not starting an argument with my spouse that might expose the separateness of our worlds.[8]

Men, too, Nelson reflects, live in their own world:

What does it feel like to be a man when your six-year-old daughter comes home from school and tells you a strange man called her to his car and exposed himself? What does it feel like to be a man when your wife reports obscene propositions from a stranger on the street? What does it feel like to be a man when your friends in the hockey arena locker room laugh at jokes about women, laughter that betrays hostility behind it?

The violence that separates the two worlds [of male and female experience] is violence to both. We are all victims when women are degraded, laughed at, abused, denied fairness, accosted, raped or murdered.

"They shall not hurt or destroy in all my holy mountain" (Isa. 11) — that is a description of how we are to live, opposing violence any way we can.

And in this case, I think we must take the initiative and the responsibility. We must first recognize the one-sidedness of our male experience and listen to that other world. We must ask ourselves some questions. What does it feel like to be a woman and walk down a dark street? What does it feel like to be a woman when an aggressive man is called a go-getter, but an aggressive woman is called pushy? What does it feel like to have a woman's body, when that body is seen as an object for male gratification?

And then we must refuse to participate in the jokes, the innuendo, the put-downs, the false male macho talk that women feel as violence against their persons. And not only must we refuse to participate, we must take responsibility for the attitudes and actions of men.[9]

NOTES

1 *Men, Masculinity and Gender Issues*, 1993.
2 *Ibid.*
3 "Murder in Montreal", in *The Eastern Synod Lutheran*, winter 1990.
4 *Crying in the Wilderness: The Struggle for Justice in South Africa*, Grand Rapids, MI, Eerdmans, 1982, p.119.
5 "Courage, Cowardice and the Abusive Male Colleague", paper presented at the Canadian Theological Society, University of Quebec, Montreal, 3 June 1995.
6 "Patriarchy, Worship, and the Subordination of Women: Some Questions about Contemporary Western Christian Practice", unpublished paper, Sept. 1994.
7 "Will Men Remain Silent?", *Groundswell*, winter 1995.
8 From his sermon preached on 10 December 1989 at St Ansgar Lutheran Church, Toronto.
9 *Ibid.*

22. Strategies for Women

KÄTE MAHN

Wanting to achieve something means different things in different cultures. In some churches and cultures it looks as if all the doors are open to us. "Women in the church, in decision-making bodies, in the bishop's meeting? No problem!" But then we encounter the obstacles: women are accused of not having enough training or experience — as if our male friends had been born with all the necessary experience. Women are not linked to the flow of information; they do not belong to the inner circle of the "powerful"; they are pushed aside and ignored. This causes loneliness and pain. I have come across women who withdrew to their hotel rooms and no longer dared to cross the threshold of the conference hall.

In other cultures, the desire to achieve something is seen as a desire for power. It is described in negative terms, as if "self-realization" can surely only mean neglecting the family. "Feminism" is often invoked without knowing exactly what the term means and an understanding of it is all too frequently based only on information from a male-dominated press. "Women's strategies" is an expression with negative associations because it smacks of communism or socialism.

In still other contexts, wanting to achieve something means rebelling against a father image, contradicting, having one's own way. I am afraid of that. It is a threat: it loosens the ground under my feet, the sky becomes limitless, and I lose sight of the horizon — both of the one fixed point towards which I was moving and of the firm post to which I was tied. Now I feel I am losing my way between the horizons; perhaps it's better for me to stay where I am.

Developing strategies

Since 1984, the Lutheran World Federation has operated with a quota for women. All things considered, it has worked surprisingly well (1947: 2 percent; 1990: 41 percent), although it is far from being met in all activities. But at least women have participated, even if many of them are amazingly calm and quiet, particularly during plenaries. In the corridors they have a lot to say, and even more in the security of a "women's room", where it is as noisy as a blacksmith's, with a lot of anvils, hammers and bellows. Women have plenty to say: why don't they speak?

— The procedural structures are really complicated and have to be learned.
— There are firmly established mechanisms relating to who speaks first; women hold back when men are speaking.
— "I'm not good at expressing what I want to say anyway; other people have already said what I wanted to say..." Men are often not so considerate.
— "I cannot speak in front of/against my bishop; I must stick to our regional agreements; I have no right to spoil the 'all is well' image of my region."
The conclusion is, you need courage and competence to speak in a big plenary.

Martin Luther talks of the freedom of the Christian, which also implies the courage and freedom no longer to accept the "bondages" mentioned above but to express one's own opinion, to support another opinion, or to contradict it.

I mean here not only competence in the areas that come under the heading of "women's questions", but also competence in the specialized fields of the LWF's work: development issues, the church and Judaism, dialogue with other churches and/or other religions, and, if necessary, even finance!

The range of issues for an assembly can serve as a springboard. It is important to study the material and get to know the questions, with the help of radio, television and publications from elsewhere (public libraries, schools, seminary libraries, etc.). If nothing like this is available, write to LWF headquarters in Geneva and ask for publications or assistance with literature from other churches. Be like a sponge: absorb everything that will make you more competent in the field that interests you.

It might be helpful if each woman had a partner (a woman or a man) so that they could look for information for one another and exchange letters and materials. There may be a language barrier but there are ways of overcoming that.

Regional meetings can be very helpful, where delegates (men and women) can share their views. Where they are difficult to implement because of distance, look for like-minded people who are interested in the same questions. When you have begun to work your way into a particular field, you will soon find that anxiety decreases and appreciation and self-confidence increase. A conference is much more fun when you know what it is about and you are competent in at least one aspect.

The situation back home

Attending an international conference just once is not sufficient. Back home in your own church there is also a field to plough. Important questions to ask and points to ponder include:

— Who is going to the assembly? Should I go or is it better for another woman to go? Examine this question very carefully; don't say "no" to yourself immediately.
— Does everyone who has a seat on the council as a member or advisor belong to a governing body of their church back home (church authorities, synod, regional structures)?
— Do these people have a level where they can report?
— Are they asked to share their experiences, to interpret the decisions, to help in their implementation?
— Don't go away from any meeting or event without sending a report to your church authorities.
— Send in your reports, enquire whether they have been read, keep the ball rolling — insist.

We all know what it feels like to be left alone at home, despite all the encouraging pats on the shoulder from those in church leadership; to hold back for fear of disturbing the peace, of disputes over competence, and also of not being loved any more. Yielding in this way, however understandable it may be, also robs the communion of something. It makes the church poorer.

Look for allies (men and women), try out your ideas at home, bring other people's ideas with you in your rucksack; the right luggage makes it easier to stay the course. They may be your friends in the church, but possibly you have friends outside too — in a trade union, among the teachers at your children's school, in human rights groups, etc. Their concerns are also the concerns of the Lutheran Wold Federation.

In the run up to an assembly it is important to have a say in the selection of those who will attend. Talk to the bishop or the dean; ask for information about the criteria for selection; indicate your interest in the content of the assembly because you want to contribute to it.

Stubbornness may not be a virtue everywhere but we need a large amount of it where we are.

23. Women and Decision-making: An Ethiopian Experience

YADESSA DABA

From the very beginning, women have been very active and made significant contributions to the Ethiopian Evangelical Church Mekane Yesus (EECMY). Today they are often referred to as the backbone of the church, and there is no doubt that women are responsible for the church's success as a religious body and in various development activities.

However, even though their activities have been appreciated, it is true that women are still not fully acknowledged, especially with regard to the decision-making processes within the church. The most obvious explanation for this is in cultural traditions, beliefs and practices.

In spite of the rather oppressive cultural influences to which women are subject, the church leadership took an important step at its ninth general assembly in 1976 to ensure that all decision-making activities throughout the EECMY should involve at least 25 percent women. Since then, church leaders have sought to motivate the various synods to comply with this decision; awards have been made to those synods which have made an effort to conform to the resolution.

At the 14th general assembly in 1993, the assembly amended its earlier decision and stated that the percentage of women involved in all decision-making activities throughout the EECMY should be 40-50. Although this quota has not yet been met, church leaders are encouraging synods to strive hard for it.

The question of ordination

Women are now graduating from the Mekane Yesus seminary, but the question of women's ordination has not been fully resolved. It remains a rather delicate issue within the church for many reasons.

Ethiopia's strong cultural traditions — faithfully followed even today — have ensured that male rather than female children have gone on to higher education, thereby endowing them with much of the authority, respect and status necessary for them to find jobs and be successful within organizations and communities. As a consequence, there have been very few role models for women to emulate, making it difficult for them to gain equality with men, especially in important positions like that of the "ordained pastor".

Despite these obstacles, the church has taken some steps to create awareness within society about the role and place of women. For example, it has organized two major workshops to discuss the issue of ordination. The topics tackled included the biblical and theological aspects of ordination, plus those cultural influences and traditional values and roles which inevitably affect decisions on the issue. Their final recommendations were that more workshops should be held in all the synods, in order to raise awareness and provide training in gender issues for both male and female church members.

Because cultural influences are so strong, awareness needs to be raised not only among men but also among women themselves. The church believes that the logical outcome of this awareness-raising should be the ordination of women. However, rather than impose this view on the various synods, church leaders decided that awareness should be allowed to evolve throughout the whole church so that a request for ordination is made eventually by the synods themselves.

As yet, no official church decision has been made about the ordination of women. We trust that through training, awareness-building and in general discussion, we shall be able to move forward and say Yes to women's ordination in the near future.

Editor's note: Since this article was written, the general synod of the Ethiopian Evangelical Church Mekane Yesus decided on 22 January 1997 that women may now be ordained to the ministry of word and sacrament.

24. The Challenge of Feminist Theologies

MUSIMBI R.A. KANYORO

Come, let us reason together

"Feminist theologies[1] are a gift to the church and a gift to women." Yet there is a danger in making such a categorical statement. To many men and women in and outside the church, the words "feminist/feminism" continue to invoke fear, inspire controversy and arouse a visceral response. Feminism/feminist are therefore dangerous words representing dangerous concepts and dangerous people. It is not uncommon to hear statements prefixed by: "I am not a feminist, but..." Thus many women and men are known to disclaim the label even when it is clear that they support feminist goals.

I write this paper as one among many women in the church for whom women's perspectives in theology have been a gift of great price. I also write it primarily as an African woman. Feminist theologies have their rooting in women's experiences in church and society. Their purpose is not to inject political correctness of the gender agenda into the church but rather to invite men and women in the church radically to examine our understanding of God and of our relationships together. Christian women's feminist theologies root their theological reflections in God's gracious gifts of creation and baptism. Men and women are each made in the image of God. We are each baptized into the death and resurrection of Jesus Christ. We are named and claimed as the offspring of God. God calls us, women and men alike, into right relationships with each other, with all creation. The women and men who raise "womanist/feminist" questions in the church are asking the church to reflect upon how gender history in our societies has shaped our spirituality, our sexuality, our worship and our interpretation and understanding of scripture.[2] Feminist perspectives invite the church to explore and discover new possibilities of *being church* and *being men and women of faith*, bound together by the good news of Jesus Christ. This is why I understand feminist theology to be a gift to the church. It is an opportunity, not a problem. It is a possibility, not a difficulty.

By our stripes we are healed

Christians claim these words of the prophet Isaiah. The wounded lives of women have formed the basis on which questions are raised by womanist/feminist theologies.[3] One of the greatest benefits of feminist scholarship has been to hear stories of women and to become aware that the subordination of women as a gender is a worldwide phenomenon defying the confines of race, class, creed or nationality. This reality was voiced loudly and clearly at the United Nations fourth world conference on women in Beijing in 1995. The conference stated that there is no single state in the world where women are safe from violence or treated as equals with men.[4] Thus despite women's diverse social, economic and political backgrounds, by virtue of belonging to the female gender women constitute an oppressed social group. The social construction of roles and status relegate women to an inferior position. This gender subordination is articulated through various institutions, both public and private. Feminist theology shows how, historically, women have experienced suffering within structures because of their gender. It analyzes the crisis of women in the church and their search for wholeness, and the transformation of the church and society.

Stories help to discover the interconnection between faith and action. Learning through stories is neither new nor strange. Communities continually explain their being through stories passed from one generation to another. The Bible is a good example: the Old Testament contains the stories of the Hebrew people and how they interpreted their experience of God in their lives. They taught their children to remember how God had liberated them and provided for their needs. The New Testament is the testimony of people who embraced a new beginning by receiving the gift of God through the message and person of Jesus the Christ. These stories are gifts left for us, not just to read and appropriate the lives of these people, but to challenge us to discern ways in which we can tell our own stories of God in our lives and times.

Feminist theologies dare to look at our histories as they are told in biblical texts, the teachings and practices of the church over centuries and in the present day. Sadly, women have found that our histories are deeply rooted in patriarchy which is part of our cultural heritage. Both Judaism and Christianity were shaped by patriarchy. Feminist theologies have shown how patriarchy has affected our experience and naming of God,[5] and shaped our structures of work, worship and decision-making. Feminist theologies name the gender injustice to women in these areas. Yet gender alone cannot define the injustices that women experience globally. While women's theologies appeal to solidarity to combat the subordination of women, they also are comprehensive enough to include the concerns of women affected by social injustices such as racism, poverty, cultural oppression, and so on. These theologies open themselves to different concerns for different women: married or single, mothers or not, poor or wealthy, of various ethnic backgrounds and religious persuasions. "Difference" is a reality. Difference can become a source of fear, bias and ignorance that results in injustice, but it can also be a platform for celebrating variety and plenty. By affirming difference women's theologies are striving to celebrate it.

Feminist theology: a pearl of great price

Culture is to African women's liberation theology what race relations are to African American womanist theologians. In both the private and public spheres, the roles and images of African women are socially and culturally defined. Within this framework of operation, women have been socialized into a state of numbness where we have lived our lives without really determining the course of it. For us women of Africa, the study of theology — any theology at all — opens doors long closed to us. A better understanding of the scriptures can affect the way women participate in group worship as well as private personal meditation. When we look critically at our cultures we know for certain that there are cases where they dehumanize women. If we relate our study of culture to the scriptures and theology, we are empowered with new courage and language to speak to new life-styles which reflect the justice of God for all people. We also contribute significantly to the theological debate by demanding serious attention to the field of cultural hermeneutics.[6]

To choose feminist theology as our method of study is to join a journey where we are in solidarity with other women rather than staying by ourselves in a desert of risks and loneliness. Our struggles as African women are in the context of global gender injustice. African women's feminist theology roots its relevance to the continent by responding to some of the issues that are oppressive to women in Africa.[7] Detractors will always choose to perceive feminist theology as Western and not conversant with our African values and religious beliefs. They tell African women to be "African", meaning to be silent and submissive in the face of injustice and oppression. This kind of strategy is outdated. Now it is our time, as African women theologians and ministers in the churches, to seek ways in which we can transform our numbness into a quest for healing and wholeness. For us, doing theology is searching for God in our villages. In choosing culture as a departure point we have the opportunity to start at home, in our bodies and hearts and in our various relations and settings. Feminist theology seeks to find the link between the level of grace, where men and women are considered equal before God, and the Christian anthropology which establishes the relationships between God and people.

Silenced by culture

Culture has silenced many women in Africa and made us unable to experience the liberating promise of God. Some aspects of our cultures which diminish women are embraced without considering their oppressive nature. Their enforcement both in the oral media and in their practice often makes women objects of cultural preservation. Culture is a two-edged sword. In some instances it is the badge or even the "creed" of community identity. In others it is used to make a distinction between different people in the community which sometimes results in oppression and injustice. If today African women are able to name the oppressive aspects of our cultures, it has not come easily. For centuries we have gone along with cultural prescriptions to such an extent that we came to believe that our lives were to be managed by the commands of our cultures. The fear of breaking taboos silenced us into a state in which we acted without questioning what we did. The family in Africa, while being the centre of the support system, also has all the potential of being a nesting place for gender subordination of women. The family is not only the nucleus of society but more importantly the power house where culture is preserved. Listen to these stories:

> *Story 1*
> I was married at the age of 19, immediately after completing form 4. We had a beautiful church wedding and I continued teaching at Sunday school in my new church just as I had done in the church where I grew up. When I could not conceive within six months, the women began to ask me what was wrong. After one year there was still no sign of pregnancy. My sisters-in-law started to make up stories that I had been a loose woman and had abortions before marriage. That was very upsetting, because it was not true.
> During the second year, my husband started coming home late and finding fault with me for everything. If he knocked at the door and I did not run to

open it, he would call me lazy and punch me. His whole family also insulted me in many ways. I talked to the pastor but he simply told me to persevere and not do anything to annoy my husband; I should know that he is the head of the family. I went to many doctors who all said that they could not find out what was wrong with me. They never asked to see my husband. For a long time I did not dare suggest to my husband that he should go to the doctor too, because it seemed normal to everybody that it was my problem. One day I dared to ask him to have a medical examination also, and my fears were justified; he beat me thoroughly. Infertility or barrenness, it was said, was a woman's issue.

Life became unbearable and I decided to return to my parents' home. My mother was embarrassed about my problem and did not want to talk about it. She welcomed me but never said anything about the situation I was running away from. For my father, I simply did not exist. He was so embarrassed that he never looked straight at me, let alone talked to me. Whenever he wanted me to do something, he would tell my mother to tell me. There were lots of chores to occupy me and keep me out of the way.

I worked at my parents' farm during the day, and in the house during the evenings until my brothers and their wives started to insult me. They said that I had come back home so as to cause problems with the land inheritance. Each of my brothers swore that he would not even bury my body on his piece of land. I spoke to my mother about these insults; she was again silent and simply said that she would talk to my brothers.

My brothers and their wives said I was a shame to the home by my life of singleness. If I answered back in protest, everybody including my mother would tell me not to be rude to my brothers when they were the owners of the home where I was getting free lodging. After some time I debated whether to kill myself or just leave. I decided to leave, although I had nowhere to go. I moved to the city... I have been doing this job for 18 years (Aliviza, Kenya).

Story 2

I went back to the hospital a week after delivery, because I could not hold urine. The doctors have not yet helped me even though I have had two operations. They say that it is because of the infibulation I had when I was 10. I am now 16 and this was my first birth. There was no money for school fees, so I did not go beyond primary class 6. My parents arranged this marriage. My husband is over 40 and has two other wives. I am the youngest (Amina, Kenya).

Go tell it on the mountain!

For generations, telling these stories of dehumanizing cultural practices was taboo. There are still many women who would not speak of their own experiences of this type, either as victims or perpetrators. Many harmful practices in society and in the family are passed on as "cultural values" and therefore are not discussed, challenged or changed. It is amazing how we hide behind culture and allow traditions such as female genital mutilation, child betrothals and marriages, stigmatization of single women, childless women and widows. In spite of the increase of HIV/AIDS, we still propagate cultural inhibitions about discussing sexuality. The World Health Organization says that the number of African women currently affected by AIDS is fast reaching that of men. African women often contract AIDS by having to submit to sex with unfaithful partners or being driven to prostitution through culture or poverty. In these and other circumstances, women are expected to bear the blame silently.

As the gospel comes face to face with African traditions, we must find another way to understand and live out our faith. Can we afford silence when people are dying, children and women are raped in broad daylight, young girls are mutilated by female circumcision? African women theologians are asking the church in Africa to be a witness of God's liberation to women of Africa. This is their "feminism"![8] African culture is the thread which strings our beliefs and social set-up together. No one would dream of condemning our culture wholesale. However, feminist theology helps women to discover that the God of the Bible is a God who liberates all people to worship and live out the promise of "abundant life".

The Bible as a book of record was written in a culture which was very much like our African culture, in which male values were exalted and female ones undervalued. This is the setting and context in which Jesus lived out his witness. There is no greater witness of faith than the Lord Jesus himself who elaborated on his own witness by announcing that he came to preach good news to the poor, release to the captives and restoration of health to those who are ill (Luke 4:16-18). In his witness here on earth, Jesus visited towns and villages and saw with his own eyes the problems facing the people. He saw the poverty, the inequality, the religious, economic and gender oppression, the unemployment, the depression, the physically ill and the socially unclean (Matt. 9:35-38). His heart was filled with pity. In his witness Jesus told the people: "The time is fulfilled, and the kingdom of God has come near; repent, and believe in the good news." This is the message that feminist theologies are reminding the church to hear and embrace.

Feminist theology: a gift to the church

The so called "feminist" views have much broader goals which beg responses from the church. The church has a pastoral responsibility to women. We who call one another sister and brother must be willing to listen, and hear the pain of women. To ignore, mock, belittle or categorically denounce feminist theology is not pastoral at all. This is the point at which ministerial formation is challenged. Those called to be God's agents for healing cannot be credible when they cast out some among the flock.

A majority of African Christian women have been raised in very evangelical churches. We therefore often find ourselves struggling with our history and our present personal situation which has changed and developed with theological studies, ecumenical exposure and encounter with other global women's analysis. We want to be relevant to our context by being agents of change in our communities and bearers of good news to our people. Yet neither the local churches nor local theological institutions are willing to welcome our thinking. The libraries in our seminaries have no books on feminist theology. There are only a handful of women teaching in the seminaries and then usually in non-theological areas. Only a few churches on the continent ordain women. The training of pastors is not yet gender-sensitive, and women pastors struggle to minister even to other women. A woman pastor raised in a Presbyterian home and church laments that her training as a pastor never equipped her to deal with social issues, let alone women's issues. Instead, she was trained to see people as souls without bodies, an aspect that made her work as a minister unrealistic if not impossible.[9] One of the challenges from feminist theology is to empower people to speak for themselves and to name their experiences. African women have for ages suffered from being spoken for. A method of theology that gives us our own voice and space is not only timely but truly a gift that can equip us for service and participation in the church. The church should re-examine the fear of feminism and start being interested in listening to what we have to say.

The fear of feminism in the church

Pioneer women in women's movements heralded the breaking of silence over the unjust treatment of women. They demanded equal treatment and recognition of the human dignity of women. This woke people up and often resulted in the popular image of feminism being negative. Questioning the status quo is never an easy matter. The women's movements were even less accepted in church circles. It is no wonder that even today being associated with feminist/womanist theologies raises suspicion, mistrust, resentment and sometimes aggression in society at large and in the church specifically. At teaching institutions feminist scholars are shunned and in some cases even risk the danger of physical attack on them and their families.[10] It is especially dangerous in the family if a woman is seen to be interested in contesting rights for women. Husbands are embarrassed by activist wives, and that alone can be a point of contention in a marriage relationship.

To seek justice is a command from the scriptures. Justice is not just us! In seeking God-given dignity for women, women also ask for justice for all other people treated unjustly. A major contribution of feminist theologies is to invite the church to consider new images of God and in so doing to discover new possibilities for men and women living together in relationship to one another and to God who created them, male and female. The witness of the church will not be credible unless we take into account the traumatic situation of millions of women and of the outcast of our societies. What meaning can faith have in churches that seek to be liberated without sharing the people's battle with the forces of oppression? These questions frighten us as churches and communities with long-established traditions and practices. They threaten our institutional comfort as churches, our invested privileges, our secure situations, and they threaten our confidence in our judgment of what is right and wrong. An experience of faith that holds itself aloof from people seeking to escape marginalization poses a serious risk for the future of the church and the church of the future.

Finally, we must ask what are the consequences to the church should it be willing to receive the gift of women's perspectives in theology. I particularly see possibilities in awakening the church to the fact that biblical history did not stop at the end of the first century. It is important for the Christian church continually to teach that the power of God still lives with us, for whom the promise of the Holy Spirit was given and fulfilled at Pentecost. In baptism we reaffirm our faith in God's power as we confess our sins and are washed clean, and accept the Holy Spirit to direct our lives and witness. Under the continuous guiding and prompting of the Holy Spirit, the gospel endlessly calls us to acts of judgment, of ourselves and our institutions, which lead to repentance, change of mind and change of structure towards an inclusive communion of saints in the church of Jesus Christ. This is what feminist theology hopes to achieve.

NOTES

1 For the purpose of focussing attention on the issues being discussed, for this paper I will use the label "feminist theologies" to affirm the plurality and difference in the content and methods of theological perspectives of women. Not all women theologians identify their issues under the label "feminist theology". There are other labels such as "womanist", "mujerista". In this paper I deliberately interchange feminist/womanist in order to affirm their legitimacy.

2 See for example Richard Holloway, ed., *Who Needs Feminism: Men Respond to Sexism in the Church*, London, SPCK, 1991.

3 For reading on the distinction on womanist/feminist, see Jacqueline Grant, *White Women's Christ and Black Women's Jesus: Feminist Christology and Womanist Response*, Atlanta, Scholars Press, 1989. This book argues that feminist Christology has not reflected the experiences of non-white women. She proposes womanist theology to account for non-Western, non-white experiences.

4 See the Beijing declaration and the Platform for Action.

5 See for example Rosemary Radford Ruether, *Sexism and God Talk: Towards a Feminist Theology*, London, SCM, 1983.

6 I strongly believe that culture needs to be analyzed and assessed for what it is. See my article "Cultural Hermeneutics: An African Contribution", in Ofelia Ortega, ed., *Women's Visions: Theological Reflection, Celebration, Action*, Geneva, WCC Publications, 1995.

7 See for example Mercy Amba Oduyoye, *Daughters of Anowa: African Women and Patriachy*, Maryknoll, NY, Orbis, 1995.

8 See for example Mercy Amba Oduyoye and Musimbi R.A. Kanyoro, eds, *The Will To Arise: Women, Tradition and the Church in Africa*, Maryknoll, NY, Orbis, 1992.

9 See Nyambura Njoroge, "Groaning and Languishing in Labour Pains... But For How Long?" This paper was first presented to the Eastern and Southern Conference of the Circle of Concerned African Women Theologians, Nairobi, 1994. It will be published in Musimbi Kanyoro and Nyambura Njoroge, eds, *Groaning in Faith: African Women Doing Theology*, Nairobi, forthcoming.

10 On 6 December 1989 Marc Lepine killed 13 women at the Ecole polytechnique of the University of Montreal "because they were feminists". In December 1994, a group of women in a church in Africa were suspended from membership for writing a letter to the synod which presented the problems of women. In 1995, students attacked a women theologian teaching at a higher institute of learning in Africa. Her family was harassed and her property destroyed because she was conducting research on sexual harassment on the university campus.

25. *The Decade as the Great Commission*

PANG KEN-PHIN

When we stress the importance of fulfilling the great commission of Jesus Christ, we should never forget that it is the responsibility of the whole church and of all believers. In other words, all the believers are the priests of God who all work together for the kingdom of God. The great commission is not limited to particular persons, times or places. The call made by the Ecumenical Decade of Churches in Solidarity with Women must go on beyond the decade.

The church is the people of God. It is never merely a particular class within the fellowship of the faithful; all believers are equal as members of the people of God. They are all "called out" by God. The church is the body of Christ, which means that all the members are important and must play their part. They all have their own dignity and their own functions on the basis of a fundamental equality. The head cannot say to the feet that it has no need of them. All have to serve each other, in mutual sympathy and affection. The idea of the priesthood of all believers can be seen in the nature of the church — the people of God, the body of Christ and the temple of the Holy Spirit.

The church is a spiritual building, the temple of the Holy Spirit; all believers, not just a few chosen ones, are filled with the Spirit. The Spirit is to be given to the hearts of the children of God. The Spirit has been poured out on the whole community (Acts 2) and on each individual (1 Corinthians 3:16). All Christians are taught and led and supported directly by the Spirit, and they are all to live by the Spirit.

When scholars talk about the "laity" they are in fact talking about the priesthood of all believers, the people who are called out of the world to belong to God. There is, then, no essential distinction between clergy and laity, skilled and unskilled, well-educated and uneducated, white and black, male and female, Jew and gentile, rich and poor. All people are equal before God. But equal does not mean identical; it means that although people have different gifts and different functions, they all come from the same source. They also have a single purpose: just as the members of the body have different functions which work together for the good of the whole, so the different gifts and functions are given to individuals for the common good, for the work of ministry, for building up the body of Christ.

No one group of people should control or exercise all the ministries in the church, but the responsibility of ministry, or service, should be shared by all in order to fulfill the calling of Christ. Jesus Christ is calling all of us to the same faith and service. Nowhere in the scriptures do we find Jesus applying different standards to women and men. He calls both to responsible discipleship in ministering to the spiritual and physical needs of the people who are working to bring about the kingdom of God. Christ did not assign one type of ministry to women and another to men: quite the contrary. We know that Christ commanded women to go and proclaim the good news. Women played a significant part in the ministry of Jesus and in the life and witness of the early church.

Once again we affirm that we are the people who are called by God to carry out Christ's great commission. We should never forget that women are part of the church. We receive the same calling for the same tasks and responsibilities as men in the renewal of our churches and the whole of society. So our spiritual gifts for ministry need to be recognized in all aspects of the life of the church. The full participation of women in ministry is important.

Practical steps to women's empowerment

We should continue to prepare ourselves for full participation in the ministry by sensitizing women to self-awareness and self-respect, promoting women's contributions and service at home, in the church and in society, and developing leadership skills. Most women are still "sleeping". Quite a number are still satisfied with the traditional image of themselves as only mothers, wives and homemakers. Most women are not aware of the needs of society (political, social, economic, educational, etc.) and their services are confined to the church. Only a few women have begun to realize that fund-raising for the church, preparing food and similar functions are not enough if women want to follow the call of Jesus Christ to creative service and discipleship.

Therefore, it is our duty to help each other as women to find the answers to the following questions: Who are we? What are the alternatives? How can we serve better? How can we develop our talents? With whom should we cooperate and what methods should we use if we want to render more meaningful service to the family, the church, and society as a whole?

The issue of women's full participation in the ministry and women's self-image should be prayerfully studied and discussed by all groups (e.g. women's fellow-ships, youth groups, men's fellowships, pastors, bishops, presidents and church council members), both separately and together through Bible study, workshops and consultations at local, national and international levels, so that everyone becomes aware of the various situations in which women find themselves. Women's recommendations should be heard by people at all levels and not simply retained by church authorities without taking action.

The proper interpretation of the scriptures should be promoted in church. We must be aware that there are different forms of interpretation, different ways of understanding the Bible. Quite often the traditional interpretation of the Bible presents women as inferior to men. What is more problematic is that the Bible is often interpreted without an understanding of its background, its social, political, cultural and religious context. Even when it is interpreted in its proper context, the perspectives of women are ignored. The way women see things and experi-ence life is often neglected for one reason or another. Thus the proper interpreta-tion of scripture should be emphasized and promoted.

Cooperation between men and women should be taught and practised from the earliest stage of life. It is usually very hard for middle-aged or elderly people to change their minds. So women have to be aware of our important role in the education of the next generation. A good family life pattern should be developed and more positive examples of women figures should be used in Sunday school. Above all, husbands and wives must be encouraged to participate in training programmes in order to bring up children to be responsible and cooperative persons at home, in church and in society.

Women should participate in theological training. We need to encourage other women in the church to develop contacts, show concern, and support them financially by sponsoring them throughout their training. For those who have already graduated, we should encourage and support them and urge them to enter the ordained ministry if they feel the call. We should influence the church to treat them equally with men in terms of work and salary. We should also encourage women to engage in further studies, conferences and workshops for their continued education, for which they should have paid leave.

Exchange programmes among women's organizations could promote better understanding and give new insights to women, helping them towards full participation in the ministry. Those churches which have ordained women pastors should have the responsibility of challenging and helping those churches that have not. Women pastors must recognize that ordination does not give us a superior status, but a special function: the ministry of word and sacrament. We should work even harder in order to contribute more to the building of the kingdom of God. The good image of a woman pastor will be the best way to convince the church fully to accept women in ministry.

Women should uphold each other in mutual understanding and love. Pride, jealousy, hatred, ignorance and narrow-mindedness are stumbling blocks to women's full participation in the ministry. We are all sinners needing and receiving God's grace and mercy. Let us examine ourselves: we can change our attitudes and see ourselves and our fellow brothers as partners in the renewal of our families, church and society.

Prayer for the future
We pray that God will continuously guide us and all churches, and give us the wisdom and courage to eliminate all the barriers before us. We all wish to live in a better world where the people of God can work together, using their different gifts and talents for the glory of God.

Contributors

Ruth Besha (Lutheran) is professor of linguistics at the University of Dar es Salaam, Tanzania.

Eugene Brand (Lutheran, USA) was until recently assistant general secretary for ecumenical affairs of the Lutheran World Federation.

Yadessa Daba (Lutheran) is president of the Ethiopian Evangelical Church Mekane Yesus.

Wanda Deifelt (Lutheran) is professor of feminist theology at the Superior School of Theology, Sao Leopoldo, Brazil.

Datuk Thu En-Yu (Lutheran) is bishop of Basel Christian Church of Malaysia, Kota Kinabalu, Sabah, Malaysia.

Elisabeth Schüssler Fiorenza (Roman Catholic) is Krister Stendahl professor of scripture and interpretation at Harvard Divinity School, Boston, USA.

Nicole Fischer (Reformed, Switzerland) was until recently consultant on the Ecumenical Decade of the Churches in Solidarity with Women at the World Council of Churches, Geneva, Switzerland.

Christine Grumm, formerly deputy general secretary of the Lutheran World Federation, is currently director of the Chicago Foundation for Women, USA.

Basa Hutabarat (Lutheran) is acting director of the Protestant Christian Batak Church, Medan, N. Sumatra, Indonesia.

Musimbi Kanyoro (Kenya) is executive secretary for the Desk for Women in Church and Society of the Lutheran World Federation.

Pang Ken-Phin (Lutheran) is lecturer at Sabah Theological Seminary, Kota Kinabalu, Sabah, Malaysia.

Manuel Larreal (Lutheran) is editor and general coordinator of Acción Ecuménica in Caracas, Venezuela.

Käte Mahn is Europe secretary for the United Evangelical Lutheran Church of Germany, Hanover.

Anna Mghwira (Lutheran) is a theologian and lawyer from Tanzania.

Ishmael Noko (Zimbabwe) is general secretary of the Lutheran World Federation.

Cuthbert K. Omari (Lutheran) is professor of sociology at the University of Dar es Salaam, Tanzania.

Elisabeth Parmentier (Lutheran) is research assistant at the Institute for Ecumenical Research in Strasbourg, France.

Péri Rasolondraibe (Madagascar) is director of the Department for Mission and Development of the Lutheran World Federation.

Ranjini Rebera is consultant on communication and gender with the Churches of Christ in Australia.

Robert Shantz (Lutheran) is chaplain of the University of Toronto, Canada.

Martha Stortz is associate professor of historical theology and ethics at Pacific Lutheran Theological Seminary, Berkeley, California, USA.

Nirmala Vasanthakumar is director of the women's programme, National Council of Churches of India.

Mariama Marjorie Williams (Jamaica/USA) is assistant professor of economics at the Fashion Institute of Technology, State University of New York, USA.